PARTICULARITIES

PARTICULARITIES

Readings in George Eliot

BARBARA HARDY

Ohio University Press
Athens, Ohio

Library of Congress Cataloging in Publication Data

Hardy, Barbara Nathan.
   Particularities: readings in George Eliot.

    1. Eliot, George, 1819–1880—Criticism and
interpretation. I. Title.
PR4688.H274   1983   823'.8   82-22584
ISBN 0-8214-0741-4
ISBN 0-8214-0742-2 (pbk.)

First published 1982
© Barbara Hardy 1982

Originally published by Peter Owen Limited, London.
First American edition published 1983.
Printed in the United States of America.

In Memoriam

Ernest Dawson Hardy

(1918–1977)

Contents

Quotations from George Eliot's works are from the Cabinet Edition (1878–80) published by William Blackwood and Sons, Edinburgh and London, with the exception of those from *The Mill on the Floss*, where the Clarendon Edition (ed. Gordon S. Haight, Oxford, 1980) has been used.

Acknowledgements

A number of the chapters first appeared in other publications.[1] Chapter 1 was first published in *The Appropriate Form* (The Athlone Press, 1964); Chapter 2 in *Middlemarch: Critical Approaches to the Novel* (ed. Barbara Hardy, The Athlone Press, 1967)[2]; Chapter 3 in *Critical Essays on George Eliot* (ed. Barbara Hardy, Routledge & Kegan Paul, 1970); Chapter 4 by the University College of Swansea, 1973; Chapter 5 in *This Particular Web* (ed. Ian Adam, University of Toronto Press, 1975); Chapter 6 in *English*, Vol. XXV, 1976; and Chapter 9 as part of '*Middlemarch*, Chapter 85: Three Commentaries',[3] in the special George Eliot number of *Nineteenth Century Fiction* (December 1980). I am grateful to the editors and publishers for permission to reprint.

I recall with great pleasure occasions when several of these essays were delivered, in a different form, as lectures; Chapter 5 at the *Middlemarch* Conference in Calgary in 1971; Chapter 6 at the *Middlemarch* Conference in London, Ontario, in 1972; Chapter 4 as the W. D. Thomas Memorial Lecture at the University College of Swansea in 1973; Chapters 7 and 8 at Princeton University in 1978 and 1979 respectively and Chapter 10 at the George Eliot Conference at Rutgers University in 1980.

I want to thank students and colleagues at Royal Holloway and Birkbeck Colleges with whom I have discussed George Eliot over many years, Barbara Brunswick and Valerie Hall for hard work on difficult manuscripts, and Thom Braun and Graham Handley for invaluable help in research and preparation of material.

B.H.

---

1. Some corrections and revisions have been made.
2. Now out of print.
3. The passage for commentary was an editorial choice.

Introduction

This book is a collection of most of the essays and lectures I have written on George Eliot in the last fifteen years. It is a miscellany; the work was often formed in response to invitations and there are certain repetitions which I have not removed. I hope that some unity is conferred on diversity by subject and by approach. There is a certain shift in emphasis: the first essay formed part of my book, *The Appropriate Form*, written in the early sixties, when there was still a felt need to spell out and argue George Eliot's artistic powers, since formal analysis of her work was defensive. Her novels, like those of the other great Victorians, had been neglected and misjudged at a period when criticism of fiction was in a relatively primitive state, comparable to that of eighteenth-century Shakespeare criticism: given to praise of natural genius rather than analysis of judgment and control. It was an oddly sophisticated primitivism, in which judgment of fiction was dominated by Jamesian standards of economy, concentration, and conspicuous elegance, and patronized the multiplicity, lavishness, and looseness of Dickens, Thackeray and George Eliot. George Eliot had always been celebrated for psychological and ethical insight, but her intellectual penetration was commonly abstracted from the art which expressed and embodied the ideas. At that time, therefore, there was still a need to defend the powers of her art.

Developments in formal interpretation and analysis since I wrote my book, *The Novels of George Eliot: A Study in Form* (1959), have made it possible - even necessary - to look at other aspects of George Eliot's genius, and these essays are linked by a concern with the affective

9

pressure of her form, language, and imagination. The two essays most evidently concerned with affectivity, Chapters Four and Five, are also attempts to see George Eliot as an analyst of the affective life, and I would want to emphasize my growing recognition of her powers of feeling and of thinking. Like many critics I have moved away from concepts of realism; rather, my emphasis would be placed on the novelist's investigation of life, made through the particularities of a literary genre.

George Eliot's imaginative achievement shows itself in triumphs of structure and language which can be examined without constant reference to post-Jamesian models of fictional art. The fact of artistry can now be taken for granted. My sense of that artistry, however, has expanded, and I have tried in the pieces of practical criticism to keep close to a full literary response, affective as well as intellectual. In Chapter 85 of *Middlemarch*, for instance, as in any part of the novel we scrutinize, there are styles and conventions characteristic of Victorian fiction: authorial commentary, the free indirect style, literary allusion, personification, psychological analysis, together with features we tend to associate with modern fiction, such as shifts of style, irony, and symbolism. Like all literature, this novel creates an affective medium, through which we are not only enlightened but also moved. As in most literature, the analysis is ethical: it presents and manipulates judgments. It becomes plain that the achievement of the chapter, in which the inner action of the character's consciousness is explored through a detailed and documented presentation we may want to praise for its realism, is to imagine the workings of the ethical, intellectual and affective life through a superb piece of character analysis. George Eliot is not simply conducting an argument or providing a hypothesis; she is trying to understand the way in which human intelligence, passion, and conscience work, through the model of an individual character (Bulstrode), imagined in a particular community (Middlemarch), at a particular time (1829-32). The method is realistic in its rendering of individual and society, but the result of the realism is knowledge.

George Eliot's art is affective, ethical, and conceptual. Form, passion, intelligence, morality, are properties of her art, and are all subjected to investigation by that art. Her fiction, however, is not merely introspective in its concern with the artistic life, but reveals a concern with the life larger than art. George Eliot's interest lies in what Coleridge called the Primary as well as the Secondary imagination.

She is constantly concerned with imagination, sometimes analysing the properties of a creative energy closely resembling her own, like that of Maggie Tulliver. There are explicit and implicit links between the imaginative experience of George Eliot and that of Maggie's immature wish-fulfilment, her attempts to assimilate external and intransigent elements, her debt to literary sources, and her mind's enlargements and dynamic process. But George Eliot does not just look at Maggie. When Maggie tries to distract Tom and praise him, to imagine a more heroic world, and a more alluring form of masculine defence for herself, she invokes an image:

> 'O, how brave you are, Tom! I think you're like Samson. If there came a lion roaring at me, I think you'd fight him - wouldn't you, Tom?'
>
> 'How can a lion come roaring at you, you silly thing? There's no lions, only in the shows.'
>
> 'No; but if we were in the lion countries - I mean in Africa, where it's very hot - the lions eat people there. I can show it you in the book where I read it.'
>
> 'Well, I should get a gun and shoot him.'
>
> 'But if you hadn't got a gun - we might have gone out, you know, not thinking - just as we go fishing; and then a great lion might run towards us roaring, and we couldn't get away from him. What should you do, Tom?'
>
> Tom paused, and at last turned away contemptuously, saying,
>
> 'But the lion *isn't* coming. What's the use of talking?'
>
> 'But I like to fancy how it would be,' said Maggie, following him. 'Just think what you would do, Tom.' (Book One, Chapter 5)

Maggie's image is made in the interests of realism: Maggie's mind is neither static nor stubborn, but gradually and flexibly adapts and extends a simple image into a story, which establishes a locale, literary authority, motivation, some comparison with habitual life, and even a little self-reflection - 'I like to fancy how it would be'. The interests of realism and plausibility improve, extend, and generate the story. Tom could easily be cast as the unimaginative realist (an Isaac Evans) rejecting the impassioned woman artist, but only by neglecting the presentation of his imagination, which is also active, though less instructed, agile, and inventive than his sister's:

> '. . . I wouldn't go halves in the toffee and gingerbread on purpose to save the money; and Gibson and Spouncer fought with me because I wouldn't. And here's hooks; see here! . . . I say, *won't* we go and fish to-morrow down

by the Round Pool? And you shall catch your own fish, Maggie, and put
the worms on, and everything – won't it be fun?' (Book One, Chapter 5)

He too looks before and after, permuting his story in at least three
versions, with appropriate foreshortenings. The details about Gibson
and the gingerbread fall out of the narrative, the self-approving
reflections do not. The technique of his personal story has considerable
interest and, like Maggie's lion fantasy, it is inspired and generated by
love and self-love. It has its element of wish-fulfilment in the plan for
the fishing-party, no less imaginative than Maggie's imaginings
because it actually comes about, and hers do not. George Eliot's art is
clearly shown in these micro-structures, whose interest is technical, but
always more than technical. The self-conscious artist, the psychologist
and the moralist show the nature of creativity, dramatizing its
tendency to be self-centred, and its tendency to reach out beyond self.
It is shown both as impassioned and ratiocinative; both children
narrate and justify their narratives with a rational persistence, by
explanatory zeal and argumentative thoroughness which would be
found congenial by Samuel Beckett, one of whose recent narrators, in
Company, asks, 'What kind of imagination is this which is so reason
ridden?' and answers, 'A kind of its own'. George Eliot and Beckett
both examine the nature of reason and imagination. She does so
through a fully detailed invention and embodiment of characters in
action, in which no detail of humdrum habitual life is alien to her large
concerns. She never looks exclusively at one kind of mind, but
accumulates and compares various kinds of specimens. She is not
crudely or simply investigating her own case, but refracting, enlarging
and generalizing personal experience, through fictional means.

To claim that art is science, is to speak of science in the broadest
sense. As Wordsworth knew, the artist's medium of knowledge may
not propose truth as its immediate end, but modestly offer pleasure, to
creator and recipient. It works through passion and particularity,
implicitly rather than explicitly. In the episode with Tom and Maggie,
the novelist is presenting realistic characters, and endowing them with
minds, feelings, conscious and unconscious drives, relationship, environment, psyche and soma. We may say that here the novelist invents
character in order to produce what the Victorian realistic novel is
expected to produce: characters who are made to seem complex and
changeable, to interact with each other, to be determined by
environment, to possess bodies, minds, passions, and to speak an

appropriate language. We can also reverse this way of thinking about realism and say that George Eliot devises a conventional mimesis of action and character in order to find out more about social and personal interaction, social determinism, the relationship and nature of body, intelligence, passion, ideolect, and change. I don't think it matters that the artist may not think of art in this way. If we value the discoveries we discover in art, then such ignorance in the artist illustrates the truth of Lawrence's dictum that we should trust the tale, not the artist, and the work of art, not what the artist tells us. This was Lawrence's reason for admitting, as he didn't always admit, the usefulness of critics. Because the discoveries of art are made implicitly, and not explicitly, the critic's interpretation can make explicit and clear what may remain expressed, but not fully elucidated, in the particularities of art.

We may, for instance, analyse the function of Philip Wakem, in *The Mill on the Floss*, referring to an aesthetically valued unity of character, or to a valued sense of control. Philip may emerge as necessary to a balanced understanding of Maggie, spokesman in the novel for that criticism of Maggie's fanaticism to which Leavis was so blind. Philip indeed has this function; but if we grasp and examine a developing intellectual topic, like that of imagination, we will see Philip, like Tom and Maggie, as making his contribution to the novelist's collection of varieties of imaginative experience. George Eliot collects her specimens, which are imagined instances of the variety of human imagination, ranging from Mrs Tulliver to Daniel Deronda. George Eliot, however, is not only examining mind, imagination, symbol-making, and ritual behaviour, but also making an affective and moral classification. She is like a natural scientist who judges and loves the specimens, and finds her cases hard to classify and impossible to stereotype. George Eliot's classifications and generalizations are dynamic and tentative, and her cases are used to investigate a number of problems simultaneously.

We become fascinated by George Eliot's elucidation of Silas Marner's gold fetishism, for instance, and come to understand his behaviour while making the responses of pity, hope and amusement which she induces in us. She uses Silas to demonstrate exactly that arrest in the flow of commodities observed and classified and explained by her contemporary, Marx, in *Capital*, but as a novelist dealing with particularities, she shows Silas's miserliness as of a piece with his catalepsy, his lack of imaginative energy in memory and anticipation, and his religious atrophy. Her presentation of character here is not realistic: misers don't have to suffer from cataleptic fits. George Eliot is mixing with her realistic conventions other devices of the not always realistic classic realistic novel, devices of stylization, exaggeration, and symbolic character. She uses her art in the interests of elucidating, not one man, but through a man, the mind of man. Similarly, if we are interested in the portrayal of Dorothea Brooke's historical conscious-ness, which I have discussed in Chapter Six, we comprehend it not in the way in which we comprehend Carlyle's account of that conscious-ness, but through George Eliot's passionate understanding of ignorance, need, vision, confusion and growth as mingled and manipulated by means of her mixed medium. She uses a rhetorical figure we call character, to concentrate, clarify, involve and invoke affective re-sponse.

In my discussions of George Eliot's interest in imagination, historical consciousness, the affective life, rituals, objects and environment, I try to show why terms such as 'vision' and 'picture of human life' seem less than adequate descriptions of George Eliot's experiments and dis-coveries. My concern with the intellectual questioning of George Eliot's novels shows itself through an analysis of particularities of language, action and character, and my sense of her enquiring enterprise is both explicit and implicit.

1

Implication and Incompleteness
in *Middlemarch*

Middlemarch provides us with a model for the expansive form, in its large scope, multiple variations, and freedom from the restrictions of either aesthetic or ideological form. Many of its structural features – antithesis and parallelism, anticipation and echo, scenic condensation – are those we also find in Meredith and indeed in Henry James, but in a restricted range. Not only is the organization of *Middlemarch* much less conspicuous and indeed less elegantly symmetrical than that of a novel by James, but there is never any sacrifice of truthfulness to the achievement of aesthetic ends. The form is the means to the ends of good story, moral argument, and the imitation of life. It is much more naturally plotted than the novels of Dickens, less dependent on coincidence and less restricted to crisis, and it shapes its moral argument tentatively through character and action, instead of shaping character and action in accordance with dogma. There are no strong climaxes like those at the end of *The Ambassadors* and *Jane Eyre* which complete a pattern or clinch an argument but distort the appearances of life.

The act of comparison is a dangerous tool in criticism. We may too easily select the material for comparison in order to back our prejudices and preferences, and if we shift the comparison, and put *Middlemarch* beside *Le Rouge et le Noir*, or *Anna Karenina*, or *Lady Chatterley's Lover*, we must modify our sense of its expansiveness and truthfulness. *Middlemarch* is a large, free, and truthful novel (to keep fairly close to James's terms but to reverse his judgment) but it has its own special restrictions. If we compare it with the novels I have just mentioned, novels which resemble it in social and psychological material to a sufficient extent to make the comparison viable, then we should use the word 'realism' more warily in our praise of George Eliot.

Middlemarch is only restrictedly truthful in its treatment of sexuality. The consequence is not only to make us use the word 'realism' warily but also to look hard at our praise of its formal unity. For one of the interesting features of this restriction is that it is uneven. The novel does not reveal a consistent restriction but a lop-sided one.

This restriction is present in George Eliot's early novels, too. It is, for instance, possible to argue that although the sexual desires of Maggie and Stephen, in *The Mill on the Floss*, are frankly dramatized, in general conception and in tense detail, the sexual implications of Maggie's relationship with Philip Wakem would have been more moving and incisive if they had gone beyond hints and implications. The sexual *lacunae* in *Adam Bede* are even plainer. Hetty's seduction by Arthur is dramatized in minute psychological detail, through the point of view of both characters. Arthur's desires are presented largely by implication and in symbol, but such symbols as the violent ride away from temptation and the unthinking ride back towards it are sufficient to give them substance. I do not have in mind an absence of physical detail but an absence of relevant emotional statement when I suggest that this sexual embodiment of Arthur throws into high relief what remains unsubstantial in Hetty. Her brilliantly recorded fantasy-life is remarkably lacking in sexual detail, but nowhere does George Eliot draw our attention to this conspicuous absence, or comment on its causes and effects, as she does with all other dramatized aspects of Hetty's mind and feelings. She tells us that Hetty is hard, but not that she is cold. The lack of sexuality seems to be the product of omission rather than of reticence, and it will not do, I think, to excuse the omissions on the ground that they are conventional or historically necessary. Hetty and Arthur are not a shadowy idyllic couple, but are subjected to the persistent analysis of both irony and sympathy. And Arthur is by no means a hero without sexuality.

It would be difficult to complain that the staled passions and live humiliations of Mrs Transome lose anything by being portrayed in a Victorian novel, though we may notice that her 'past' is shown retrospectively, in the novel's past, which possibly removes some of the difficulties of sexual delineation. The important thing, as I have already stressed, is not the absence of sexual realism achieved through a detailed clinical report, but the absence or presence of that psychological realism which makes the characters appear as sexual beings. And in spite of conventions of reticence, I would claim that George Eliot writes about Maggie and Mrs Transome and Gwendolen, Arthur, Stephen and Grandcourt, as creatures of sexual vitality, desire, and commitment. It is because of their sexuality that they are vulnerable, moved, aggressive, or threatened: sex enters not only into the 'portraits' but into the causality of the action. The passions and conflicts of these characters are sufficiently vivid and particular to make her moral argument meaningful despite changes in sexual morality.

In the earlier novels she handles sexual situations which she is able to make fairly explicit. There is no doubt that Janet is driven to drink by a sadistic drunkard, no doubt that Hetty is seduced and becomes pregnant, no doubt that Mrs Transome has committed adultery, even though George Eliot does not always give names to the situations and relationships. Her refusal to give names is probably less a matter of social decorum than a matter of dramatic effect. Our curiosity and tension, and our troubled identification with secrecy, privacy, or anxiety, is brought about by local evasiveness and lack of explicit naming. We do not know immediately what Mrs Transome has done, nor do we know immediately that Hetty is pregnant. Our lack of information is justified by their furtiveness or pride. Our mere suspicion matches their understandable retreat from the subject. In these instances George Eliot withholds information in order to create tension and shock or decorously follows the reticence and evasiveness implicit in the situation.

In *Middlemarch* George Eliot is dealing with a situation which she cannot even name, and her evasiveness and suggestiveness, her retreat and approach, deserve close attention. Her refusal to be explicit is so marked that many readers do not even notice that there is anything which she is refusing to be explicit about. She is reticent - not, I claim, silent - about the Casaubon marriage. This reticence, because it is not silence, is compatible with a truthful and complete account of what it was like for Dorothea to be married to Casaubon, and what it was like for Casaubon to be married to Dorothea. We may not see the point at once, but when we do, I suggest, everything fits. But the novel's truthfulness is not sustained. In Dorothea's relationship with Will we have much more than a refusal to name the passions. We have a refusal even to suggest them. She is reticent about Dorothea and Casaubon, but she leaves things out in her treatment of Dorothea and Will. The omission is both an unrealistic element in an unusually realistic novel and the cause of imbalance. We can make the criticism in terms of truth and in terms of form. *Middlemarch* has often been praised as a great realistic novel and, more latterly, as a triumph of unified organization, but both its realism and its, unity are flawed.

This flaw has to be uncovered in some detail. There have been many commentaries on the novel, but its delineation of sexuality has been glanced at very shyly or neglected utterly. Critics may have sometimes assumed that the sexual implications of the Casaubon marriage are obvious. It is true that they form only a part of the moral and psychological action and are easily subsumed in a general account of the great trials and smaller triumphs of Dorothea Brooke. I do not want to give the impression that the novel has been misunderstood because critics have not recognized the impotence of Casaubon. This is a part of the story, but not the whole. But I want to bring out this part, and for several reasons. Some readers interpret this reticence as omission, and their view is encouraged by a generalized notion about the absence of sex in Victorian fiction, and in turn encourages this notion to persist: only in a Victorian novel could we have such an asexual view of a marriage. Some readers think that the omission is there, but is unimportant: the question does not come up, the failure of the marriage has nothing to do with sex. Some even respond rather perversely to what clues and cues we are given, and see Casaubon as physically repulsive, like Hardy's Phillotson, or even sadistic, like Grandcourt in *Daniel Deronda*. These are some of the views I have met - though not in print. One published view is that of John Hagan, in an article in *Nineteenth Century Fiction*: '*Middlemarch*: Narrative Unity in the Story of Dorothea Brooke' (Vol. XVI, June 1961, pp. 17-31). Mr Hagan calls Casaubon 'a sterile ascetic'. We can all agree as to his sterility, but I think George Eliot tells us something about its cause. Calling Casaubon 'ascetic', however, seems as appropriate as calling Sir Clifford Chatterley ascetic. Neither of them has to make any effort to subdue the flesh.

George Eliot never tells us that Casaubon is impotent. Like most English novelists of her time, she is reticent, sometimes evasive, about sex. *Middlemarch* appeared twenty years before *Jude the Obscure*, and if we compare it with contemporary novels in France and Russia, it leaves out a lot. Everybody knows that Dickens was interested in the social aspects of sex, but contrived to write at length about a prostitute, in *Oliver Twist*, without giving her a local habitation or a name which would be unpalatable in family reading. Sex as an aspect of personal relations scarcely comes into Dickens, but George Eliot is plainly giving her action some sexual substance in *Adam Bede*, *The Mill on the Floss*, and *Daniel Deronda*. Her domestic drama seems restrained when we compare her with Tolstoy, but restraint is not the same thing as omission, and if we confuse the two when discussing *Middlemarch* we are surely imprecise when we proffer the favourite words of praise like 'adult' and 'realistic'. I am not claiming sexual realism for George Eliot. D. H. Lawrence allows himself total explicitness and is moreover interested in aspects of sexual behaviour which do not concern *Middlemarch* in any way. George Eliot writes within a restricted convention of reticence, and is emphasizing sensibility rather than sexuality. But if we look at the sexual implications of Casaubon, and see what they contribute to the moral and social pattern of the novel, George Eliot's dramatization of the conflict between life-values and death-values – Eros and Thanatos – will appear to have a good deal in common with *Lady Chatterley's Lover*. Certain Iliads, as Carlyle reminds us in *Sartor Resartus*, acquire new extrinsic significance over the years, and it is possible that the twentieth-century reader of *Middlemarch* sees this correlation of sexual and social values with exaggerated clarity. When we isolate a theme we invariably appear to exaggerate its prominence, but I hope I am isolating something which is an important and neglected part of the novel. *Middlemarch* uses the sexual theme not merely in order to confront life more truthfully, but in a significant bracketing of social criticism and individual moral affirmation. The rescue into love, which is a theme in many novels besides *Middlemarch* and *Lady Chatterley's Lover*, involves some social diagnosis of personal failures in feeling and relationship. It makes a symbolic equation of social and sexual energy in ways which hold both terms in equal tension. The virile rescuer can be a vivid symbol of social revolution; the decadent society can be seen as a cause of individual sterility; the failure of love can be explored causally – in the condensed causality of symbolism – and generalized. Such symbolism is condensed: it is not necessarily true that reactionaries are sexually impotent, and in these novels their impotence functions as metaphor. But this is more than rhetoric. There is some literal truth in relating the capacity for loving individuals to the capacity for loving humanity, and although the sexually impotent may be capable of love, the novelist can use both kinds of impotence and energy as mutual reinforcements.

Unfortunately, *Middlemarch* does not make this reinforcement in a sufficiently complete fashion. The rescue and its implications are blurred and softened by an inadequate rescuer. One of the many reasons for discussing the Casaubon marriage is the light it has to throw on the character and role of Will Ladislaw. But this is to anticipate. The first thing to look at is the Casaubon marriage itself.

It would be misleading to say that the first real crisis in Dorothea's development is the sexual failure of her marriage. George Eliot's main emphasis is emotional, not physical, and though this emphasis may be in part attributable to the reticent treatment of sex, it is mainly caused by George Eliot's chosen situation – the frustration and collapse of a general marital failure. Casaubon's impotence is part of a larger incapacity for life, an incapacity we also find in Sir Clifford Chatterley. There is, however, one important difference between the two characters. In both the novelist is using physical impotence – I suppose 'unrealistically' – as a sign of basic sterility. Sir Clifford's impotence, caused by a war-wound, is made the cause of his imaginative and emotional failure. Lawrence uneasily combines an account of psychological causality with a metaphor. George Eliot avoids this causal account. Casaubon's physical impotence is seen neither as cause nor effect of his general impotence. It is one of many symptoms. And even if we recognize that its appearance in the cluster of other symptoms is metaphorical and not realistic – there are presumably intellectual egoistic failures, incapable of proper human relations, who are sexually potent – his impotence is a fine stroke, which does more than complete a total picture of failure. It brings out Dorothea's ignorance and ardour, and society's irresponsibility in 'smiling on propositions of marriage from a sickly man to a girl less than half his own age' (1st edition, 1871-2; dropped in later editions).

Unless we see the sexual implications of Dorothea's crisis in Rome, George Eliot must seem to be vainly expending much of her satire and her sympathy. The author's reticence finds dramatic reason (or excuse) in the character's reserve: 'No one would ever know what she thought of a wedding journey to Rome.' But by the time we reach this enigmatic comment on Dorothea's reticence we have heard many frankly explicit doubts and fears about her marriage. Such doubts are voiced by several characters, though never to Dorothea. Each point of view is isolated and tempered by the prejudice of the speaker into a local effect of vagueness or ambiguity. Such ambiguity disappears as the impressions converge.

Let us look at some of these separate but converging points of view, noticing that they appear in several ways. There is the author's analysis of Dorothea's consciousness, ironically neighboured by an analysis of Casaubon's which is deliberately non-committal on first appearance. There is the spirited commentary of some biased and unreliable spectators.

Dorothea has been frequently analysed and I will therefore merely pick out one or two relevant features. She is healthy, ardent, idealistic, young enough to be Casaubon's daughter, and very innocent. Her innocence is brought out strongly in her misunderstanding of the motives and affections of Sir James Chettam and in the explicit contrast between her and her sister, the more knowing and 'worldly-wise' Celia. It is Dorothea, not Casaubon, who tries to be an ascetic. She tries to renounce and rationalize her response to the glow of jewels and the joys of riding. Like Maggie, she knows too little about her own instincts to be able to adopt the ascetic role with safety. She has theoretical ideals of marriage ominously expressed in references to fathers and teachers, Milton and Hooker. She creates an image of her own nature and an image of ideal marriage which matches Casuabon's with fatal perfection. She defends his 'great soul' against Celia's distaste for his looks and habits. There is, of course, the additional irony that even measured by this theoretical ideal of marriage, Casaubon falls short: he is not a Hooker or a Milton in intellect or scholarship, and his soul is a little one, if we can fall into George Eliot's way of measuring souls. But this irony is not immediately relevant to my argument, and I mention it only to stress the selective analysis I am making. If Dorothea were right about her own emotional needs – which she is not – she would still be in for intellectual and moral disillusion. It is the emotional and physical shock which I want to bring out here.

When we see her in Rome, through Naumann's shrewd perception, she is standing in her Quakerish garb beside the statue of Ariadne, then thought to be the Cleopatra. George Eliot deliberately reminds us of both Ariadne and Cleopatra, and the association with Ariadne, forsaken after all her efforts in her maze, is as relevant as the sensual association with Cleopatra which gives extra point to Naumann's comment on the 'fine bit of antithesis'. The girl and the statue are not as different as all that, despite appearances.

Next we see her weeping, feeling a tendency to 'fits of anger and repulsion', disturbed by the violence and incoherence of Rome and by

Casaubon's deficiencies of sensibility and explanation. Both she and
Casaubon are irritable and nervous, and when she begs him to let her
help in his work, 'in a most unaccountable, darkly-feminine manner
. . . with a slight sob and eyes full of tears', she explains that she 'can be
of no other use'. She asks if he is 'thoroughly satisfied with our stay – I
mean, with the result so far as your studies are concerned'. Before
Ladislaw's scepticism has made her doubt the value of Casaubon's
research she has already begun to feel doubts about the future years 'in
her own home', realizing that 'the way in which they might be filled
with joyful devotedness was not so clear to her as it had been'. The main
action of disillusionment is expressed in the response to Rome, which
startles and bewilders her, while Casaubon comments 'in a measured
official tone', quoting authoritative opinions on Raphael, for instance,
with Cupid and Psyche picked out for special illustration. There is
direct comment too, when George Eliot observes, with meticulous
qualification, that this frustration and disappointment might have
'remained longer unfelt' if there had been ardour and tenderness:

> if he would have held her hands between his and listened . . . or if she could
> have fed her affection with those childlike caresses which are the bent of
> every sweet woman, who has begun by showering kisses on the hard pate of
> her bald doll, creating a happy soul within that woodenness from the
> wealth of her own love. That was Dorothea's bent. With all her yearning to
> know what was afar from her and to be widely benignant, she had ardour
> enough for what was near, to have kissed Mr Casaubon's coat-sleeve, or to
> have caressed his shoe-latchet, if he would have made any other sign of
> acceptance than pronouncing her, with his unfailing propriety, to be of a
> most affectionate and truly feminine nature, indicating at the same time by
> politely reaching a chair for her that he regarded these manifestations as
> rather crude and startling. (Chapter 20)

This describes a failure in feeling, and though there seem to be
physical implications, it is certainly no clear indication of impotence.
But this account is set in a context of highly critical comment which is
frankly physical, and not primarily concerned with Casaubon's
failures in tenderness or sensibility. The initial physical contrast
between Dorothea and Casaubon is presented in descriptive detail:
Dorothea's health, her 'grand woman's frame' and – at a significant
point, just before Mr Brooke is to announce Casaubon's proposal –
'maternal hands', contrast with Casaubon's poor physique, white
moles with hairs, and so forth. The inequality of the physical match is

not left to the reader's inferences. Almost everyone who comments on the marriage reacts in protest and disgust. The exceptions are the over-tolerant and detached Cadwallader, and vague, self-engrossed Mr Brooke, who feels that the complications of women are equalled only 'by the revolutions of irregular solids'. Brooke's own reasons for never marrying are scarcely calculated to evoke respect and his hints about 'the noose' and a husband's desire for mastery are carefully placed in a very personal context. The fastidious Celia shrinks, but we see her response in the context of her limited egoism and superficial common sense. Sir James Chettam, as the Cadwalladers point out, speaks with the partiality of a young, handsome, and rejected suitor: 'Good God! It is horrible! He is no better than a mummy,' and 'What business has an old bachelor like that to marry? He has one foot in the grave,' and 'He must be fifty, and I don't believe he could ever have been much more than the shadow of a man. Look at his legs.' He calls him 'a parchment code' and claims that 'he has got no good red blood in his body'. The outspoken Mrs Cadwallader, connoisseur of 'blood and breeding', calls Casaubon 'A great bladder for dried peas to rattle in!' She reassures Sir James that Celia will now be the better match, since 'this marriage to Casaubon is as good as going to a nunnery', and winds up her comment on his blood, 'Somebody put a drop under a magnifying glass, and it was all semi-colons and parentheses.' Will's early hostility to Dorothea makes him conclude that there 'could be no sort of passion in a girl who would marry Mr Casaubon', but he soon comes to rival the jealous eloquence of Sir James and thinks of Casaubon as having 'got this adorable young creature to marry him, and then passing his honeymoon away from her, groping after his mouldy futilities' calls him 'a cursed white-blooded pedantic coxcomb', thinks of 'beautiful lips kissing holy skulls', and sees the marriage as 'the most horrible of virgin-sacrifices'. Will's reaction is the only one based on compre-hension of Dorothea's motives in marriage, and he uses the word 'fanatic' to cover both these and her rejections of art.

The implications of this chorus of disapproval go beyond a distaste for mere outward disparity of body and age. Incidentally, Casaubon is no obvious case of senile impotence,[1] and he may even be nearer forty-five than Sir James's suggested fifty. Mr Brooke tells Dorothea that 'He

1. The actual age of characters who strike the modern reader as old is often surprising in earlier novels. Adam Verver, in *The Golden Bowl* (1904), is only forty-seven, though he makes a more elderly impression and Charlotte says that he is responsible for the infertility of their marriage.

is over five-and-forty, you know.' Mrs Cadwallader is unambiguously thinking of sterility, from whatever cause, and although this aspect of the Casaubon marriage is dealt with reticently, it is an important thread in the pattern. It is much less prominent than it would be in the life of a heroine who had staked less on marriage as an education and a vocation, and it is true that nowhere does Dorothea long for children or lament their lack. But the subject is present everywhere except in Dorothea's actual words. It is alive, for instance, in the ironical contrast of her frustration with Celia's maternal complacency and Rosamond's miscarriage. It is alive, too, in imagery: there is the image of the elfin child withered in its birth, the strong image of the judgment of Solomon, in which Dorothea figures as the true mother and Rosamond as the false, and perhaps in this image used on one occasion for Casaubon's unresponsiveness to Dorothea: 'it is in these acts called trivialities that the seeds of joy are for ever wasted' (Chapter 42). Dorothea's lament is vague – it is for 'objects who could be dear to her, and to whom she could be dear'. On one occasion she is thinking of Casaubon's will, which has provided for issue, but at no point in her innocent scheming for sharing the estate with Will, nor in Casaubon's reactions, nor in her discussion with Lydgate about having nothing to do with her money, does the obvious question of heirs come up. It is a marriage without ardour, without children, and, most significantly, without the expectation of children.[2]

Casaubon does contemplate his possible heirs in drawing up his will, 'made at the time of their marriage' as we are told in Chapter 37. It is now time to consider his expectations and reactions to marriage. George Eliot endows him with 'chilling rhetoric', both in love-letter and speech, but draws our attention to the possibility that this may not mean 'that there is no good work or fine feeling in him'. She also warns us of the unreliability of Casaubon's critics, forcing us to keep pace with the slow development of her action by her usual omniscient author's disclaimer of omniscience. But as soon as we enter the mind of Casaubon her irony and her pity confirm suspicion.

Casaubon, like many lovers, is looking forward to 'the happy termination of courtship', but for his own peculiar reasons – he will then be able to get on with his work. He has expected more from

---

2. This point is not dealt with by Gordon Haight in his article 'Poor Mr Casaubon' (*Nineteenth-Century Perspectives: Essays in Honour of Lionel Stevenson*, ed. Clyde Ryals, Durham, North Carolina, 1974, pp. 255–70) in which he concludes that Dorothea has had a 'violent and painful' initiation into matrimony.

courtship. Relying, as later in Rome, on the appropriate authorities, he 'determined to abandon himself to the stream of feeling, and perhaps was surprised to find what an exceedingly shallow rill it was'. Authority is discredited in the sad ridiculous conclusion, 'that the poets had much exaggerated the force of masculine passion'.[3] His own deficiency is the only uncanvassed explanation: 'It had once or twice crossed his mind that possibly there was some deficiency in Dorothea to account for the moderation of his abandonment; but he was unable to discern the deficiency, or to figure to himself a woman who would have pleased him better; so that there was clearly no reason to fall back upon but the exaggerations of human tradition'. Doubt continues:

> For in truth, as the day fixed for his marriage came nearer, Mr Casaubon did not find his spirits rising . . . though he had won a lovely and noble-hearted girl he had not won delight. . . . Poor Mr Casaubon had imagined that his long studious bachelorhood had stored up for him a compound interest of enjoyment, and that large drafts on his affections would not fail to be honoured. . . . there was nothing external by which he could account for a certain blankness of sensibility which came over him just when his expectant gladness should have been mostly lively. . . . (Chapter 10)

The imagery of low vitality covers his egocentric feeling for his wife and his work, his marital and his scholarly jealousies – a cloudy damp engenders all. George Eliot turns from such satirical comment to a straight unironical account of his conflict. He cannot tell Mr Brooke that he would like Ladislaw to leave Middlemarch because this would be a public admission of deficiency: 'To let anyone suppose that he was jealous would be to admit their (suspected) view of his disadvantages: to let them know that he did not find marriage particularly blissful would imply his conversion to their (probably) earlier disapproval. . . . on the most delicate of all personal subjects, the habit of proud suspicious reticence told doubly' (Chapter 37).

Although the self-regard is still the same, a new note has entered since his earlier assumptions that the failure in delight was attributable to poetic exaggeration. Even though Casaubon now has rather more grounds for blaming the failure on Dorothea, who has proved unexpectedly critical and independent, it is in fact hinted that he at

---

3. The motto for this chapter (7) is 'Piacer e popone Vuol la sua stagione'.

least sees the possibility of other people thinking in terms of his 'disadvantages'.

This is the failure of ardour seen from his point of view. The question of issue is touched on only once in his internal commentary. This is in Chapter 29, after their marriage, when George Eliot interrupts the expected sympathetic analysis of Dorothea to consider instead the 'intense consciousness' of Casaubon. Included in his marital balance-sheet are thoughts which go back to his previous expectations:

> On such a young lady he would make handsome settlements, and he would neglect no arrangement for her happiness: in return, he should receive family pleasures and leave behind him that copy of himself which seemed so urgently required of a man – to the sonneteers of the sixteenth century. Times had altered since then, and no sonneteer had insisted on Mr Casaubon's leaving a copy of himself; moreover, he had not yet succeeded in issuing copies of his mythological key; but he had always intended to acquit himself by marriage. . . .

This account, moving backwards and forwards in time, is interesting in its ellipsis and juxtaposition. Casaubon's failure to leave a copy of his mythological key is ironically placed between the lack of any demand for him to leave another kind of copy and his (past) intention to acquit himself in marriage. It is a suggestive item, at least, and it is followed by an account of his lack of capacity for joy, which is in part a physiological explanation:

> To know intense joy without a strong bodily frame, one must have an enthusiastic soul. Mr Casaubon had never had a strong bodily frame, and his soul was sensitive without being enthusiastic: it was too languid to thrill out of self-consciousness into passionate delight; it went on fluttering in the swampy ground where it was hatched. . . .

George Eliot insists on the lack of passion, claiming pity, not contempt, for such a 'small hungry shivering self', and ending with the mention of 'the new bliss' which 'was not blissful to him':

> And the deeper he went in domesticity the more did the sense of acquitting himself and acting with propriety predominate over any other satisfaction. Marriage, like religion and erudition, nay, like authorship itself, was fated to become an outward requirement, and Edward Casaubon was bent on fulfilling unimpeachably all requirements.

Whatever ambiguity and evasion may at times come from the convention of reticence, the double emphasis on emotional and physical deficiency, on the one hand, and sterility, on the other, appear to converge in only one probable explanation. It may be that the adult Victorian reader found the suggestion more plainly pronounced than the modern reader, having fewer cases of sexual frankness before him, being more accustomed to implicit rather than explicit sexual themes, and having no hardened prejudices about the limitations of the Victorian novel.[4] Our expectations and prejudices may well blind us to the implications of this reticent mode of suggestion, but if we look carefully at these implications I think we must say that Casaubon is sexually very inadequate.[5] We cannot definitely say that the marriage is never consummated, but since Dorothea's nervous misery begins in Rome, this seems highly probable.

As I said at the beginning of this chapter, I do not think that the truthfulness of *Middlemarch* is impaired because George Eliot does not tell us outright that Casaubon is impotent. The very technique of implication has dramatic advantages. Mrs Cadwallader might be expected to talk to Sir James in knowing metaphor. Casaubon might be expected to avoid naming his deficiencies. Dorothea would only weep in silence. On the other hand, I do not want to exaggerate this dramatic decorum. It could have been combined with explicit naming, by the author or one of the characters, and there is no doubt that social and literary restraint governs the novel's reticence. There is no doubt, too, that the sexual failure is only a part of Casaubon's generalized failure of mind and feeling. But the author does not distort the facts of nature and marriage: if we do not see the point, all is not lost, and the novel makes sense. If we do, then many of the small hints and details, as well as the larger tensions, make better sense, are more coherent and complete.

But where the novel shows the unhappy consequences of the restricted treatment of sex is in Dorothea's relation with Will Ladislaw. Here is the psychological and structural flaw in *Middlemarch*.

4. Since writing this I have seen David Daiches' little book on *Middlemarch* in which he discusses Casaubon's impotence, making the comment that 'no doubt the Victorian reader failed to see in the relationship between these two the matching of impotence and sublimation' (*Studies in English Literature*, No. 11, p. 21). This conclusion strikes me as very odd.
5. Perhaps the most interesting interpretation of Casaubon's sexuality was made by Richard Ellman in his study of Casaubon and Ladislaw, 'Dorothea's Husbands' (*Golden Codgers*, London, 1973).

It is a psychological flaw because of a failure in truthfulness, a structural flaw because of the vivid presence of truthfulness elsewhere. I do not insist on describing the flaw in psychological and structural terms merely because of an interest in structure, but because I think the successes and failures which are combined in *Middlemarch* afford an interesting model for the formal critic. If we limit our definitions of form in fiction, as we so often do, to the organization of symbols, imagery, and ideas, then we may well pass over this failure. Recognition of this kind of failure forces us to review our ideas of form, especially our ideas of unity. It is possible to demonstrate the thematic and poetic unity of the novel: the themes cohere and persist throughout, and there is a mobile unity of imagery and symbol which has been analysed by several critics. But if we regard form in the largest sense, and think not merely of unity but of a more useful and less popular word, completeness, then we have to qualify our praise of the form of this novel.

The structural relationship of Casaubon and Ladislaw takes us on to James, and suggests that there is some point in his 'law' that the antithesis should be direct and complete. Up to a point the fable which lies at the heart of *Middlemarch* is clear enough. The three main characters are Casaubon, Dorothea, and Ladislaw. The fable may be called the rescue into love, and it has many forms in fiction. It is present in James's *The Bostonians*, in Gissing's neglected novel *The Emancipated*, in E. M. Forster's *A Room With a View* and *Where Angels Fear to Tread*, in several of D. H. Lawrence's stories and novels, and in Meredith's *Lord Ormont and his Aminta* and perhaps in *The Egoist*. In all these novels the sexual rescue – from an old man, a woman, a sterile aesthete – has social implications. The rescuer is something of the Noble Savage and something of the Outsider, representing not only personal passion and fertility but the new blood needed and feared by the old establishment. Casaubon is, like Sir Clifford Chatterley, a cluster of different kinds of impotence. His futile mythological research, his nominal clerical function, his birth and property, all combine with his physical and emotional deficiencies to give him a significant place in the unreformed society. Like Sir Clifford, his assumption of Providential grace and favour for self and class gives him more than a merely personal deadness and egoism, though both in *Middlemarch* and *Lady Chatterley's Lover*, this is only an indirect generalization in a novel containing a great deal of overt political and social discussion. George Eliot's advantage over Lawrence, despite her sexual reticence, is that she creates an individual as well as a symbol, a man who feels the internal strain and loneliness of his position, a man torn by doubt and anxiety and pride, a man capable of stepping briefly outside this clearly marked and moral category and on one occasion speaking to Dorothea with surprise and humility and recognition, capable of responding as a human being and certainly created out of sympathy and fellow-feeling. There is no possibility of an even identification with the characters in *Lady Chatterley's Lover* because they are not evenly animated, but Casaubon is presented as part of his environment, having a history, having the register of his differentiated consciousness, made of the same stuff as everyone else though warped, hardened, and self-regarding.

Ladislaw completes and answers these social implications. He is 'a kind of gypsy', defiantly déclassé, grandson of a woman who rebelled against the Casaubon values of class and money, son of a woman who rebelled against the Bulstrode values of a Nonconformist respectable thieving line. His father is a musician, his mother an actress, and he is a dilettante and a Radical. As a Radical, of course, he also rejects the superficial and feeble liberalism of Brooke. Like Matey Weyburn in *Lord Ormont and his Aminta*, and Mellors in *Lady Chatterley*, he is a social misfit, a man seeking his vocation, and the poor man who wins the lady. But the mere absurdity of the comparison with Mellors or with Forster's Gino makes his deficiencies plain. As a Noble Savage he is a little fragile.

It may be objected that the very comparison itself is artificial, that I am complaining that Ladislaw fails to meet a standard set up by other novels and inappropriately applied to *Middlemarch*. Though I think the social implications of the love-story in *Middlemarch* are usefully brought out by this classification, I am not judging Ladislaw by the general and external standards I may have implied, but by the expectations set up within the novel itself. Ladislaw and Casaubon make an excellent social antithesis in their roles, but an unequal sexual one.

The pattern is worked out very satisfactorily in terms of symbol and image. Dorothea is imprisoned in the stone prison of melancholy Lowick, in the labyrinth, in the dark tomb. Casaubon is the winter-worn husband, and the Minotaur. Ladislaw has a godlike brightness, is irradiated by images of light, is the natural daylight from which Dorothea is shut off. Images of darkness and light, aridity and water, enclosure and space, are strong. If Mellors turns up in the grounds of dismal Wragby in answer to Connie's question, 'What next?', Ladislaw is the unexpected 'someone quite young' found painting in the garden of Lowick. The generalized fertility symbols and more precise Persephone motifs are very subdued in *Middlemarch* when we compare it with *Lady Chatterley's Lover*, but they are present. But poetic unity is not enough. The unity and antithetical completeness of the imagery and symbolism of place and weather and appearances are not endorsed by the characters. Ladislaw is presented in terms of sensibility, not sensuality. The sexual implications of the imagery are substantiated in Casaubon – of course he can only refer to the opinions of *conoscenti* when he shows Dorothea *Cupid and Psyche* – but not in the rescuing hero. At times, indeed, the imagery itself takes on and contributes to Ladislaw's idyllic colouring: there is a sexual implication when Casaubon concludes that the poets have overrated the force of masculine passion which is sadly lacking when we find Will 'verifying in his own experience that higher love-poetry which had charmed his fancy' (Chapter 47). Those 'tall lilies' which he associates with Dorothea are more like a romantic detail from a Pre-Raphaelite painting, disturbing in their chastity, than like the shooting daffodils of *Lady Chatterley's Lover*. When the Cupid and Psyche symbol finds its antithetical completion, after Casaubon's death, the image is delicate and innocent, not strongly passionate:

> She did not know then that it was Love who had come to her briefly, as in a dream before awaking, with the hues of morning on his wings – that it was Love to whom she was sobbing her farewell as his image was banished by the blameless rigour of irresistible day. (Chapter 55)

The appropriate comment seems to be that at this point in the story she should have known. There are some Victorian novels in which it might seem captious not to accept such a lack of self-knowledge but *Middlemarch* is not one of them. George Eliot spends a fair amount of energy criticizing Dorothea's ignorance and short-sightedness but here remains romantically identified with this innocence.

Henry James is one of the few critics of Ladislaw to discuss his 'insubstantial character' in the appropriate terms. If his meaning is ambiguous when he complains in his review of *Middlemarch* (*Galaxy*, March 1873), 'He is really, after all, not the ideal foil to Mr Casaubon which her soul must have imperiously demanded, and if the author of the *Key to all Mythologies* sinned by lack of order, Ladislaw too has not the concentrated fervour essential in the man chosen by so nobly strenuous a heroine,' it is clear that he is not merely thinking of Dorothea's soul when he later says more outspokenly, in the person of Constantius, 'If Dorothea had married anyone after her misadventure with Casaubon, she would have married a trooper' (*'Daniel Deronda:* A Conversation', *Atlantic Monthly*, December 1876).

I do not mean to suggest that our impression of Will is entirely romantic, innocent, and radiant. In his private thoughts about Dorothea's marriage, in his discussions with Naumann, in his excellently convincing relationship with Lydgate (especially where their 'masculine' solidarity puts Rosamond's narrow femininity in its place), in his quarrels with Bulstrode and his differences with Brooke, he is detached, honest, and touchy. The relationship between Dorothea and Casaubon is presented in terms of sexuality, but that between Dorothea and Ladislaw is shown as denying it, and it is here that his sensuality falters. George Eliot is not hampered by the difficulties of describing actual love-making, though it is worth noticing that when Dorothea and Will touch each other they are at their most innocent and childlike. In the relationship between Maggie and Stephen, or the relationship between Lydgate and Rosamond, in this same novel, tension and desire are conveyed without physical detail.

In this novel sensibility acts as a surrogate for sensuality. This comes out in the presentation of Will as an artist, less marked by his ability than by impressionability. It comes out too in the sustained aesthetic debate which is the beginning of Dorothea's acquaintance with Will, and which has many implications. Dorothea is presented as a Puritan, and this makes for a special irony in her marriage – her self-abnegation has made the innocent blunder possible, but her ardour is there to suffer. It is Will who points out this ignorance and sees the paradox, as Philip did for Maggie. He preaches ardently on behalf of the art he loves, which Dorothea distrusts, because of its obscure relation to the hard realities, because of its apparently trivial delight in beauty. Will's attempt to convert her to the aesthetic attitude is most ironically placed in Rome, on her wedding-journey. Will is presented as an aesthete of a special kind. His impressionability is both praised and doubted: if it shows itself in his response to art and in his restless trials as poet and painter, it shows itself also in his sensitivity to other people – to Lydgate, for instance, as well as to Casaubon and Dorothea, where his understanding is less impartial. But although he is carefully seen as

a creature 'of uncertain promise' (like Fred Vincy), he is given much
more than an effeminate aestheticism. His arguments in defence of
beauty are largely realistic attempts to persuade Dorothea into 'a
sturdy neutral delight in things as they were'. In Dorothea's first
bewildered impressions of Rome is, I suggest, a reaction to sensuality,
though this is muted if we compare it with Strether's response to the
sensuality of Paris or the reactions of Forster's heroines in his Italian
novels. A neglected novel which probably owes much to *Middlemarch*
and which makes a very explicit use of the landscape and art of Italy in
the education of the senses is George Gissing's *The Emancipated* where
Miriam, the Puritan heroine, is prepared for her rescue into love by the
sensual challenge of painting. Miriam, like Dorothea, changes her
views on art, but after Mallard, the Bohemian hero, realizes that she is
still alarmed by sculpture, there comes an interestingly explicit
dialogue between Mallard and another male character in which this is
expressly accounted for by the mention of nudity. Mallard rejects
Philistinism in a brave picture of a domestic circle where family
reading will involve 'no skipping or muttering or frank omissions' and
where 'casts of noble statues . . . shall stand freely about'. Journeys to
Italy in the last century presented special problems to Podsnaps and
others.

Middlemarch was written twenty years before *The Emancipated*, but
there are more than aesthetic implications in Dorothea's reaction to
Rome:

> Ruins and basilicas, palaces and colossi, set in the midst of a sordid present,
> where all that was living and warm-blooded seemed sunk in the deep
> degeneracy of a superstition divorced from reverence; the dimmer but yet
> eager Titanic life gazing and struggling on walls and ceilings; the long
> vistas of white forms whose marble eyes seemed to hold the monotonous
> light of an alien world: all this vast wreck of ambitious ideals, sensuous and
> spiritual, mixed confusedly with the signs of breathing forgetfulness and
> degradation, at first jarred her as with an electric shock, and then urged
> themselves on her with that ache belonging to a glut of confused ideas
> which check the flow of emotion. Forms both pale and glowing took
> possession of her young sense, and fixed themselves in her memory even
> when she was not thinking of them, preparing strange associations which
> remained through her after-years. (Chapter 20)

The vague sensual implications here, and elsewhere, are related to
her 'tumultous preoccupations with her personal lot', but not picked

up in the ensuing debate with Will. This debate is indeed not continued throughout the novel, and lacks the clearer suggestions to be found in James or Gissing, who both correlate aestheticism with sensuality in their Bohemian characters. Will's Bohemianism[6] and his political activity are both related clearly enough, by opposition, to Casaubon's class-values, to Bulstrode's respectable Nonconformity, and to Brooke's brand of Radicalism, but they are less convincingly related to each other. If the idyllic and romantic innocence of Will's love for Dorothea is one weakness, his movement from art to politics is another aspect of his character which does not ring quite true. There is a slackening in the novel with the disappearance of the aesthetic debate which has carried so much of the antithetical play of social and sexual values. Will's political activity alone has a slighter reference, leaving his role as lover conspicuous and inadequate. We can see why the debate drops out. Once Dorothea sees her error in marriage, once she sees exactly where her fanaticism and self-ignorance have led her, the aesthetic debate is no longer required, and there are other ways of showing her aversion to her marriage. Her problem ceases to be one of bewilderment and becomes one of clear vision. Once she sees her marriage for what it is - which takes some time - her problem is chiefly that of accepting it, and living with it in activity and not mere resentment and despair. Dorothea cannot find Connie Chatterley's solution, and has to live with her sterile marriage until her author provides the solution with Casaubon's death. Death often has to provide a substitute for divorce in Victorian fiction.

The weakness of the novel, and the weakness of Will Ladislaw, are located in his relationship with Dorothea. It is when they are together, physically or in thoughts of each other, that the romantic glow seems false and the childlike innocence implausible and inappropriate. In Will's other relations George Eliot can scarcely be accused of romantic softness, or of glossing over sexual problems. She keeps her heroine clear of any emotional conflict in her feeling for her husband and her feeling for Ladislaw, and here the moral scheme strikes the modern reader as being worked out at the expense of truthfulness. But although Will is shown as romantically rejoicing in the purity of Dorothea and in the impossibility of his love - 'What others might have called the futility of his passion, made an additional delight for his imagination'

6. George Eliot's use of art to express social value owes much, I suspect, to *Culture and Anarchy*.

(Chapter 47) – this is only a part of the analysis of Will's emotions. In his relations with Rosamond the 'romantic' glow is strikingly absent.

His rejection of Rosamond is violent, shocked and fearful, and he deals a hard blow to her strong sexual vanity when he tells her that he loves Dorothea: 'I never had a *preference* for her, any more than I have a preference for breathing. No other woman exists by the side of her' (Chapter 78). His declaration is a fine example of George Eliot's psychological truthfulness at its best, and it is neither exclusive nor obsessed, as declarations of love tend to be in many Victorian novels. George Eliot shows us the present, in William James's words, as more like a saddle-back than a razor-edge, for Will's confident rejection and words of love and loyalty are darkened by the shadow of the possible future. He looks over the edge of the present, though with pain and not with desire. Feeling, moral commitment, and time, are truthfully confused:

> When Lydgate spoke with desperate resignation of going to settle in London, and said with a faint smile, 'We shall have you again, old fellow', Will felt inexpressibly mournful, and said nothing. Rosamond had that morning entreated him to urge this step on Lydgate; and it seemed to him as if he were beholding in a magic panorama a future where he himself was sliding into that pleasureless yielding to the small solicitations of circumstance, which is a commoner history of perdition than any single momentous bargain.
>
> We are on a perilous margin when we begin to look passively at our future selves, and see our own figures led with dull consent into insipid misdoing and shabby achievement. (Chapter 79)

Those critics who find Will Ladislaw a weak romantic conception, the under-distanced product of the author's fantasy, might reflect on the fact that few Victorian heroes are shown as contemplating adultery, and so clearly and miserably, in the moment of passionate commitment to the pure heroine. George Eliot is restricted in her handling of the central relationship in this story, but her treatment of the relations of Will and Rosamond, like her treatment of the Casaubon marriage, shows not merely her ability to admit realities commonly left out of the novels of her time, but to recognize uncomfortable truths often evaded or denied outside literature.

Middlemarch is full of such uncomfortable admissions. There is Mary Garth's moment of fantasy about Farebrother, when she glimpses possibilities of a relationship which might have advantages which marriage with Fred, whom she loves, will lack. There is the extreme irritability of Dorothea, punctuated by her impulse to love, but not removed by it. There is the hard truth which Caroline learns in *Where Angels Fear to Tread*, 'that wicked people are capable of love', shown with much less explicitness and fuss in the extreme case of Bulstrode. This kind of acceptance of the mixture of things is not confined to the hard truth. There is the comforting truth that we recognize with Lydgate, that even in the moment of passion, 'some of us, with quick alternate vision, see beyond our infatuations, and even while we rave on the heights, behold the wide plain where our persistent self pauses and awaits us' (Chapter 15). If Will is capable of tolerating his vision of adultery with Rosamond, there is another shift of mobile moral category when Rosamond for one brief moment responds to Dorothea, or when Casaubon recognizes Dorothea's gesture of patient love. The recognition of human complexity blurs the clearly established moral categories, if temporarily, and can work in the interest of moral optimism and pessimism. George Eliot's choice of the tentative word 'meliorism' is clearly illustrated in her sense of the close neighbourhood, in human nature, of possibilities of the good and the bad.

Middlemarch, like most novels, has its formal simplifications and omissions which are determined by social and personal factors, but its expansiveness allows for many moments of surprising truth. We cannot say that there is a strict organization of category, of parallels and antitheses which breaks down in the free admission of change and complexity. In describing the form of the novel we have to confront not a neat symmetry and clear unity with some additional details which seem to be added on, like grace-notes (if we admire them) or as wasteful and arbitrary strokes (if we do not approve), but a highly complex and mobile pattern. But this does not mean that we are left with no standards with which to judge formal success, and in at least one respect, as I have tried to show, it is necessary to criticize *Middlemarch* for a lack of balance and completeness. The demand for unity and the demand for truth are here inseparable. The inadequacy of the word 'unity' is suggested in this attempt to analyse form and truth as inseparable constituents of the good novel, for it would be true to say that *Middlemarch* would be a satisfactory unity if the asexual presentation of Dorothea's relation with Will were matched by a similar omission in the presentation of her relation with Casaubon. Completeness seems to be a better word than unity, including as it does the formal concept of equality of strengths with the concept of truthfulness. Who would exchange the flawed *Middlemarch* with its omissions made conspicuous by its suggestive reticence, for a novel where truth were reduced and mere aesthetic balance retained?

1964

2

The Surface of the Novel:
Chapter 30 of *Middlemarch*

The whole has undoubtedly had a better press than the part, 'unity' as William James observed in *Pragmatism*, 'being more illustrious than variety'. There is no need to labour our recent concern with unity in theoretical and analytical criticism, but what is perhaps slightly surprising is the neglect of parts and details even in Victorian criticism. Variety is appreciated, and details are mentioned, but in too random and unsystematic a way to throw light on the qualities of randomness itself. Henry James, the most sophisticated contemporary critic of *Middlemarch*, never really explained what he had in mind when he called it 'a treasure-house of detail'. He made it clear why he considered it 'an indifferent whole', but the detail he praised rather than appreciated. My concern in this essay is with the detail.

I start with the assumption, more easily accepted than acted upon in critical practice, that some details are more local and more superficial than others. The objects, events, and images in this treasure-house of detail are not all equally profound, microcosmic, or symbolic. Some details lie casually on the surface, taking their place in a rendering of people, feelings, places and ideas. The casualness may be true or deceptive: some very unnoticeable details come to pick up colour and resonance from connections and repetitions, some do not; some arresting images do not belong to an elaborate network of metaphor and symbol. When we first move over the surface of the novel we tend to be less observant of relative complexity. When we come at a later stage to analyse the novel we may tend to treat details too evenly and uniformly as epitome and symbol, as surface details sinking the same kind and size of shaft into depths of generalization and association. The locally simple detail is frequently ignored or distorted.

One of the disadvantages of the critical tendency to over-generalize is its remoteness from reading experience. The preoccupation with the part as representative of the whole tends to back away from a fully responsive reading. In speaking of this kind of reading I should like to remain deliberately vague, hoping to include the experience of an unprofessional but sensitive and intelligent reader and a critic's more alert and distanced reading which has not passed quite beyond empathy into note-taking. The note-taking stage is, in my experience, particularly difficult in the novels of George Eliot. Even when searching or checking in a highly reductive way, to find images or phrases belonging to a series, I have found myself dragged back into an absorbed reading of the story and its characters, the analysis arrested. The same kind of reductive checking of similar details in Dickens and Meredith, for example, has been much easier and less interrupted, though the experience will obviously vary from critic to critic as well as from author to author.

This personal detail will perhaps serve to declare my own interest in structural analysis. It is in no anti-formal spirit that I set out to look at parts in their own right, not just as complex epitomes. I think it is indeed impossible to acknowledge the importance of local and simple effect without being interested in the total structure. Henry James said nothing of interest about the details in this treasure-house because he saw no figure in the carpet. Victorian criticism was fairly inept at appreciating wholes, and James was inept at appreciating wholes which did not resemble his own ideal of concentration and total relevance, so it is in fact only slightly surprising that neither part nor whole should have been properly discussed in nineteenth-century criticism. We have to perceive the structure of imagery in order to see what lies within the main series, what lies on the edge, and what seems to lie outside. I began with the intention of looking at the part rather than the organization but came to conclude that looking hard at the part also brings out other aspects of organization – the local configurations of scene and chapter which are also neglected in most structural analysis. I want to say that some parts are simple and not symbolic, but that other, larger units are more intricately and systematically organized than I had imagined. If we look hard at each detail in a particular chapter, for instance, we learn more about the structure of the chapter than if we simply hop from key image to key image, placing our details on the very large scaffolding of the novel 'as a whole'. It is with local form as well as with small detail that I am here concerned. My starting-point was the small detail. It is plain, I imagine, to most readers of Samuel Beckett, that there are sources of narrative power which lie outside the scheme of formal analysis. Beckett constantly disturbs any search for unity by his intransigent and opaque particulars, which strike us violently as baffling, disconnected, mysterious, odd, leading nowhere or certainly not where we had expected. More conventional novelists also convey more through individual moments of sensation and feeling than we allow, not because they are driven to express despair, doubt, nihilism or absurdity, but in simple apprehension of the quality of individual experiences. The ways in which Victorian novelists convey particular sensations and feelings are more easily subsumed and more easily lost in an account of 'unity' or 'theme' than the ways of Beckett, but I have a strong feeling, composed of reverence and of irreverence, that most critics of earlier fiction could learn something from getting lost for a while in *Watt*. Reading Beckett is a good way of losing old bearings. If we are sufficiently moved by a detail or event without placing it in a pattern or progression it is a short step to being moved by the surface of detail even if it does take its place in a coherent pattern and conventional progression. It is necessary to appreciate *Middlemarch* 'superficially' as well as symbolically.

When we sit down and read a novel for the first time, it is, I suggest, with a feeling for local life. When we look up and verbalize our responses, it is 'this bit' that we appreciate, rather than structure and symbol. It is true, of course, that an atomized response is characteristic of unawareness, of impressionistic selection, and of incomplete understanding, but it seems to be also true that at mature stages of reading, there are some simple effects that remain simples and not part of a total 'gestalt', not at least in any tidy or obvious way. Those simples that are seen to become symbolically expressive are often reduced and hardened in critical analysis, the first vivid impact lost and discarded in the process of perceiving and restating generalization. Formal analysis tends to strip off surface in order to reveal symbol, and in so doing may give a stark and unreal account both of the art of the novelist and of the pleasure of the reader. In an appreciation of the conceptual and ordered pattern of events in *Middlemarch* we should be able to recognize that the symbolic pressure is made through particular feeling and sensation. When Dorothea returns to her disenchanted room, to see its furniture shrunken, its tapestry ghostly, its volumes of polite literature 'more like immovable imitations of books', the outside uniformly white in snow and uniformly low-hanging in cloud, it is plain that her emotional disenchantment on her wedding journey is taking a symbolic shape. What one should also acknowledge, I believe, is the sensational quality of the symbol. The visual and physical pressures are strong, in imagery like 'the unlit transparency' but also in the primary rendering of actual landscape and objects. It really is winter, and winter really is like this. The room's faded charm is its individual quality, not there for purposes of equation through metaphor. The scene is made particularly vivid by the subtle incorporation of objects that in fact lie outside the symbolic equation: it is easy enough to render desolation, disillusionment and emotional sterility through the uniform land and sky, through the faded tapestry, the pale stag, and the dull polite books, but the picture includes also 'The bright fire of dry oak-boughs burning on the dogs' and George Eliot, as elsewhere, makes her generalization by insisting on what will not translate into the appropriate emotional tones, and observes that the bright fire 'seemed an incongruous renewal of life and glow'. One can of course schematize even this effect by suggesting that the bright fire with its renewal of life and glow attaches itself to Dorothea, and represents her future renewal and her potential resilience. One might well hasten to attach the 'pale stag' to Casaubon, but the haste would be rash. When one actually reads the passage, what is important and conspicuous is the full acknowledgment of the appearances of the room. The physical impact, too, of Dorothea's presence, as she comes in, glowing from her toilet, can be symbolically related to imagery and action elsewhere, but is important as *particular* vitality. Her vitality is checked and chilled in this room, it is superfluous in these neutral surroundings and George Eliot makes us feel this. This account is, true, part of a so-called 'undramatic' author's commentary, and it is perhaps still essential to say that the materials of fiction should not be too crudely divided into commentary and drama. The commentary in this novel achieves much of its concreteness and vitality through sensation. The force of the general representation is inseparable from the sensuous feeling of this and other moments. George Eliot's symbols are effective in this way, rendered in the vitality of such individual moments. When Dorothea feels the impact of the red hangings in St Peter's 'like a disease of the retina', an image which is clearly related to major themes, situations, and other images, it is essential that we first recognize the pressure of the surface: *this* sight, *this* physical impact. Once the dependence of symbol on particular sensation and feeling is admitted and described, it is easier to recognize and expect the unpurposive detail, whose effect is simply local and immediate. Structural criticism has to precede an analysis of detail, so that we can relax the effort to burrow below the surface, to generalize the particulars. The broad-meshed net is necessary but through it can escape the vitality and rhythm of actual response.

The innocent first reading is one in which we register ends rather than means. It moves from one impression to another, not in the big leaps of distanced analysis but in a continuous flow. Both the moments and the process too easily get forgotten. While we read we move through a continuum which is made up of many components, some emblematic, some simple, some transparent, some opaque, some arresting, some scarcely noticeable. Such a motion is less unlike the process of moving through an ordinary day's experience than formal analysis can afford to admit. A novel like *Middlemarch* surely makes sustained identification impossible, and ordinary egocentric living involves much observation and feeling of a vivid but detached kind. In life we are often on the fringe of personal involvement, responding to events, people and sensations in ways which can interrupt action, the dialogue of the mind with itself, and the streamy train of reverie. Much sensuous experience is not only fairly detached, but also fragmented and localized. Fiction offers us the inside of experience which is normally unavailable except in relation to ourselves, and it does so in a medium composed of a continuous but unpredictable set of stimulae. The continuum is certainly more ordered and lucid than the forms of actual living, but the most realistic fiction keeps some faith with the solid, discrete, and unpremeditated nature of actual experience through which we move while we wake. George Eliot presents the vivid impact of the present moment, and the process of *Middlemarch*, in authorial report and in dramatic scene, is a series of such moments, alive to sense and feeling, mutable and continuous.

The mutability is lost even in the kind of verbal analysis which both appreciates and classifies detail. The structural critic may stride over particular effects to draw an outline-map of scenes, images, symbols and persons, but the analyst of language crawls faithfully over the page. Perhaps he crawls so slowly that the word 'faithfully' becomes a little imprecise. His snail's pace may strike us as necessary, like the camera called in to determine the photo-finish, but as too slow to give a full record of the impressions of responsive reading. Reading speeds vary, but the linguist's pace is plainly much slower than the pace of the slowest reader, just as the image-tracker's seven-league boots move him much faster than the fastest reader. The snail's pace keeps us close to the word, to its nuances, associations, typicality, and particularity, but it has to stop for a long scrutiny which regards each part while unnatural arrest takes place, while moments are attenuated or cut in sections, while the cellular structure is revealed and the surface removed. The analyst of language moves slowly, the analyst of total structure moves fast: one gives an exaggerated close-up, the other a long-shot. Both standardize and falsify, neglecting the completeness, movement, and complexity of reading experience. Both lose touch with the surface of the novel.

Such distortion is necessary. To object would be to object to the microscope or the telescope, to methods and machinery which reveal and discover. I wish only to say that we need to admit the distortion, and not to pretend – as we sometimes tend to do – that an analysis of syntax or typical vocabulary or imagery is a total analysis. I do not agree with Spitzer[1] that one can get at the heart of the work of art from many directions. Direction and method may well determine result. I do not want to claim that a close look at detail will tell us much about total structure, but only that it takes its place in the investigation of the nature of fiction, and especially of the novels of George Eliot. I would however, claim that an analysis of the surface should counteract the necessary distortions of linguistic and formal analysis, despite the restrictions of its discovery.

There are, no doubt, many ways of organizing a study of detail. We might proceed by taking one or two striking and symbolic images and then looking at their local and particular effect in relation to and in distinction from their function as epitome. We might choose some striking but apparently isolated images, and look at them in their local context. We might take the presentation of minor characters or minor events, or look at 'background' material like description of places, objects, or gestures. I decided to choose a chapter and look at the various details it contains. I chose Chapter 30 at random since any part will do to represent the continuous surface of the novel. It so happens that it is an interestingly mixed chapter, more relaxed and heterogeneous than, say, Chapter 28, which presents Dorothea's disenchanted

---

1. *Linguistics and Literary History* (New York, 1962), p. 18.

awakening, or Chapter 80, which presents her vigil after she has seen Ladislaw with Rosamond, or Chapter 83, her last scene with Ladislaw. These are all scenes of crisis in action, but all also highly compressed and pregnant. Chapter 30 is also less blatantly and totally symbolic than other scenes which do not mark such crises of decision, but are plainly summaries and potent expressions of idea and feeling, like the scene in Rome where Casaubon takes Dorothea on a tour of significant works of art, or the scene of Featherstone's funeral, or the scene where Mary Garth and Rosamond look together in the mirror. Chapter 30 does however mark a very important stage in the action: in it Dorothea is told that Casaubon's illness is fatal and must change his way of life, and it ends with Brooke's decision to invite Ladislaw to Middlemarch. It is morally important, involving Dorothea's declaration of unselfish love and desire to help, her cry to Lydgate, and his warm but helpless response. It uses symbolism, but in a diffuse and unarresting way, as I shall try to show.

It is difficult to find a chapter in this novel which contains neither a crisis in action nor a crisis in vision. Although the texture is more dense and the epitomes less glaring than in the novels of Henry James, there is very little relaxation of tension in *Middlemarch*, very much less assertive comic play, casual filling-in and local colour than in the Victorian-Gothic structures of Dickens or Trollope. *Middlemarch* has its choric scenes of gossip and crowd-reaction presenting the character of the community, as in the scene of the auction, for instance, or the talk of the guests at Mr Brooke's second dinner-party, but these passages are parts, not whole chapters, and usually share the chapter with more crucial and symbolic material. Nearly all the chapters have the same form of organization. There is a dominance of dialogue and action, and this is usually grouped into one, two, or three scenes, separated and steadily bridged by exposition or report. There is a frequent change of scene, of persons, place, and time, but within a fairly restricted framework. We move from one room to another but very often stay in the same house, or move from one part of the day to another but with the same people. Sometimes time is indefinite, faintly and usefully blurred. There are some chapters which have very little exposition, but there are none with no scenic material. Exposition overlaps with scene, for it is dotted with scenic images, and is often vividly and immediately sensational, while scene is seldom purely dramatic but uses commentary and description as well as dialogue. George Eliot's typical chapter, in *Middlemarch*, achieves a loose unity, often with a local concentration of ideas, atmosphere and symbol, as well as of time and place. She often uses her varied and modulated materials to push on time and action *during* rather than *between* chapters.

Chapter 30 begins with a very brief scene between Casaubon, Lydgate, and Brooke, at Lowick, which is followed by the long and central scene between Lydgate and Dorothea. This modulates into a report of Dorothea's thoughts and doings after Lydgate goes, and eventually, after a longer and rather indeterminate interval, presents Brooke writing the crucial letter asking Ladislaw to come to Middlemarch. The very beginning of the chapter moves us on from the point at which we left Casaubon at the end of Chapter 29, when he had his first heart attack. In Chapter 30 we are told how 'in a few days' Casaubon 'began to recover his usual condition'. Then there follows an uncommitted past tense in which Lydgate sits and watches by the sick man, obviously on more than one occasion. At last a particular occasion is singled out to make the first scene, in which Lydgate advises Casaubon 'to be satisfied with moderate work, and to seek variety of relaxation'. Next comes another vague past-continuous tense, going back beyond the scene to various times when Dorothea had been present 'by her husband's side'. Lydgate 'had determined on speaking' to her, and when Brooke makes the suggestion as they stand 'outside the door' of Casaubon's sickroom, he decides to do it there and then, asks for her, is told that she is out, and waits until she comes in.

Then we reach the central scene, long, detailed, chronicling every word and movement and feeling, co-terminous with the whole experience and leaping over nothing. It deals very fully and faithfully with the present but has one or two moving flights into the past (Dorothea's 'if I had known') and into the future ('For years after Lydgate remembered'). Lydgate goes and time moves on slowly as Dorothea, still in the library, reads the letters on the writing-table and then ends by giving Ladislaw's letter to 'her uncle, who was still in the house'. He writes the reply to Will at Lowick and apparently on the same day: we are told that 'he went away without telling Dorothea what he had put into the letter, for she was engaged with her husband, and - in fact, these things were of no importance to her'.

Time moves on, at first quickly, then very slowly indeed, foreshortening nothing. Elsewhere this forward progression covers much larger periods, as for instance in the next chapter, though here George Eliot uses the same device of picking up exactly where we left off in the previous chapter and making the leap within the chapter. In Chapter 31 we begin on the evening of the same day and we have Lydgate off duty with Rosamond, to whom he talks about the day's happenings – in particular about Dorothea's reactions and the strong impression they have made on him. In the following section we return to the indefinite past-continuous, 'Aunt Bulstrode, for example, came a little oftener', and thus we proceed a fair distance in time. My chosen chapter provides less exciting examples of this form of movement than others, including its successor and its predecessor, but it does reveal what I think is the typical pattern: overlap or coincidence of time, foreshortening by a past-continuous, movement within rather than between the chapters, and smooth transition. This kind of structure is one of the things revealed by a close look at detail.

George Eliot's central events, however, take place within a unity of time and place, and local unity is another important feature of her manipulation of time. In this chapter there is great compression, and in others there is more variety and movement. Here we have three or four conversations and events, all involving the same people, and taking place on the same day in the same house. George Eliot's timing presents not only a slow and detailed chronicle but a very natural, almost casual, flow. Events and dialogue appear to be connected by proximity, not by careful selection. The transitions themselves are often unexciting, undramatic, and inconspicuous, and the structure is superficially episodic, not appearing as prologue, main action, and epilogue, as it usually does in a Jamesian chapter. This episodic and almost casual appearance *is* only an *appearance*, since of course selection is taking place all the time. The structure is governed by the relations of proximity, the appearance suggests the loose unity of 'everything that happened at Lowick on that day' but crisis is present at each stage. Casaubon is more or less told to give up his work. Dorothea is informed, and grasps the loss and desolation for him, and the awful helplessness involved for herself. The action leading up to Ladislaw's invitation, the beginning of another crisis, is all strictly necessary and plausible. The crises are all revealed and relaxed by the insensitivity of Brooke, whose suggestions of shuttlecock and Smollett and final almost automatic writing to Ladislaw are splendid instances of what Henry James called the fool's ministrations to the intensities of others. In the first scene Brooke lays bare the intensity he cannot grasp, in the last he shows himself as the only person sufficiently unaware to summon Ladislaw to Middlemarch. He is an ironically chosen maker of destinies. Action pushes ahead at each stage: most important, the reader looks ahead with the characters to the obscure future where Casaubon must relax, where Dorothea will try to help him. This is not just a matter of looking forward, since involved in the look is uncertainty and question: how can he possibly relax, how can she possibly help him? We are left too with the growing attachment of the book title, 'Waiting for Death', to Casaubon and Dorothea as well as to Featherstone.

The book title makes itself sharply felt in this and in the previous chapter, not simply in the subject of the grave illness but also in the emphasis on waiting in general. Looking at single chapters brings out this kind of local emphasis, which I should prefer not to call 'theme' or 'motif', since it scarcely reaches the level of generalization and is really not very conspicuous. However, it is there, and naturally enough. It plays its part in the feeling of the chapter, where watching and waiting are thoroughly explored through many aspects. We observe frustration, fear, anxiety, understanding, insensitivity, love, sympathy, and professional detachment blended with that good humane curiosity informed by imagination. It is not just the action of waiting with which many of the chapters in this book are concerned, but the feelings with which human beings may wait. Lydgate is the first to watch and wait, and we are carefully told that he does this in different ways: he uses the newly invented stethoscope but he also sits quietly by the patient and watches him. His quiet watchful patience, and his conversation with Casaubon about being satisfied with moderate work, are among those details of professional character which make us feel that Lydgate is a good doctor, and that being a good doctor has something to do with being a good man. A little later we are told that he also watched Dorothea as she watched and waited:

> . . . but she was usually by her husband's side, and the unaffected signs of intense anxiety in her face and voice about whatever touched his mind or health, made a drama which Lydgate was inclined to watch. He said to himself that he was only doing right in telling her the truth about her husband's probable future, but he certainly thought also that it would be interesting to talk confidentially with her. A medical man likes to make psychological observations, and sometimes in the pursuit of such studies is too easily tempted into momentous prophecy which life and death easily set at nought. Lydgate had often been satirical on this gratuitous prediction, and he meant now to be guarded.

Unlike so many watchers in *Middlemarch* Lydgate is concerned to observe Dorothea, to learn about her, to make no predictions about her marriage, feelings, and future. His imaginative tact in this scene shows the delicacy and tenderness in his character (ironically neighbouring the spots of commonness) which are to emerge so significantly in the shaping of his and Rosamond's destinies. This delicacy is brought out more plainly in the following chapter when he tells Rosamond how moved he has been by Mrs Casaubon's strong feeling for a man thirty years her senior, and when Rosamond's brashly conventional and ignorant rejoinder makes another strand in the web of irony. All the characters in Chapter 30 watch and wait. Casaubon has to wait, to try to 'relax', to pass time. Dorothea has to wait, feeling remorse, responsibility, and helpless love. She who has been a great collector of lame dogs, and has met the hardship of finding no lame dogs to nurse in Lowick, now finds herself faced by a great need and can do little. Here Dorothea finds a cause, but cannot battle. The only character who is not centrally involved in watching and waiting is Brooke, whose reactions frame the central scene, whose role here is his role elsewhere in the novel, that of the fool who rushes in but avoids all real commitment. His comments are benevolently maladroit. The ironies of his reference to toy-making (in this house and this family) and the words 'a little broad, but she may read anything now she's married, you know', are embedded in his flow of well-meaning futile chatter. This barely touches the real conversation between Casaubon and Lydgate, who have little enough in common but are both serious men, here brought together by their understanding of professional seriousness and values. Brooke never actually comes into real communication with anyone in this chapter, and his detachment shows at its beginning and at its end.

The decisive event which is comically and ironically framed by Brooke's detachment is Dorothea's reaction to Lydgate's bad news. The form of the chapter reflects in some ways the form of the novel. George Eliot has chosen to call this book, 'Waiting for Death', and to spend most of her imaginative energy showing the waiting done by Dorothea. Throughout the novel the significant departures from Dorothea's point of view – 'why always Dorothea?' – emphasize the normative function this performs. It is she, not Casaubon, who is central in the chapter and in the novel. There are withdrawals, opacities, and foreshortenings in the treatment of Casaubon, very few in the treatment of his wife.

Dorothea comes in to hear the tragic news, from her walk with Celia, radiant and glowing. The 'glow' has been established already, and represents her vitality and her physical youth and health. She comes in from the outside world of health and light, and these vital qualities recede as she goes into the library with Lydgate. What follows is the breaking of the news and a moral crisis. Dorothea does not consciously weigh and choose, as on some occasions before and after, but here spontaneously chooses love. She has stopped resenting, wanting, and criticizing, and she thinks of herself in relation to Casaubon only as a possible and frail source of help. She has broken with the past Dorothea who has usually spoken and acted from a sense of her own trials, has stopped listening to her own heartbeats and thinks only of the feeble ones of her husband.

If it is, in George Eliot's terms, an 'epoch' for her, so it is for Lydgate. There is yet another strand in the contrast between Dorothea and Rosamond: 'Women just like Dorothea had not entered into his traditions.' He makes no rash predictions, but waits with rare sensitive concern, then 'wonders' about her marriage. He is that unusually imaginative man who does not impose categories and who does not gossip. This is a novel where George Eliot is concerned to show how character fits (or does not fit) profession, and how profession shapes character. Lydgate is a fine example of the consistency and subtlety of her psychological and professional detail. Dorothea's spontaneous cry, 'Tell me what I can do' is to be picked up on several later occasions but here it marks very sharply that naked contact of real feelings which makes a crisis in many different kinds of relationship in the novels of George Eliot.[2] Here Dorothea's helplessness meets Lydgate's helplessness, but the communication makes a living and lasting relation between them.

In action and in feeling, the chapter is crucial, and we see George Eliot underpinning it to past and future, not just in the references to time but also in its symbolic associations. We pick up tones of light and dark from past scenes where Dorothea has stood out from Lowick, from past scenes in the library. We hear tones which are to resound and accumulate in later contrasts between Dorothea and Rosamond, and later scenes where Dorothea's moral energy is seen to be linked with the 'epoch' here marked. If we consider this chapter as 'an organ to the whole' there is abundant material: the recurring antithesis of light and

2. See *The Novels of George Eliot* (London, 1959), pp. 104-5.

darkness, the particular forms of Lowick and the dim room, the small windows, and the world outside, all connect with many interwoven series of images and symbols in the novel. So too does the cry 'Tell me what I can do', the significantly expressive use of clothes, and the image of a marble statue. I should like to take some of these familiar structural symbols and to bear in mind both their place in the pattern and their local impact in this chapter.

Only one of these images is made conspicuous by being generalized within the chapter. This is the contrast of darkness and light. I should add that it is also the image which has already been most fully developed before we meet it: in many small metaphors and in the elaborately expressive description of Lowick in Chapter 9, and in Ladislaw's violent conspicuous extensions. What additional impressions are made in Chapter 30? The library is dark, because it has been left shuttered: 'But there was light enough to read by from the narrow upper panes of the windows.' The light which is let in is described by a tiny arbitrary reminder of its scholarly occupier; it acts as preparation – if the room were too dark Dorothea would not be able to read Will's letter later on. But there is no immediate question of anyone wanting to read. The 'narrow' is also a detail which seems redundant in the immediate context, but makes a link with the associations already established in the early descriptions of 'small-windowed and melancholy-looking' Lowick. The first description of the library itself, ironically placed in the radiantly optimistic vision of Dorothea before her marriage, mentions 'dark book-shelves', 'curtains with colours subdued by time'. The small windows, birds-eye views on the walls, and Casaubon's revelation of his own 'sufficiently large' views of women, are contrasted with the bow-window of Dorothea's room, and make their small but unmistakable contribution to the details of visionary symbol. (Chapter 9 is full of imagery of views and darkness and light from which I have merely chosen a few examples.) We are told that Lowick is the kind of house 'that must have children, many flowers, open windows, and little vistas of bright things, to make it seem a joyous home', and we have also met Casaubon's lack of interest in houses for people to live in, and his preoccupation with narrow Egyptian dwellings, tombs and catacombs. The library itself is later to be dubbed 'a caticom' by Tantripp. It is obviously the centre of what Will Ladislaw calls the stone prison and the labyrinth, the room most darkened and subdued by Casaubon's sterile and isolated gloom. Will is of course associated with light and colour, Dorothea with open

windows and outward gaze, and the symbolic antithesis of light and
dark is to cover many implications of fertility and sterility, breadth and
narrowness, life and death – in value and expression natural and
common and not confined to this novel or this novelist. How do we
read the images of darkness here?

I do not think that we read them simply as expressive of Casaubon,
in spite of the details that attach them to the main pattern of value and
feeling. For instance, when Dorothea says to Lydgate, 'You will not
mind this sombre light', this is, I think, to be taken at its face-value,
with some appropriate and immediate associations with Lydgate's
habituation to the valley of the shadow of death. Death does, after all,
hang over this book. Her words about the sombre light stand also for
Dorothea's acceptance of gloom. But they are primarily an indication
of Dorothea's trusting, genuine casualness and informality in dealing
with Lydgate in this situation. We are told that Lydgate remembered
for years after Dorothea's cry of appeal: 'this cry from soul to soul,
without other consciousness than their moving with kindred natures in
the same embroiled medium, the same troublous fitfully-illuminated
life'. Here the dark and the light are generalized and stand for the
variegation of human life, and the darkness is that of suffering, death,
obscurity, the light perhaps of hope, joy, lucidity. The antithesis acts
like the image of the lighthouse in *To the Lighthouse* and does not belong
to the Casaubon/Ladislaw or the Casaubon/Dorothea contrast.
George Eliot has established a pattern to which she can refer briefly
and reliably, as in the easy association in the previous chapter between
Casaubon's mood and 'the foggy morning', but it is not a rigidly
insistent pattern, and the primary impressions of light and dark in
Chapter 30 are likely to be falsified if we are concerned only to pluck
them out of context.

Another image which we have already met before is the image of a
marble statue. When Lydgate tells Dorothea that Casaubon may live
for years, with great care, but that 'it is one of those cases in which
death is sometimes sudden', Dorothea's physical reactions and feelings
are described in this way:

> There was silence for a few moments, while Dorothea sat as if she had been
> turned to marble, though the life within her was so intense that her mind
> had never before swept in brief time over an equal range of scenes and
> motives.

The most famous of the images of marble lies ahead, in Farebrother's dictum, 'Character is not cut in marble,' to which Dorothea makes the incisive reply, 'Then it can be rescued and healed.' But we have met it before, in many forms, in many actual casts and statues. There are the incomprehensible casts brought home by Brooke, 'Whose severe classical nudities . . . were painfully inexplicable, staring into the midst of her Puritanic conceptions', and the marbles of Rome, on the wedding-journey, where 'the long vistas of white forms whose marble eyes seemed to hold the monotonous light of an alien world' make on Dorothea an indelible impression. (Incidentally, the accuracy of 'marble eyes' is another instance of a symbol working through precisely realized sensation – 'marble eyes' holding 'monotonous light' is a superb description.) In the Vatican, she 'walked with him through the stony avenue of inscriptions', and she passes on listlessly to the Museum, while he goes to the library. She stands in the hall, where Naumann and Will Ladislaw find her:

> . . . where the reclining Ariadne, then called the Cleopatra, lies in the marble voluptuousness of her beauty, the drapery folding around her with a petal-like ease and tenderness. They were just in time to see another figure standing against a pedestal near the reclining marble: a breathing blooming girl, whose form, not shamed by the Ariadne, was clad in Quakerish grey drapery. . . . (Chapter 19)

Naumann makes explicit what he sees as the antithesis:

> 'What do you think of that for a fine bit of antithesis?' said the German, searching in his friend's face for responding admiration. . . . 'There lies antique beauty, not corpse-like even in death, but arrested in the complete contentment of its sensuous perfection: and here stands beauty in its breathing life, with the consciousness of Christian centuries in its bosom.' (Chapter 19)

In each of these examples, and in Farebrother's metaphor too, marble is brought into contrast with life, not as a form of death but as something fixed, arrested, and unconscious. Look again at the metaphor of marble in Chapter 30, remembering that Rome and Naumann are mentioned in the chapter, so that resonance from the earlier scene might well be expected and effective:

There was silence for a few moments, while Dorothea sat as if she had been turned to marble, though the life within her was so intense that her mind had never before swept in brief time over an equal range of scenes and motives.

It is a purely local simile, though a few lines later we have a reminder of Dorothea's 'pallid immobility'. What are we to say about this image? The art/life antithesis is a very important subject in *Middlemarch*, not merely because it forms the ambience for the character and career of Ladislaw, but because George Eliot is discussing the nature of asceticism and the function of art, as belonging to the analysis of society, as continuing Arnold's exploration in *Culture and Anarchy*, as relevant to the problems of Dorothea's feelings and values. Many characters are defined and even tested by their response to art, and art itself is defined and even tested by its relevance and meaning for human beings of different kinds. If we were making an analysis of artistic images in the novel, we might well include the simile in Chapter 30, and observe that it belonged to the symbolism of aesthetic value. If, however, we look at it in its context, it adds absolutely nothing to that theme, except in automatic reminder, for what that is worth. What is vivid here in this image is the local expression of Dorothea's shocked stillness and pallor, contrasting with the racing pulse of thought and feeling within. It is an image which shows both the transformation of feeling and the contrast between outside appearance and inner passion. It is this local vividness that is primary, not the structural contribution to patterns of imagery and to dominant themes of life and art. The superficial impression is the most important one.

This is probably a fairly uncontroversial example. More difficult is the symbol of clothes in this chapter. Dorothea first comes in with Celia, 'both glowing from their struggle with the March wind'. When Lydgate speaks to Dorothea, as we have seen, she behaves quite spontaneously, and opens the library door, 'thinking of nothing at the moment but what he might have to say about Mr Casaubon'. She leaves her outdoor clothes on, but a little later takes off her bonnet and gloves. There is the comment that she throws off 'her bonnet and gloves, with an instinctive discarding of formality where a great question of destiny was concerned'. The informality extends also to her action of sitting down, and her 'Sit down' addressed to Lydgate. Her actions and attitudes are typically informal and unselfconscious, but here there is a particular pointing. This is not just Dorothea's usual genuine disregard for social formality, but the informality produced by the crisis, the simplicity and unaffected impatience that are the understandable response. This is also felt after Lydgate has broken the news about Casaubon's illness: 'Lydgate rose, and Dorothea mechanically rose at the same time, unclasping her cloak and throwing it off as if it stifled her.' Here we go beyond the unstudied impatience and spontaneity of the earlier detail: this action of throwing off the cloak is also expressive of violent feeling. In this chapter George Eliot uses Dorothea's clothes not as symbols of value but as changing and highly expressive properties. Clothes are certainly important symbols in this novel, as associated with Dorothea, Celia, Rosamond and Mrs Bulstrode, and in larger traditional ways which draw on the aesthetic and social values with which history has invested clothing, ways which have been emphasized by Swift and Carlyle. People's attitudes to their clothes symbolize surface and appearance, vanity, exhibitionism, flaunting of sex, of class, over-decorativeness, materialism, extravagance and so on. There are local nuances: Dorothea does not 'deck' herself, Celia and Rosamond do, Dorothea changes from deeper mourning to light, Mrs Bulstrode takes off her ornaments.[3] It is attitudes to clothes, rather than the actual clothes, which are important. This scene in Chapter 30 is particularly interesting because in it nothing at all is said about what the clothes are like. It is what is done with them that matters. Dorothea's informal throwing off her garments is in perfect keeping with her neglect of appearances, conventions, propriety, and vanity. It is in perfect keeping with her relationship with Lydgate. And it is in perfect keeping with the grave crisis, when polite formality is too slow and too fussy for deep feeling. Ceremony has broken down. We grasp the expression of these values, but grasp also that the actual gestures are expressive of strong feeling, of impatience, urgency, desire to break out and breathe or do something, need for relief, action, getting down to essentials – this unwieldy list comprises many reactions we might lump together under the reaction from frustration or tension. The last casting off of the cloak is attached to the other gestures and movements in the chapter, and this again is part of the continuum we are likely to ignore and break up if we jump from image to image. Dorothea's attitude to her clothes belongs to the whole presentation of her person and personality and character in this place at this time.

 She sets the tone with 'You will not mind this sombre light.' When

3. See *The Novels of George Eliot*, op. cit., p. 104.

she addresses Lydgate she is 'standing in the middle of the room' and she does not invite him to sit down for some little time. When she does, she speaks rather abruptly. She begs him to speak plainly, she reacts quickly, her words come out 'like a cry'. The word 'quick' is used of her 'ear', which detects significance in the doctor's tone of voice, and of her 'prevision' of Casaubon's wretchedness. Her voice is described in detail: it is imploring, like a cry, then low, then has 'a childlike despondency' while she actually cries, and her last appeal to Lydgate, 'Think what I can do' is made 'with a sob'. George Eliot is following the detail of voice and movement: we know what Dorothea sounded like, where she stood or sat, how she moved or stayed motionless. We know too how each sound and movement came from the last. The movement of feeling, so much more detailed here than in the framework which begins and ends the chapter, is composed of simple straightforward non-figurative description as well as of metaphors. The metaphor of the marble statue and the cry of 'soul to soul' are placed in a very precise and physical record of movement and speech, some of which is expressive, some apparently there to make a natural flow of acting and doing. People talk, take off their outdoor clothes, come in from walks, notice or do not notice their surroundings, sit down and stand up. Rooms have been changed or left alone since the last time we saw them. The continuum is natural, but it allows for climax. The ordinary actions stop when Dorothea makes her cry for sympathy, which comes quite naturally out of all that has gone before, but strikes the reader, like Lydgate, as a baring of feeling in a crisis presented in decorous and far from unusual terms: after all, people do keep doctors standing up while they put their questions, and do weep in their presence.

After Lydgate goes, the natural track of movement continues, variously and fluently. Although she is alone, she stops crying at the thought that she must keep her tears from Casaubon. She goes to the table, looks at the letters, and reacts to Will's outpoured 'young vivacity' by seeing that it is 'impossible to read' it at that time. The very lack of comment is masterly. Nothing is said about her feelings, she just sees what kind of letter it is and sees that it has nothing to do with the here-and-now. She passes on to give the other letter, addressed to Casaubon, to her uncle. Even the ironical introduction of 'her want of sturdy neutral delight in things as they were', as Will sees it and puts it, meets the reader unemphatically, with no need for comment on the present crisis which has made everything different, and rendered their debate in Rome theoretic and very far away. It is a most beautiful showing of her control and her commitment, unemphatic and restrained in form as in content.

This central scene is composed of many incidents, tones, and narrative methods. The author's commentary, for instance, is often dramatically appropriate, as in the comments on Lydgate's watching or his withdrawal from rash prediction, or on Dorothea's marble appearance and passionate feeling, or on the process of Brooke's decision to ask Will to Middlemarch, made less by Brooke than by his pen: none of these comments, if we reflect, could have been dramatized or expressed directly through character. The author's voice here, as so often in the later novels, is broken up, and is used functionally, to present and punctuate the dramatic scene. It does not hold up movement but facilitates it, filling in the movement backward or forward in time, standing back and staying silent, condensing urgent feeling into an image, or making a nice stroke of *erlebte Rede*,[4] as in the very last sentence in which Brooke goes away without telling Dorothea what he had 'put into the letter' since 'she was engaged with her husband, and – in fact, these things were of no importance to her'. The many small steps which we take here are made up of some material we call 'dramatic' and some material we tend to call 'undramatic'. My contention is that once we see the continuity and movement, especially of feeling, these divisions seem inappropriate. Voice of author and of characters blend in a naturally moving sequence which gives even to a scene of crisis the appearance and motion of life. The flow attaches us to the parts rather than to the whole, and makes a whole of a stanzaic unit, of the chapter itself.

In this chapter, carefully organized into a fluent but intricate three-part unit, George Eliot has concentrated on crisis and feeling. This is how certain people react to dying, their own and other people's. The detached attitudes of Brooke and Lydgate are delicately observed, and a spectrum of feeling is organized, though Casaubon's unanalysed response makes a stubbornly opaque streak, here as elsewhere. It is one of George Eliot's beautiful movements of decorum, that she withholds the internal commentary of Casaubon, and makes his questions and frustrated comments represent feeling, while the reactions of Lydgate and Dorothea are made fully available to us. She

4. See Derek Oldfield's discussion of this technique in *Middlemarch: Critical Approaches to the Novel* (ed. Barbara Hardy, London, 1967), pp. 81-4.

is in a later chapter (42) to follow Casaubon to 'the dark river-brink' in one of the most moving, solemn, and pathetically accurate movements of feeling and reflection, but as yet he is literally the patient, not knowing the implications of Lydgate's watching, which he is later most courteously to praise for its 'scrupulous care', in a phrase which takes us back to this chapter of watching.

Other scenes are more strikingly subtle and novel in their psychological analysis, for here George Eliot is relying on impressions already built-up and consolidated, though we should notice the new stroke of Lydgate's relationship with Casaubon, forming over the obtuse chatter of Brooke, and that of Lydgate's developing relationship with Dorothea. Both strokes add to character, and are also very important in the creation of local feeling. A character created by George Eliot is made up not only of a carefully arranged sequence of moral choices but also of a variety of feelings. Those feelings are very important in our experience of characters as 'real'. They are not always arranged in the carefully sequential pattern of the moral crisis. For instance, once Lydgate has chosen to vote for Tyke rather than Farebrother, we recognize his susceptibility to the varied pressures of Middlemarch, and we can all eventually nod wisely when he makes a similar choice in the matter of Raffles's death. In this kind of regular development the characters in the novel are much more schematic and steady than real people. But perhaps we accept this kind of moral schematism because it is truthfully presented in the solid and directly expressive forms of feeling. It is not true that Lydgate's strong feeling for Dorothea in Chapter 30 changes anything he does: in the very next chapter we see the fatal ease with which he can absorb, or scarcely notice, Rosamond's prettily and dishonestly phrased words about Dorothea and Casaubon. But for the reader he is changed: we have felt, not just been told, that those spots of commonness are really spots in a very delicate and responsive substance, because we have felt his reactions to Casaubon and to Dorothea. This is the full response to character, and it should be made plain that it is a response to feeling which exists in its own right, as it does perhaps most lucidly and movingly in poems which do not give elaborate histories and causalities. In discussing plot and theme and character, we often overlook feeling, but in discussing local detail we stay close to the track of feeling.

When we encounter these characters subsequently, it is with the felt experience behind us. This seems to be important to the total life of the novel. If we compare the scenes of feeling involving Romola and

Daniel Deronda, for instance, they will, I suggest, show themselves as lacking in this kind of continuous creation, where all creatures respond and move fully, not only in major ways, plainly functional and purposive, but with the implication of total availability. The gestures and tones of Romola and Daniel are fewer and cruder, more intensively symbolic. There is a lack of the kind of detail I have mentioned here, which is so marvellously typical of *Middlemarch*. I cannot substantiate this kind of comparison in a short study nor can I substantiate what I have called the typicality of this kind of detail. As I said earlier, this is a crucial scene, and there are many scenes in the novel where the detail is looser and freer, in feeling, gesture, and sensuousness. This scene contains few objects, for instance. Some of the scenes in Dorothea's room, or in Mrs Garth's kitchen, or in the Lydgates' drawing-room, are filled with prolific examples of the detail which is neither totally symbolic nor painstakingly naturalistic, but which has a superficial vividness which plays a strong part in the life of the novel. The surface is not evenly transparent, the detail sometimes does and sometimes does not create an epitome. The surface is continuous, made up of a complex structure which our larger analysis can only touch on. The divisions in that continuity are many, and the units within book and chapter cannot be appreciated unless we look at them in a close and individual way. It is the detail of sense and feeling, the continuous flow, and the subtle organization within chapters, which I have tried to bring out in this examination of Chapter 30 as a specimen of the neglected surface of the novel.

1967

3

The Mill on the Floss

I take it that *The Mill on the Floss* is the novel most visibly close
to George Eliot's life. As in many novels loosely classed as autobiographical, this closeness to life has advantages and disadvantages,
and shows itself in various ways. It creates the loving and seemingly
accurate chronicle of actual events; the successfully externalized
conscious and unconscious disguise and transformation; and the glib,
inventive fantasy of dreaming and wishing. I am separating these
processes for the purpose of announcing my analysis, but the novel
blurs the edges and blends the kinds. It is a novel where the author is
recalling the landscape and feelings of her childhood, in ways both
gratifyingly indulgent and rationally analytic. As she dwells on the
relationship between a brother and sister we can discern an understandable and undisfiguring nostalgia; a need to explain and justify in
concretely imagined terms; and the falsifying pressures of a wish-
fulfilling reconciliation. Where she modifies experience, in order to
hide or reveal, we can find resemblance with difference: she brings out
order and meaning, discovers and argues her case, by summoning
variety and antithesis, by trying out her particular conclusions and
experience in the generalizing process of ordered invention, which
accumulates and patterns fresh particulars. The submission to pressures
of wishing and dreaming shows itself in a failure to particularize, in a
movement away from the scrupulous testing process into simplifications
of symbol and plot. *The Mill on the Floss* is especially interesting as a
novel because it sets up an expressive form which betrays itself, and

because in so doing reveals the varying relationships between the work of art and the materials of life.

The uneven and complex relation between the work of art and its sources – which we can usually only guess at – is perhaps most clearly introduced by taking a look at some similar cases in the art of fiction. Like *The Mill on the Floss*, Charlotte Brontë's *Jane Eyre* and Dickens's *David Copperfield* also combine a strongly contrasted particularity with an uncontrolled submission to fantasy. Not surprisingly, all three novels sharply betray this submissiveness in the testing ground where the novelist solves his problems and reaches his conclusions – at the end of the story. At the end of novels of education the novelist stands back and defines the nature and meaning of the process, the development, the *Bildung*. His conclusion is a conclusion in both senses: an end and an arrival at meaning. Behind such problem-solving lies the more or less invisible pressure of the artist's personal problems, and it is characteristic of such mid-Victorian novels that they should arrive at conclusions which are affirmative, reconciliatory, and final. Charlotte Brontë, Dickens, and George Eliot do not exactly create simple fables for their time, but achieve affirmation and finality by crushing a complex experience into narrow simplifications of plot and symbolism. The endings of all three novels are religious or quasi-religious, and are marked by a strong emotional crescendo which betrays the uncontrolled urge to reach an end. They make an under-distanced appeal which can command the assent of tears or the dissent of stony recognition – or both. Charlotte Brontë kills off Rochester's mad wife, and brings him through the fire, mutilated and penitent, to Jane's arms: there is the triumphant reconciliation after all that pain, and the triumphant discovery of meaning. Dickens kills off David's child-wife, Dora, and brings him through visionary experience in the high and lonely Alps to Agnes's arms: there is the triumphant reconciliation after all that pain, and the triumphant discovery of meaning. George Eliot kills off Tom and Maggie, bringing them through the waters of the flood into each other's arms: there is the triumphant feeling after all that pain, and the triumphant discovery of meaning. Each novel ends with a double Eureka feeling: the final embrace of the loved-one and the vision of meaning. The blinded Rochester now sees the pattern in his life and Jane's; David ceases to be metaphorically 'blind, blind, blind'; and Tom Tulliver at last sees (and Maggie sees that he sees) 'the depths in life, that had lain beyond his vision which he had fancied so keen and clear'. The imagery of blindness and good vision is there in each novel.

In *Jane Eyre* and *David Copperfield* the fantasy runs as a vivid unreal thread through the novel, and is particularly associated with Rochester and Agnes. In both novels there is an increase in authorial magic at the end, but the wish-fulfilment also shapes a kind of character who will make for that end, fantastically idealized and simplified. In *The Mill on the Floss* there is no such character – not even Maggie – and the drop, or rise, into the heights of the false Sublime and a false catharsis is therefore especially violent. All three novels show a controlled and controlling particularity *and* an abrupt movement into unparticularized consolations and conclusions. Whether we see the novel as an imitation of reality or as an expressive form creating virtual experience, it seems right to speak of partial failure. Each novel seems to fail for a good reason: the solutions and conclusions are so visibly needed by the artist, not by the tale. Each novel is an instance of technique acting, not as discovery, but as obscuring fantasy.

Perhaps all we can really say about autobiographical novels is that they are novels which reveal this connection between the life-need and the completed form. Novels which seem more objectified are often novels which we simply cannot check against biographical data. The weakness in Coleridge's distinction between the Shakespearian or Spinozan imagination which becomes all things and the Miltonic imagination which brings all things into itself, or in Keats's distinction between the chameleon poet and the Wordsworthian or egotistical Sublime, is their reliance on the distinction between an artist's life about which little is known and an artist's life about which a great deal is known. We happen to be in a position to say that Charlotte's sexual and social experiences may well explain her need for a sexual and religious solution like the one provided by the conclusion to *Jane Eyre*, to see that Dickens's marriage encouraged fantasy, and to see that George Eliot's break with family and society shaped the form and content of her solution. The actual prayers of Jane, David, and Maggie all correspond closely with the needs of their authors, and the needs produce the facile sublimity of the answers. But we do not find that the novel is totally falsified, wholly shaped by the fantasy of wishing and dreaming: each novel challenges the notion of an evenly objectified and totally realized work of art.

Each novel happens not only to betray wish-fulfilment, but to discuss it. If there is the self-indulgence of fantasy here, it is not the gross indulgence of ignorant artists, but the fine indulgence of intelligent artists, alive to the nature and dangers of romantic fantasy.

Dickens creates a comic inflation and deflation of the fantasy and romantic imagery of David's immature loves. Charlotte Brontë has an intense analysis of the nature and the origin of fantasy in Jane's deprivation and ennui before she meets Rochester. George Eliot discusses and dramatizes Maggie's needs for various opiates – in daydreams, literature, religion, and personal relationships. The existence of this discussion of fantasy could mean no more than the unsurprising combination of rational insight with irrational blindness, but it happens also to be accompanied by a very strenuous effort to shape experience, to distinguish between dreaming and waking, and to break with the simplifications and stereotypes of fantasy.

The Mill on the Floss explores the realities of character and event by exposing human beings to life without opiate, but in the end it succumbs itself, as a work of art, to the kind of unreality it has been criticizing. The process by which it succumbs is not a simple one. I do not see the novel in terms of a polarity of soft dream and hard, daylight experience. There is a toughness and openness, a kind of pragmatism which shows itself especially in a movement away from heavy plotting and shaping of character development; there is a successful and transforming use of the personal experience of religious crisis and conversion; there is a successfully particularized though more personally interested transformation of George Eliot's sexual crisis; and there is a final unsuccessful resort to solution by fantasy. I want to take these four aspects of the novel in reverse order, beginning at the end.

The case against the concluding Providential fantasy has perhaps been won too easily, whether by Henry James or Joan Bennett or Dr Leavis, who have all written finely but not lengthily on the subject. I assume that all readers of George Eliot will agree on the importance of a sense of unity and continuity in her life and her novels. The two major crises of her life, the one a crisis of belief and the other a crisis of ethical choice, and many less climactic occasions of depression and anxiety, were all marked by a frightening sense of dislocation and loss of identity. Behind the loving chronicle of childhood and the fantastic problem-solving in The Mill on the Floss lies the estrangement from her early past. The breach with her brother Isaac was not mended until 1880, when she married John Cross, and received the famous letter of forgiveness:

I have much pleasure in availing myself of the present opportunity to break the long silence which has existed between us.

To which she replied:

It was a great joy to me to have your kind words of sympathy, for our long silence has never broken the affection for you which began when we were little ones.[1]

It is no act of wild speculation which finds personal pressures at work in the childhood scenes of *The Mill on the Floss*, in the nostalgic and analytic treatment of brother and sister, in some aspects of Tom's character, and in the subject of the break and the reconciliation. The emotional centrality of the relationship is significant, and so is the intensity of the final embrace – 'In their death they were not divided'.

The conclusion still needs to be closely evaluated. We can only defend it, I think, on very restricted aesthetic grounds. We may say that the novel's ending is prepared from its beginning, in the doom-laden references to death by drowning, in the river-imagery, and in the threads of pagan and Christian lore that run through the reminiscences of past floods, the legend of St Ogg and the folk-superstition that 'when the mill changes hands, the river's angry'. George Eliot is all too plainly preparing for her dénouement. This is what Henry James had to say about the dénouement in his essay, 'The Novels of George Eliot', in *The Atlantic Monthly*, October 1866:

The dénouement shocks the reader most painfully. Nothing has prepared him for it; the story does not move towards it; it casts no shadow before it.

James is wrong about nothing preparing us, wrong too about no shadow being cast, but he is quite right to say that 'the story does not move towards it'. Almost everything moves except the story. Even the characters are ingeniously though artificially involved in the pre-echoes as Mrs Tulliver fretfully worries about her children being brought home drowned, or about Maggie tumbling in some day, and as Philip teases Maggie about selling her soul to the ghostly boatman

1. *Letters*, VII, pp. 280 and 287.

on the Floss. The foreshadowings strike us as artificial because they are uninvolved with action. There is the sense of a restless preparation in rhetoric which does not move dynamically with events and characters. Mrs Tulliver's nagging worries attach themselves clearly enough to the Maggie who pushes Lucy into the mud, but scarcely to the flood and the heroic rescue. If Maggie were to fall in carelessly, or throw herself in recklessly, there would be a relation between prolepsis and action. Or if those legends about the river and the great set-piece descriptions of its transiently tamed powers were part of a presentation of man at work in and against Nature, there could have been such a relation. But such descriptions remain figures in the frame, not in the picture. The imagery that Henry James uses of Isabel Archer not only hints at danger, but is fully related to the action: Ralph does something very like putting wind in her sails, and the audacity, responsibility, freedom, and danger involved in the figure are fully worked out in event and character. The animation that Thomas Hardy bestows on Nature is revealed throughout *The Return of the Native* or *Far from the Madding Crowd*, and Nature and Man are related at every turn of the action. But the river-imagery and the descriptions of Nature in *The Mill on the Floss* expose instead of disguising those gaps in the action. Most of the hints and images and descriptions could be cut without much loss of lucidity; Tulliver is a marvellous study in reduced pride and love and temper, but not the hero or victim of a story of man against nature. The novel has a unity in imagery, and this has a strong mnemonic force, but it does not prepare us for the part played by the river in reaching the conclusion and solving the problem. What we are prepared for is the struggle between the energetic human spirit and a limited and limiting society: such struggles are not settled by floods.

The flood is the Providence of the novel. It would not be quite true to say that religion is rushed in at the end without being earlier involved with action and character. The community of St Ogg's is most carefully analysed as a mixed pagan and Christian society, and a very large number of the characters are placed in religious tradition, belief, and feeling. Maggie's religious experience is central to the novel, but I do not think it prepares us for the miraculous aura, however delicately adjusted, which surrounds her in the last pages. It is interesting that a scholar who has made a special study of George Eliot's treatment of religion, Martin J. Svaglic, observes that 'Maggie and Dorothea, in their moments of greatest crisis, do not pray.' Gordon Haight rightly corrects him about Maggie (in a footnote to the reprinted article in *A Century of George Eliot Criticism*). Yet there is a sense, I think, in which we can see why Svaglic can say that Maggie, like Dorothea, does not pray. Her prayer is in no way formal, her God can merge into the God of our anguished cries to no God, her voice is not raised to be heard – only compare her prayer with Jane Eyre's. But he is wrong, for the vague appeal is instantly answered, pat, like the prayers in *Jane Eyre*, with comfort and solution. When she is faced with a crisis of decision (which is what Svaglic may have meant by her moment of greatest crisis), she does not make her decision by referring to any laws or values that are not human. Dorothea's critics knew very well that her decisions and values were revealingly humane, void of supernatural reference, and Maggie feels, thinks, and chooses in the same humanly reliant way. True, there is the conversion by the aid of Thomas à Kempis, but there is absolutely nothing in it that does not pertain to George Eliot's Feuerbachian creed. Here is the third Positive, Duty, which she allowed to Myers in the garden of Trinity, Cambridge, but no trace of the first two, God and Immortality. If we look carefully, we see that George Eliot makes the religious conversion insistently human: the value is that of selflessness; there is a conversion of ethic, not of belief. George Eliot's emphasis is on the human agents, on Thomas himself, but also on the conveying human agent, whose 'hand' made the marginal marks and helped Maggie read and emphasize. There may be some slight trace of her own Evangelicalism in Maggie's adolescent histrionics, and it is, of course, interesting that this is the part of the conversion that is criticized and rejected. But the chief emphasis is human, though by this stage George Eliot could take and indeed represent human duty and fellowship in a solvent of religious symbolism and association. What is emphasized in the conversion is the human element, but what is emphasized at the end in the final chapter, despite the tactful and tactical ambiguities of 'almost miraculous divinely-protected effort, and the dream of the Virgin in the boat, is the superhuman:

Her soul went out to the Unseen Pity that would be with her to the end. Surely there was something being taught her by this experience of great need; and she must be learning a secret of human tenderness and long-suffering, that the less erring could hardly know? 'O God, if my life is to be long, let me live to bless and comfort—'

At that moment Maggie felt a startling sensation of sudden cold about her knees and feet: it was water flowing under her.

What turns a great psychological novel into a Providence novel at the end is not simply this magical coincidence of prayer and answer in the 'water flowing under her': it is the appearance of exactly the wrong kind of problem-solving. Throughout the novel there have been two chief implications in the action and relationships – implications which at times rise into explicit formulation: one, the Novalis aphorism that 'character is destiny', which is qualified by George Eliot's words 'But not the whole of our destiny', emphasizing not only social determinism and large human influence, but the sheer chanciness of life; the other, that 'The highest "calling and election" is to do without opium',[2] a belief central to George Eliot's rejection of Christianity, which remained with her all her life, which is fully and strongly borne out in all her novels, and which seems to be the standard by which maturity is described and measured in The Mill on the Floss. Maggie's 'process' is more complex than any extracted pattern, but one of the strands in the extracted pattern must be her rejection of the opiates of daydream, literature, and religion. When she is able to make no dream-worlds any more, and when literary dream-worlds fail her, she finds a new and subtly effective drug in the religion of self-denial. Philip – and the novel's course – make it plain to her that she is now substituting another harder fantasy for the older fragile ones. She acts her renunciations, and Philip prophesies, while the novel's course reveals that she has fallen into the fantasy of choosing renunciations – little ones that will not hurt too much. The final experience is the lengthy painfulness of renunciation, and George Eliot takes great pains to show this, even in the last foreshortened book of the novel, by making Maggie try to live with the renunciation, and by making her go through it a second time. She dramatizes most movingly the difference between giving up passion in passion and giving it up in deprivation. Laurence Lerner, in The Truthtellers, seems to me to be right off the track when he says that the second renunciation is theoretic, because the actual presences of the victims have gone. The second renunciation is, on the contrary, a proof of the untheoretic nature of her choice: she has lived with it. Imagination can people Maggie's world with her victims, just as it makes her 'hear' Stephen's voice as she reads his letter – a true

2. Letters, III, p. 366.

and acute touch about the physiological pressures of imagination. George Eliot is showing implicitly what she made Philip tell Maggie explicitly - that renunciation hurts, that pain is unpleasant, that deprivation is destructive. My reason for making such an elaborate attack on the end of this novel is not a high regard for aesthetic unity and distress over an unprepared ending; it is an objection to the bad faith that contrasts so strongly with the authenticity of everything that comes before. George Eliot insists that renunciation does not make you feel noble and striking and secure, but empties life, depresses the spirit, and disrupts a sense of meaning. Little renunciations and sacrifices, such as doing plain sewing and being nice to your mother, are enjoyable because painless, and are no kind of rehearsal for the real thing. George Eliot makes this point as toughly as James was later to do in *The Portrait of a Lady*, but she then goes back on it, softens it, tacks on the least appropriate conclusion. She gives Maggie rewards and triumphs after all, not just by answering the despairing prayer, but by taking her to Tom and allowing her, before they drown together, to see that change of vision in his eyes. The novel has been about living without fantasy and opiate, and ends with a combination of several strong fantasies. There is the fantasy of death, the fantasy of reconciliation, and the fantasy of being finally righted and understood. Henry James's suggestion that Maggie might call back Stephen was nowhere within range of the novel's contingencies: Maggie could either have thrown herself into the river or carried on, and the point which the whole novel had been sharpening would then have been driven against the reader's breast.

I do not see this novel as sharply divided into 'realism' and fantasy. We can see the way the end undermines the strength of the analysis of moral choice, and we can see personal reasons behind the shift into such blatant fantasy. In the rest of the novel there are other visible personal pressures at work, which are far from being destructive and falsifying. If the final fantasy is a response to her personal break with the past and her brother, so the crisis of renunciation seems also to be propelled by a personal need. There is some relation, at each stage in the novel, between a great personal need and the artistic shaping. The renunciation of Stephen seems to me to be a typical and successful instance of personal problem-solving: in it George Eliot transfers the ethical issues involved in her own sexual choice to a different situation which will generalize, justify, and explain. George Eliot violently and predictably rejected the renunciation in *Jane Eyre* - a renunciation made in the interests of 'a diabolical law which chains a man soul and body to a putrefying carcase'.[3] *The Mill on the Floss* reverses the situation in *Jane Eyre* in a way that can be seen as an argument with Charlotte Brontë. But I would scarcely wish to put it so theoretically. George Eliot went to live with Lewes in what was technically an adulterous union; her heroine refuses to marry a man who is unofficially engaged. George Eliot is not affecting moral delicacy (as some hostile readers thought) but inventing a situation which brings out her own defence, which eliminates all the personal particulars and invents new ones which generalize her argument. In her own case there is the breaking of a social, moral and religious 'law'; in Maggie's case nothing approaching law or contract. In her own case there are no human victims, but George Eliot's own freedom and isolation, and Lewes's already wrecked relationship with his unfaithful wife; in Maggie's case there are two human beings, Lucy and Philip, out of whose painful deprivation would be taken her joy. The novel's apologia says, in effect: had human ties been involved, I would not even have broken the faintest commitment; since there were none, I was prepared to break social laws and commandments. Here is another personal pressure shaping the novel, but it works lucidly, logically and imaginatively: the argument is sharpened as artistic argument must be, through particulars of feeling and relationship.

George Eliot's presentation of sexual-ethical choice is very far from being disinterested, but it in no way distorts the solidity and effective particularity of the novel. The same may be said for her presentation of religious conversion. Here we have something which seems also to have a source in personal experience, though George Eliot's change of faith is probably further 'behind' Maggie Tulliver's conversion than her sexual choice lies 'behind' Maggie's. At this point in the novel, we are midway between invention and experience, and it is, of course, true that crises of decision and vision which are to be found in most of the other novels can also be so described. Romola's decision to reject Savonarola's rigid doctrine for her human ethic is very close to George Eliot's arguments for Maggie's renunciation, but the situation in which Maggie is placed is plainly closer to personal experience. There is the continuity and stability of the ethic: her moral arguments are not purely pragmatic, and her reasons for living with Lewes are perfectly compatible with her humanist ethic as reasons, not as rationalizations.

3. *Letters*, I, p. 268.

But just as the inventions are closer to the personal crises elsewhere, so they are, I think, in the religious crisis. Once again there is involvement, but no loss of clarity. The artist seems to be using invention in order to see experience straight, or in order to validate fantasy. Maggie's conversion to an ethic of love and sacrifice draws on George Eliot's own conversion from Christianity. As in *Silas Marner*, the religion to which she gives fullest sympathy is a religion of personal love, so that it is not true to say that experience is reversed. Characteristic of her own experience is the sense of false conversion and the restoration to continuity: George Eliot dramatized her 'conversion' in much the way Maggie does, by refusing to go to church, by taking the risk of a break with her father. Afterwards came not only a loving need to compromise and conform, but a tolerance which refused to draw lines between right and wrong belief. The element of egoism in Maggie's altruism, of new fantasy in her apparent rejection of fantasy, makes the presentation psychologically alive and morally interesting.

But this interestingness depends on much more than the ability to criticize and generalize moral experience. It depends also on the imaginative representation of ethics and psychology, on the ability to make us feel that the artist is enlarging investigation, not restricting it. At the end of the novel we feel this restriction with particular force, not simply because it goes against the grain of the truths the novel is trying to utter, but because the presentation of character has been remarkably open and unformed by the usual *Bildungsroman* conventions. E. S. Dallas, in his review of the novel in *The Times* (19 May, 1860), spoke with fine penetration of George Eliot's 'effortlessness', observing that 'even when she has reached her climaxes she is entirely at her ease'. Maggie's character is presented in the medium of pity which has made it possible for Dr Leavis and other critics to see in it elements of indulgence and self-gratification, but it also comes very close to an existential openness, freedom, and pragmatism. Right up to the bad faith of the conclusion, we are presented with characters who are defined by the process of experiencing. Such closeness to experience is a rich theft from life by art, and all too rare in the great Victorian novelists. There is a tendency in modern critcism to argue or assume that closeness to life has the disadvantage of imperfect externalization, but it may also bring with it the advantage of unformed experience – of intransigence and a denial of form. The characteristic formal movement of novels of education is a progressive and evolutionary one, but even though *The Mill on the Floss* is a very Darwinian novel, its debt to Darwin is to be found in its hard and pessimistic look at struggle and survival, rather than in its optimistic treatment of personal evolutions. If we feel effortlessness in the climaxes, this is to some extent the result of a refusal to let climax determine and change character too markedly. To compare the process of Maggie Tulliver with the process of Janet Dempster or Adam Bede is to see George Eliot presenting character still sunk in the inchoate eddies of living.

Maggie is a character who believes herself to be converted and transformed, but who is incorrigibly herself. I speak relatively: of course, she does learn to live in a reserved and controlled way, but this lesson is scarcely a dramatic change, being a part of social education hard for sane and sensitive creatures to escape. But her change is minimal. George Eliot creates a pattern of apparent *Bildung*, but undermines and flattens its gains and crises. I do not know what Lady Ritchie had in mind when she said in her essay on Mrs Gaskell (*Blackstick Papers*) that George Eliot seldom becomes subject to her creations, but seems to watch them from afar, except in the case of Maggie, where for once she is apparently 'writing of herself'. Apart from the sources of personal experience I have been speaking of, there is this lack of patterning, which also seems to have come out of the closeness to life. Writing out of personal dreams and urges has many effects, moves art in contrary directions. Here perhaps it moves it in the direction of a static concept of moral character in marked opposition to the models of development and deterioration found in earlier and later novels, where the heroes and heroines seem smoothly and steadily to ascend and descend their moral staircases.

It is possible to describe Maggie's progress in the diagrammatic form of such an ascent: her childhood is marked by the habit of creative and drugging fantasy, by the need to be loved and admired, by recklessness and absentmindedness, by pride and masochism; she moves to more subtly effective fantasies, in art and religion, her need to be loved and admired is controlled and subdued, and modified by her need to argue her values, she softens her pride; but the final stages show the weakness of her masochistic and unreal religiosity, and recklessness and dreaminess are finally triumphed over in the renunciation of Stephen: Maggie emerges from illusion and self-love. My account of her process is the more distorting for being faithfully close to the climaxes of the novel. What happens, however, is that the climaxes are reached and then denied. Maggie ascends and descends. It is a process more like an eddy than a directing current. It is true that Maggie is 'converted' to self-abnegation and the life of duty, and true, too, that Thomas à Kempis brings into her life something which changes it and does not entirely disappear. But it is a much weaker influence than we may remember. Before Philip tells her that fanaticism brings its own perils and that renunciation may have a terrible backlash, she is already moving out of that violent act of histrionic repression. She is very easily persuaded by Philip to move into a world of emotional and intellectual gratification, but a world that is the adult equivalent of her old dream-worlds. George Eliot shows the backward movement very gently and unfussily. The climax of vision and decision is not utterly undone, but its effects are largely erased:

(Could she really do him good? It would be very hard to say 'good-bye' this day, and not speak to him again. Here was a new interest to vary the days – it was so much easier to renounce the interest before it came.) (Book Five, Chapter 1)

This mild and muted irony does not hold up its hands and exclaim in horror that on the preceding page Maggie had been saying 'it makes the mind very free when we give up wishing, and only think of bearing what is laid upon us, and doing what is given us to do'. George Eliot does not shirk showing the dividedness of Maggie's mind, and the shifting dialogue between the two voices, one sweet, one stern, which comes close on the passage just quoted, is Clough-like in its refusal to set a good angel against a bad. Maggie postpones conflict and drifts with the conversation, until she hits against 'an old impression' revived 'with overmastering force'. Philip offers to lend her *The Pirate*, and she feels the old wind blowing on her from Scott's rough sea, and puts the book aside: 'It would make me in love with this world again . . . it would make me long for a full life.' Philip tempts her then with sacredness and purity of 'Poetry and art and knowledge', relying ruefully on the lack of sexual temptation his friendship offers. Maggie replies with fair self-knowledge, and a better instinct about the sacredness and purity of the arts, 'But not for me. . . . Because I should want too much. I must wait – this life will not last long.' The debate is lengthily repeated once more in the third chapter of Book Five, and once more there comes an interval in which it is dropped. In the less intense and argumentative talk in the interval there is another aesthetic temptation as Philip sings 'Love in her eyes sits playing'. The argument and the song end very undramatically, with little comment from the author, as Philip offers his sophistry, 'If I meet you by chance, there is no concealment in that?' which Maggie snatches at. The long, reflective passages which follow do not exclaim at the shortlived nature of Maggie's renunciations, but are given up to Philip. And in the following chapter, which moves on nearly a year, Maggie is back again reading Scott, identifying with the dark-haired heroines, telling Philip that their renewed friendship has indeed made her restless and occupied with 'the world', and referring to the time when she was 'benumbed' as past time. What happens next is one of those unexpected eddying movements: Philip asks her to love him, she accepts and assents, and what has seemed a source of dream and love and richness for the mind is set out as a new renunciation: 'if there were sacrifices in this love, it was all the richer and more satisfying' and 'The tissue of vague dreams must now get narrower and narrower'.

The web is a complex one: just when Maggie seems to be most enticed by the old voice 'that made sweet music', George Eliot shows that the relation with Philip is made up of renunciation as well as indulgence. At each step of apparent progress, when Maggie says most confidently that she has made up her mind, she is shown, very quietly, as moving back on her word. This eddying process shows itself not only in each detail of apparent change, but throughout the whole broad pattern of growing up. The Maggie who pushed Lucy into the mud, who ran away, who used her doll as a scapegoat, who cut off her hair, who wanted to give Tom the bigger half of the jam-puff and immediately forgot his existence in devouring it, this Maggie is still present in the older Maggie, with adult appetites, adult control over trivial acts, and adult lack of control over grave ones. The strength of personal love which animates her sense of duty as she renounces Stephen owes something to the stern voice she listened to in Thomas à Kempis, and forgot, and heard again, but much to the generous lovingness that was there in the little girl. Her *experience* changes: she finds that renunciation is hard and destructive, but her *character* is not transformed by this discovery. Character is not cut in marble, George Eliot tells us in *Middlemarch*, but although the motion of Maggie's character is dynamic, it is no case of progress, like Silas Marner's. It is not very easy to say what George Eliot is doing in creating this oscillation and eddy. It may be that she saw herself as writing a tidy *Bildungsroman*, as she was in her other novels, but that the very closeness to life, so falsifying at the end, paradoxically broke the pattern by its fidelity to the stubborn and unchanging nature of human character. It may have been Maggie's refusal to be a tragic and evolutionary heroine (like Morel's refusal to be a villain in *Sons and Lovers*) that brought about the final swing into dreaming and wishing.

One last word. It is not a novel where one character shows this openness and freedom while others remain conventionally grouped around that live centre. The stubborn and unchanging nature of character is shown dynamically, not statically, and the whole psychological notation of the novel keeps us in touch with mobility and complexity. This stubbornness is seen outside Maggie, for instance, in Tom, and perhaps most movingly in Mr Tulliver. One of the finest examples, to my mind, comes in two adjacent scenes, which show Tulliver's recovery after his stroke. One marks a crisis of change, the other undercuts and makes an almost cancelling movement. 'Almost cancelling' – it is necessary to say 'almost', because although the novel is constantly showing characters apparently changing and thinking themselves changed, it is also showing that what seemed so influential is not utterly to pass without trace. Maggie does hear the stern voice at the end. And though Mr Tulliver feels the Christian sacramental demands of his family Bible, and is led to an action which he tries to cancel in an act of pagan revenge, set out in that same Bible, the first submissive act does hold good, does affect events. It is rather that George Eliot shows people acting out of character, in obedience to strong external pressures, and then shows the recoil, in obedience to the principle of self. In Book Three, Chapter 8, Mr Tulliver is apparently transformed, rather like Maggie, on the day when he comes down from his sick-bed to face the daylit emptiness of his house after the bankruptcy and sale. He picks up the family Bible and traces in it the cyclical history and ritual of birth, marriage, and death: his mother's death, his own marriage, his children's births. His wife wails in terms reduced to sacrament and proverb, speaking in the urgent voice of traditions larger than herself:

'. . . we promised one another for better and for worse. . . .'
'But I never thought it 'ud be for so worse as this. . . .'

and

'Then we might stay here and get a living, and I might keep among my own sisters . . . and me been such a good wife to you, and never crossed you

from week's end to week's end . . . and they all say so . . . they said it 'ud be
nothing but right . . . only you're so turned against Wakem.' . . .
'Let her be,' said Mr Tulliver.

There is a strange unreality and foreignness in Tulliver's feelings in
this chapter: he speaks in a voice of feeling unnaturally enlarged by
awe and suffering and responsibility and illness. What George Eliot
knows, and clearly shows that she knows, is that such high tide-marks
of feeling, as she calls them elsewhere, when speaking of Maggie's
deceptive acquiescence in Philip's love, may take us out of character,
but do not transform us. It is the same intuition about moral change
which lets her show Rosamond briefly and warmly responding to
Dorothea, then living on to be Lydgate's basil plant. In the very next
chapter Tulliver's return to health and routine, his habituation to
what shocked him out of character, makes him speak and act from the
feelings of an older and for him more native religion of vengeance,
curse, and feud:

- That first moment of renunciation and submission was followed by days of
violent struggle . . . he had promised her without knowing what she was
going to say. . . .

Here again it is easy to set out a plain, unblurred antithesis, missing the
nuances. George Eliot does not show a straight swing of the
pendulum, any more than she does with Maggie's 'submission' to
Philip. Tulliver's old vigour returns, not simply to show him the
difficulty of that vow made out of character, but also to bring up
feelings that argued on the side of that vow, feelings that were not
relevant when it was made, but which crop up later to arrest the
pendulum, feelings of practical advantage, feelings of love for his past
and his home. Here too, George Eliot uses her authorial reserve, saying
nothing to interrupt the swing from tugging nostalgia to the violent
decision to curse Wakem. There are times when her refusal to
comment on the relation between two contrary states of mind points to
the subterranean workings of conflict and decision. Tulliver repeats
that vow out of character, 'I'll be as good as my word to you,' but
makes Tom write - in that same Bible whose ritual influence helped to
take him out of character - the words of unforgiveness and hate: 'I wish
evil may befall him.'

The novel whose chapters and divisions are so marked by quotations
and images from Bunyan is no simple pilgrim's progress, but is indeed

the least progressive of all George Eliot's studies in character and morality. This denial of progress in character, this flattening and erasing of the conventional diagram of moral evolution (conventional in moral thinking as well as in art) is a source of the truthfulness of a great but flawed novel, a novel whose merits and flaws show how art can tell difficult truths and consoling lies.

1970

4
Rituals and Feeling

Rituals are ceremonies which mark some special or crucial occasion. They often involve worship, as in weddings, christenings, churchings and funerals. Their action and properties are usually symbolic, as in the giving of a ring, baptism by water, and the donation of presents. They are prescribed by traditions, which are usually religious or social, and they give rhythm, record and meaning to the memory of a society, a family, an institution, or a person. Rituals frequently draw their form and action from art, drama, music, dance, poetry and fable; they are activities of the community, collective dramas and actions. Art, such as lyric poetry, tragedy and comedy, often has a ritual origin, and the work of art may indeed resemble ritual in many ways.

Ritual plays an important part in Victorian novels, especially those which present a view of society distanced by several years of history. Most of George Eliot's novels are set about thirty or forty years before the date at which they were written. Society was, of course, changing fast, and with the growth of industry and communications came changes in ritual. Although George Eliot was less inclined than Thomas Hardy to lament the erosion or disappearance of ritual, she was drawn to the clearly marked rituals of small rural or semi-rural communities, and she was very sharply aware of both the strength and the fragility of such traditions and dramas. Such sensitivity, however, is a trait of the author rather than the form of the rural novel; despite her chronicling of village life, Jane Austen is scarcely concerned with presenting such a record. All George Eliot's novels record rituals: weddings, funerals, feast-days, Christmases, birthdays, harvest festivals, and church services stand out strongly in her fiction as occasions when she dwells with veneration on the collective history and drama of the society she portrays. Such collective scenes give range, solidity, and depth to her presentation of communities, as well as noting and exploring historical perspective.

George Eliot had special needs for such reverence. We know of three occasions in her personal life when ritual seems to have been of crucial importance to her. When, as a young woman, she discovered that she could no longer accept the Christian faith in which she had been brought up, and decided that the honest public act was to stop going to church, her decision caused great family anguish, and she eventually revoked it. She rejected and then accepted the ritual of churchgoing (though not its faith) for what she valued in family feeling and personal continuity. Much later, when she decided to live with George Henry Lewes without the benefit of the marriage ritual, it was not from a doctrinal belief in free unions, but because Lewes could not get a divorce from his wife. This act too caused a breach with her family, and especially with her brother, Isaac. After Lewes's death George Eliot accepted the ritual of marriage with a man much younger than herself, John Walter Cross. After twenty years of silence Isaac wrote to forgive, and she replied to accept forgiveness, in a real-life version of the reconciliation at the end of *The Mill on the Floss*. These breaches and healings go a long way towards explaining the habitual concern and reverence for rituals in her novels. We know that she was particularly anxious not to write anything which might weaken or disrupt the faith she did not share, and so her use of religious ritual is solemn and tender. She was equally anxious not to appear to undermine family life, and so conspicuously celebrates the rituals of marriage, home and family.

Her novels and stories follow the rhythm of rituals, each in its appropriate fashion and form. She uses ritual to invoke a special sense of a life in touch with the seasons, as in *Adam Bede*, and to stress the value of religious ceremony, as in *Scenes of Clerical Life*, where church services play a large part in creating the atmosphere of the community. She uses ritual to show the strengths and unity of the family, and its seasonal and primitive roots, in *The Mill on the Floss*. She calls on ritual, in *Silas Marner*, to show the psychological response of a man whose narrow and ritually-dependent religious life is suddenly broken, forcing him into a new, personal, and secular set of binding rituals. In *Romola* ritual is part of an historical record, and the crowd scenes, which draw vitality from religious procession and carnival, help to dramatize the archaeology and anthropology of a past Florentine life. A growing secularity and individuality of ritual marks the action of *Middlemarch*, where the recognition of change and reform, while conservatively and quietly treated, involves a sense of shifting values. *Daniel Deronda* continues this personal creation of ritual, but there is also, of course, the lavish use of Jewish ritual, conferring dignity on the common Cohen family, and awakening kinship and feeling in Daniel.

When Daniel visits the synagogue in Frankfort his curiosity is balanced by his reverence, and he finds in its liturgy a model for ritual participation, which combines a sense of tradition, community, and personal meaning:

> The most powerful movement of feeling with a liturgy is the prayer which seeks for nothing special, but is a yearning to escape from the limitations of our own weakness and an invocation of all Good to enter and abide with us; or else a self-oblivious lifting up of gladness, a *Gloria in excelsis* that such Good exists; both the yearning and the exultation gathering their utmost force from the sense of communion in a form which has expressed them both, for long generations of struggling fellow-men. The Hebrew liturgy, like others, has its transitions of litany, lyric, proclamation, dry statement and blessing; but this evening all were one for Deronda: the chant of the *Chazan's* or Reader's grand wide-ranging voice with its passage from monotony to sudden cries, the outburst of sweet boys' voices from the little quire, the devotional swaying of men's bodies backwards and forwards, the very commonness of the building and shabbiness of the scene where a national faith, which had penetrated the thinking of half the world, and moulded the splendid forms of that world's religion, was finding a remote, obscure echo – all were blent for him as one expression of a binding history, tragic and yet glorious. He wondered at the strength of his own feeling; it seemed beyond the occasion – what one might imagine to be a divine influx in the darkness, before there was any vision to interpret. (Chapter 32)

Daniel is responding fully to the features of ritual; its memorial function, its communion, its sensuousness, its unity, and its variety. Daniel hears the music and makes general associations. He cannot identify the particular liturgy for the Day of Reconciliation, and so the special occasion and symbol are not understood. But he is made to feel moved in an almost mystical way because he is, although he does not know it, a Jew. He also notes that many members of the congregation are not moved and concludes that for most of them the ritual is mere routine. All George Eliot's novels have a particular interest in showing that vitality of rituals which is the very opposite of routine, and they do so through the individual human response. This response makes the tradition clear. It may be selective, but it is not null or false. Amongst the most striking of the many instances of such selective personal response is that of Adam Bede, at his father's Sunday afternoon funeral service. Adam, like Daniel, is strongly and appropriately moved, but in his case there is no mysterious superfluity of response. His participation in ritual is perhaps the most individual and at the same time the most complete of any of George Eliot's characters:

> . . . a certain consciousness of our entire past and our imagined future blends itself with all our moments of keen sensibility. And to Adam the church service was the best channel he could have found for his mingled regret, yearning, and resignation; its interchange of beseeching cries for help, with outbursts of faith and praise – its recurrent responses and the familiar rhythm of its collects, seemed to speak for him as no other form of worship could have done: as, to those early Christians who had worshipped from their childhood upward in catacombs, the torchlight and shadows must have seemed nearer the Divine presence than the heathenish daylight of the streets. The secret of our emotions never lies in the bare object, but in its subtle relations to our own past. . . . (Chapter 18)

Adam, the grown man, mingles his personal praise, faith, resignation and yearning in the old familiar ritual he has known since he was a child. George Eliot makes it highly individual as Adam first re-members how he has been intolerant of his father, and then lovingly remembers him at his best. He is most responsive when, for the first time in his life, emotion stops him from joining in the psalm. It is a response all the more individual and effective for its being not the only one on view. We also see the clerk, Joshua Rann, conceited, narrow, with rusty spectacles and a big head, marvellously in control of the strong calm melancholy of the responses, and passing to the choir to sing the solemn minor strain of the funeral hymn, 'Thou sweep'st us off as with a flood;/ We vanish hence like dreams –', to which

> mother and sons listened, each with peculiar feelings. Lisbeth had a vague belief that the psalm was doing her husband good; it was part of that decent burial which she would have thought it a greater wrong to withhold from

him than to have caused him many unhappy days while he was living. The more there was said about her husband, the more there was done for him, surely the safer he would be. It was poor Lisbeth's blind way of feeling that human love and pity are a ground of faith in some other love.

Seth, the younger son, not an Anglican but a Methodist, is easily touched and weeps, trying hard to hope that his father has had a single moment of consciousness which might obtain him pardon and reconcilement, 'for was it not written in the very psalm they were singing, that the Divine dealings were not measured and circumscribed by time?' Finally, however, the sermon reminds all the listeners that it is only the present that we have for mercy, righteousness, and family tenderness, and the congregation breaks up and leaves the church in kindness and sympathy, streaming through the old archway into the green churchyard to begin 'their neighbourly talk, their simple civilities, and their invitations to tea', in ritually appropriate Sunday-best clothes and a Sunday-best humour.

Even in this beautifully rendered communion and ritual, not everyone is responsive. Hetty Sorrel is oblivious of the act of collective worship, memory, and sympathy, and thinks only of what she looks like in her best clothes, and how hurt she is that Arthur Donnithorne, the young squire, is not present. Her rejection and neglect of the ritual emphasizes her isolation and weakness. She is rootless, easily torn from her soil, and, in her small and unimaginative way, defiant of order. To be a deviant from the community is to be in serious personal danger – and George Eliot makes it implicitly clear that such deviation will ultimately endanger and disturb the community itself.

Deviations exercize George Eliot again in *The Mill on the Floss*, where she analyses the pagan strengths of the small rural community, which swears its oaths of vengeance in the family Bible. Mr Tulliver and Tom join in a pagan ritual, the more marked for being crossed with Christianity. It is preceded by a moving instance of Christian ritual, but unlike a response to public ceremony, this involves an individual version and a personal re-making of ceremony and ritual. Just before the swearing of vengeance, the family Bible is used more orthodoxly by Mr and Mrs Tulliver. Mr Tulliver, after his stroke, finds that he has been sold up, and that only a few of his sacred objects remain on the family hearth. Amongst those which do is the family Bible, and he looks at it and slowly reads, in the hesitant tones of his stricken and convalescent speech:

'They've left the big Bible,' he said. 'It's got everything in – when I was born and married – bring it me, Tom.'

The quarto Bible was laid open before him at the fly-leaf, and while he was reading with slowly-travelling eyes, Mrs Tulliver entered the room, but stood in mute surprise to find her husband down already, and with the great Bible before him.

'Ah,' he said, looking at a spot where his finger rested, 'my mother was Margaret Beaton – she died when she was forty-seven – hers wasn't a long-lived family – we're our mother's children – Gritty and me are – we shall go to our last bed before long.' (Book Three, Chapter 8)

Slowly the hesitating voice and finger trace the human cycle, moving from birth and marriage to death, then back to his own marriage:

'Ah . . . Elizabeth Dodson . . . it's eighteen year since I married her. . . .'

'Come next Ladyday,' said Mrs Tulliver, going up to his side and looking at the page.

Her husband fixed his eyes earnestly on her face.

'Poor Bessy,' he said, 'you was a pretty lass then – everybody said so – and I used to think you kept your looks rarely. But you're sorely aged . . . don't you bear me ill-will . . . I meant to do well by you. . . . We promised one another for better or for worse. . . .'

'But I never thought it 'ud be so for worse as this,' said poor Mrs Tulliver, with the strange, scared look that had come over her of late; 'and my poor father gave me away . . . and to come on so all at once. . . .'

'O mother,' said Maggie, 'don't talk in that way.'

In *Adam Bede* and *Daniel Deronda* George Eliot writes most exaltedly of our response to ritual and tradition, but in this revision of ritual there is something more poignant and complex. The ritual is the ground, the very basis of life, and counterpointed against it is the change in feeling and circumstance. We are aware of the movement in time which the ritual anticipated, but which the participants did not foresee, in the words 'for better or for worse'. In a sense, the ritual is unimpaired, even effectively reinforced, for with its aid Mrs Tulliver forces on her husband a new vow to stay and work for Wakem, the man he hates. But in the next chapter Mr Tulliver adds a new (and old) ritual with the oath of revenge. Human beings are defined in many ways by ritual, but its norms are sometimes too small or too big for human passions, its binding-power sometimes too frail. The ceremony and form of ritual sometimes need revision.

While deviations still show the form of order, they also show the process of necessary, if painful, change. When Arthur Donnithorne comes of age in *Adam Bede*, we sense the irony of the young squire drinking the health of Adam, his new agent. Arthur, after all, comes of age in another sense by seducing Hetty, whom Adam loves. This discord is only one part of a false harmony. All the tenants are there, carefully ranged in a graduated and stratified ritual feast, which has various defects: the expenditure is curbed because the old squire is mean and because drunkenness amongst the lower orders is not to be encouraged; the races are run but young Bessy Cranage gets a heavy middle-aged grogram gown as a prize; Wiry Ben dances with verve but is laughed at by the gentry; and the gentry themselves do not always know the people to whom they present the prizes. When we look closely, the feudal ritual shows within it the seeds of its own destruction. This destruction is sometimes seen in implicit observation, and sometimes articulated as an explicit theme. The people who live in Hayslope are fatally close to each other, incapable of escaping or containing the consequences of lust and selfishness. But at the same time they are also fatally separate, drinking each other's health, but knowing nothing of each other's lives. Neither Arthur, for all his patronage and benevolence, nor the Reverend Irwine, for all his sympathy and interest, knows that Adam loves Hetty. The ignorance is deeply wounding, even fatal. The community is brought together in ceremonies and festivities, but these rituals also mark the dangerous divisions of class and rank which the novel reveals as injurious. George Eliot is not writing a revolutionary novel where the rituals of conservatism and feudalism are treated with strong radical irony, but neither is she always idealizing such rituals. Her criticism is made apparent when the rites and ceremonies of a community speak anachronistically from time past to time present, without the adaptation necessary in a changing society. Sometimes what the rituals symbolize is no longer quite strong enough.

The same criticism of separateness in the community is made through the funeral ritual in *Middlemarch*. Some of the gentry (not including sensible Philistine Celia, who 'doesn't like funerals') are watching the villagers from the window of Lowick Manor. Mrs Cadwallader laughs, comparing them with 'jugs', and condescendingly remarking on Mrs Vincy's good looks. Dorothea voices her distress that someone should die and leave no one to mourn. As she speaks Casaubon joins her, and she is silent. Later on, when he is about to die, George Eliot invokes the classical ritual of Lethe's verge to suggest something of the tension, sorrow and fear he must feel when the doctor tells him that he is to die – when the words 'we must all die' change to 'I must die – and soon':

> Here was a man who now for the first time found himself looking into the eyes of death – who was passing through one of those rare moments of experience when we feel the truth of a commonplace, which is as different from what we call knowing it, as the vision of waters upon the earth is different from the delirious vision of the water which cannot be had to cool the burning tongue. When the commonplace 'We must all die' transforms itself suddenly into the acute consciousness 'I must die – and soon', then death grapples us, and his fingers are cruel; afterwards, he may come to fold us in his arms as our mother did, and our last moment of dim earthly discerning may be like the first. To Mr Casaubon now, it was as if he suddenly found himself on the dark river-brink and heard the plash of the oncoming oar, not discerning the forms, but expecting the summons. (Chapter 42)

Almost as soon as George Eliot invokes this dark solemnity, she cuts violently across it by telling us that his attitude to death has not changed his character, but that he felt only the jealous need to possess his wife even after death. The rituals are not always there to confer dignity. They also mark its absence, when human beings and societies are unable to rise to the ideal sublimity or intensity. George Eliot constantly surprises us, in ways small and large, as we follow the emotional track of her characters, and one source is her measurement of individual feeling against the expected, preferred, or ideal pattern which is formed, recorded and exalted in rituals.

Many of these rituals are religious and social, and they are acted out in public ceremony. But life is ritualistic in many ways, and while some of them are concerned with smaller and more private institutions like the family, others are even more solitary. Ritual may be felt as crucial in the breach rather than in the observance, as when Adam Bede rejects the precious evening meal his mother makes and offers. Adam's rejection acts as ritual, for in rejecting the meal he is symbolically rejecting the family, in fury with his father who has not done the promised job of making the coffin. Critics sometimes hasten to interpret the small ritual act as a larger symbol, as when they read the bread and wine offered by Bartle Massey to Adam as a symbol of the Last Supper. This interpretation seems insensitively redundant, since the meal rather shows the way life often needs to become personally and individually ritualistic, in private ceremonies of loving or unloving.

What these two meals in *Adam Bede* show is the way symbolic behaviour conspicuously attaches itself to well-known rituals of feasting and offering. This can also be seen in individual acts, as in a ritual use of clothing, which, as George Eliot observes of Dorothea, is felt to be appropriate to a new phase of experience. Dorothea, usually indifferent to dress, puts on lighter mourning as she proposes to renounce and subdue her own jealousy through an unselfish action, and the ritual act consists in the wearing of fresh garments for a fresh life. Mrs Bulstrode, who has always loved dress, takes off her frills and furbelows to wear simple Quakerish dress when she goes to stand by her husband after he has been publicly shamed. These two women behave half-consciously in a way which seems to lean on a larger tradition. What they feel is strengthened by an external symbol, a public display of their acts of renewal and change. At times the support of ritual is not enough. Gwendolen Harleth, in *Daniel Deronda*, is always conscious of her appearance and, because she intends to refuse to marry Grandcourt, attires herself in a plain black gown without ornaments. But she overestimates her resolution, despite the attempt to proclaim it and strengthen herself by the ritual act of putting on plain clothing, and finds herself accepting his proposal. She repeats this ritual action later in the novel when she is about to meet Deronda, and realizes that, although she is wearing a plain dark dress, it is too becoming to her white neck and head, and so she hastily throws over her shoulders some black lace. This second time the ritual act is more solidly and successfully expressive of her whole attempt at subduing vanity. Her habitual self-consciousness about dress is finely and subtly used by George Eliot to show the private person's ritualistic behaviour and the need for support from tradition.

Ritual is again shown realistically as an aspect of character, when Silas Marner turns from a life filled with ritual to one where he is cut off from the community and religion. He finds in his weaving a formally reassuring repetition, he worships the hoard of gold coins, and he has a fetishistic but tender feeling for his water-jug:

> Yet even in this stage of withering a little incident happened, which showed that the sap of affection was not all gone. It was one of his daily tasks to fetch his water from a well a couple of fields off, and for this purpose, ever since he

came to Raveloe, he had had a brown earthenware pot, which he held as his most precious utensil among the very few conveniences he had granted himself. It had been his companion for twelve years, always standing on the same spot, always lending its handle to him in the early morning, so that its form had an expression for him of willing helpfulness, and the impress of its handle on his palm gave a satisfaction mingled with that of having the fresh clear water. One day as he was returning from the well, he stumbled against the step of the stile, and his brown pot, falling with force against the stones that overarched the ditch below him, was broken in three pieces. Silas picked up the pieces and carried them home with grief in his heart. The brown pot could never be of use to him any more, but he stuck the bits together and propped the ruin in its old place for a memorial. (Chapter 2)

Similar instances of ritualistic behaviour in the individual are present in Mrs Tulliver's lament over her household goods (the sprigged china, table linen, and silver teapot with her maiden initials), and in Maggie Tulliver's ritualistic hammering of her wooden doll, which both expresses and controls feeling. Human feeling is given clarity and definition by ritual, and shown at crucial moments to feel itself a part of a larger tradition.

One of the oldest rituals is storytelling, and we are especially conscious of this ritual as we read George Eliot. Like most novelists, she takes care to make storytelling play an important part in the whole tale. Her stories contain the large and crucial narratives of dreams and hopes that the characters tell to themselves and to each other, narrating in order to know, to love, and to survive. But there is also conventional storytelling, like the tale of Rumpelstiltskin which Mary Garth tells to the children at the Vincys' ritual Christmas party, 'in her neat fashion'. We are bound to feel that George Eliot was amused to mention such small-scale but effective storytelling within the monolithic and far-reaching narrative of *Middlemarch*. She also pays a general self-conscious ritual homage to art and craft through certain aspects of her form, making clear that they belong to a great tradition. She uses the musical terms 'Prelude' and 'Finale' for the beginning and end of *Middlemarch*, and by means of ancient literary ritual she salutes, praises, and invokes in various novels the appropriate Muses, Fielding, Goethe, Wordsworth, and Bunyan, to bless her art, theme, and contribution to the mystery of storytelling. Most interestingly, the particular events of her stories invoke a larger life, a larger myth, a larger ritual which generalizes and supports character, theme, and action, as with Silas and Dorothea and the Bulstrodes. Dorothea's struggles with love are shown through the figures of Cupid and Psyche, Bacchus and Ariadne, Pluto and Persephone; and the novelist's imagination works back to the meaning of such myths, to the awakening of spring after wintry deadness, and fertility after sterility, thus enlarging and solemnizing her story. Ritual effects like these are, of course, found in most good stories where the individual life is most intensely realized. In Joyce's *Ulysses* we are aware of Homer's *Odyssey*, and an ordinary Dublin funeral moves out of time to become more sinister, dignified, and resonant. A layabout in Beckett's *More Pricks than Kicks* becomes a soul in purgatory. A frustrated wife in Lawrence's *Lady Chatterley's Lover* is Persephone, 'out of hell on a cold morning'. Such ritual enlargement reveals the ancient, common life behind and within the individual story. The ordinary clocks and calendars of realistic fiction are stopped by such timeless moments, which confer awe, and remind and involve the reader, in ritualized awareness, of the common lot shared by genius and ordinary mortals, authors and readers, in and out of fiction. Great art creates ritual.

1973

5
Middlemarch and the Passions

How shall we even begin to educate ourselves in the feelings?

Not by laying down laws, or commandments, or axioms and postulates. Not even by making assertions that such and such is blessed. Not by words at all.

If we can't hear the cries far down in our own forests of dark veins, we can look in the real novels, and there listen-in. Not listen to the didactic statements of the author, but to the low, calling cries of the characters, as they wander in the dark woods of their destiny.

(D. H. Lawrence, 'The Novel and the Feelings,' *Phoenix*)

The strange thing about life is that though the nature of it must have been apparent to every one for hundreds of years, no one has left any adequate account of it. The streets of London have their map; but our passions are uncharted.

(Virginia Woolf, *Jacob's Room*)

In the 'Spanish Gypsy' there are seven arguments of about fifty pages each. This is the way she describes passion.

(W. B. Yeats in a letter to F. J. Gregg, quoted in R. Ellmann, *The Identity of Yeats*)

One of the less obvious sources of the greatness of *Middlemarch* is its charting of the passions, in ways that sometimes come close to Lawrence's recognition of the complexity and inarticulate eloquence of the life of feeling. Still, we cannot entirely ignore the author's didactic statements. Yeats was both right and wrong: *The Spanish Gypsy* does describe passion through argument, but George Eliot's novels are more responsive to the life of feeling than her poetry. Even in *Middlemarch* she uses statements about the passions as well as passionate enactment, needing words that classify psychological experience as well as words that stay faithfully and subtly close to the movement of feeling, in inner life and outer expression.

To begin with the didactic statement and argument. George Eliot usually introduces her major characters, not always right at the moment of dramatic entry, but fairly near it, in words that are clearly analytic, taxonomic, and instructive. Here are the discursive accompaniments to what is shown, as well as told, about Rosamond, Dorothea, and Lydgate.[1]

> If you think it incredible that to imagine Lydgate as a man of family could cause thrills of satisfaction which had anything to do with the sense that she was in love with him, I will ask you to use your power of comparison a little more effectively, and consider whether red cloth and epaulets have never had an influence of that sort. *Our passions do not live apart in locked chambers,* but, dressed in their small wardrobe of notions, bring their provisions to a common table and mess together, feeding out of the common store according to their appetite. (Chapter 16)

and

> Into this soul-hunger as yet all her youthful *passion* was poured . . . (Chapter 3)

and

> All Dorothea's *passion* was transfused through a mind struggling towards an ideal life . . . (Chapter 5)

and

> . . . that distinction of mind which belonged to his intellectual ardour, did not penetrate his feeling and judgment about furniture, or women, or the desirability of its being known (without his telling) that he was better born than other country surgeons. (Chapter 15)

1. The italics in the immediately following passages are mine. George Eliot uses the term 'passions' as freely as Fielding.

In each analysis George Eliot attends to the place of the passions in the psychic unity of character. She observes the difficulty caused by the proximity of passions and by their separateness. Rosamond seems to emerge as a case of insufficient discrimination, of a common but dangerous 'messing together'; Dorothea too as a more intensely serious and ardent case of similar merging; Lydgate as a counter-example of emotional segregation. All show a similar confidence and innocence about their strong feelings, illustrating in their sharply individual ways D. H. Lawrence's insistence on our brash creation of categories of feeling which are not only inaccurate but lead to illusions of simplification and control. 'We see love,' he observes in the essay already quoted, 'like a woolly lamb or like a decorative decadent panther in Paris clothes: according as it is sacred or profane. We see hate, like a dog chained to a kennel. We see fear, like a shivering monkey. We see anger, like a bull with a ring through his nose, and greed, like a pig.' George Eliot is not dealing with such emblematic simplifications, but what she sees and shows is very similar.

The shift from the characters' inadequate knowledge to the author's didactic analysis exposes the dangers of ignorant confidence. It is an ignorance commonly encouraged by literature, like Casaubon's expectations about the nature of 'masculine passion', which are pathetically and abstractly grounded in his reading of the classics, and confounded by the experience of his own disappointing ardours. He concludes that 'the poets had exaggerated the force of masculine passion', but George Eliot's parallels startle as often as they settle expectation, and just as the altruistic Dorothea and the egocentric Rosamond are equally led astray by the fatal association of feeling, so both the cold Casaubon and the febrile Ladislaw are similarly misguided and let down by literary expectation. The novel's discriminations are nice, and insist in many ways that the names we commonly bestow on emotional experience are inadequate: 'there are many wonderful mixtures in the world which are all alike called love, and claim the privileges of a sublime rage.'

The power of the passions in *Middlemarch* resides not only in the telling but in the showing. The presentation of feeling is continuous, running right through explicit commentary, behaviouristic description of action, movement, gesture, and the drama of human relations and inner life. Each chapter has its trajectory of strong feelings. In Chapter 42, for instance, George Eliot joins the emotional analysis of character with the inner drama of feeling. Both analysis and inner flow are marked by variety and motion. The conversation between doctor and patient, in which Lydgate tells Casaubon the diagnosis and prognosis, is marked by the mobile registrations of complex feeling. Lydgate feels 'a little amusement mingling with his pity' as he responds silently to Casaubon's pathetic and ridiculous speech about his life's 'possible importance', but the author moves on to place this response through the irony of her foreknowledge: 'He was at present too ill acquainted with disaster to enter into the pathos of a lot where everything is below the level of tragedy except the passionate egoism of the sufferer.' This rash immature amusement is a silent one, and it is a sensitive sympathy which urges his question, ' "You refer to the possible hindrances from want of health?" he said, wishing to help forward Mr Casaubon's purpose, which seemed to be clogged by some hesitation.' Lydgate's controlled and measured sympathy is registered at the same time as Casaubon's clogging hesitation, doubt, fear, and anxiety. Perhaps the most poignant moment in this reticent passage is the comment that 'Mr Casaubon winced perceptibly, but bowed' as he begins to understand the drift of Lydgate's speech. When it is finished, the doctor's sympathy is registered once again, this time more purely, as an imaginative gesture of tact unmixed with amusement: 'Lydgate's instinct was fine enough to tell him that plain speech, quite free from ostentatious caution, would be felt by Mr Casaubon as a tribute of respect.' The emotional medium is full and fluent. Lydgate does not exactly feel respect, but feels the need to speak respectfully, and the nuance is movingly and candidly registered. What is not said is as important as what is said.

From this mute intercourse of feeling, we are drawn into Casaubon's solitude:

> Lydgate, certain that his patient wished to be alone, soon left him; and the black figure with hands behind and head bent forward continued to pace the walk where the dark yew-trees gave him a mute companionship in melancholy, and the little shadows of bird or leaf that fleeted across the isles of sunlight, stole along in silence as in the presence of a sorrow. Here was a man who now for the first time found himself looking into the eyes of death – who was passing through one of those rare moments of experience when we feel the truth of a commonplace, which is as different from what we call knowing it, as the vision of waters upon the earth is different from the delirious vision of the water which cannot be had to cool the burning tongue. When the commonplace 'We must all die' transforms itself suddenly into the acute consciousness 'I must die – and soon', then death grapples us, and

his fingers are cruel; afterwards, he may come to fold us in his arms as our
mother did, and our last moment of dim earthly discerning may be like the
first. To Mr Casaubon now, it was as if he suddenly found himself on the
dark river-brink and heard the plash of the oncoming oar, not discerning
the forms, but expecting the summons. In such an hour the mind does not
change its lifelong bias, but carries it onward in imagination to the other
side of death, gazing backward – perhaps with the divine calm of
beneficence, perhaps with the petty anxieties of self-assertion. What was
Mr Casaubon's bias his acts will give us a clue to. He held himself to be,
with some private scholarly reservations, a believing Christian, as to
estimates of the present and hopes of the future. But what we strive to
gratify, though we may call it a distant hope, is an immediate desire;
the future estate for which men drudge up city alleys exists already in
their imagination and love. And Mr Casaubon's immediate desire was
not for divine communion and light divested of earthly conditions; his
passionate longings, poor man, clung low and mist-like in very shady
places.

This passage is startling in several ways. George Eliot is brilliantly,
almost terrifyingly, imagining what can only be imagined, the
moment of belief in one's own imminent death. Like her other
moments of deep feeling, this combines something piercingly individual
with an invocation of communal feeling, through the words 'We', 'us',
and 'our mother', through the common experience of childhood and
death, memory and expectation, and through the solemn enlargement
of the myth. Awe, loneliness, fear, passivity, are invoked through the
culture and the myth, when George Eliot draws on Lethe, as Joyce was
to do in his great summons of the myth of death in Paddy Dignam's
funeral in *Ulysses*: 'the dark river-brink and . . . the plash of the
oncoming oar'. But just as the resonance unnerves us, we leave it in a
staggering return to particulars it cannot register. For the myth of
Charon is invoked in order to be rejected. We rise to the awful occasion
of death, but only for a moment. The sublime is deceptive, although it
briefly permits pity and terror. Casaubon does not rise to the occasion.
With the quiet and ironic comment on his beliefs, 'He held himself to
be, with some private scholarly reservations, a believing Christian, as
to estimates of the present and hopes of the future,' begins the return to
what George Eliot calls elsewhere in the novel 'habitual self'. The
beginning registers a scholarly Christian conformity which may
temper the awfulness of Charon and Lethe. It is followed by a more
devastating displacement of awe, fear, and suffering, in the return to

Casaubon's jealous possessiveness. His passions as he faces Lethe are not
those we have been led to imagine. Fear of death is weaker than fear of
his widow's freedom, pity is just what his pride cannot accept, Lethe is
just what his jealous egocentricity cannot entertain:

> Consider that his was a mind which shrank from pity: have you ever
> watched in such a mind the effect of a suspicion that what is pressing it as a
> grief may be really a source of contentment, either actual or future, to the
> being who already offends by pitying?

Out of this analysis, necessarily conducted within and beyond the
character's inner action, comes the well-known response to Dorothea's
pity. She brings to Casaubon a sympathy that he cannot read, and as
we move back from his solitude to the world of relationship, the
conflict between his passions and Dorothea's takes its course. She
makes her sensitive, loving movement of silence and contact; he keeps
his hands rigid behind him so that her 'pliant arm' clings to his 'with
difficulty'. So the chapter proceeds from the dumb show of hands and
arms to Dorothea's solitude, where her anger and pity conflict in a
morality play of passion invoking not a classical but a Christian myth.
The drama shows Dorothea's capacity to check her feelings, and
measures the distance she has travelled from that early time when her
passions had been innocently in unison. What torments her is the
knowledge that her best feelings cannot be communicated or received,
that 'her best soul' is shut 'in prison'.

The last part of the chapter sets its scene in the familiar boudoir
whose significant 'open bow-window' lets in 'the serene glory of the
afternoon'. George Eliot uses the natural symbolism with apparent
effortlessness, contrasting the serene glory with the unserene and
inglorious human passions, while using sunshine to register Dorothea's
distressed carelessness of comfort: 'She threw herself on a chair, not
heeding that she was in the dazzling sun-rays: if there were discomfort
in that, how could she tell that it was not part of her inward misery?'
The passions are recorded with due attention to the physical
sensations. First is the generalized 'inward misery', then 'the reaction
of a rebellious anger stronger than any she had felt since her marriage.
Instead of tears there came words: – "What have I done – what am I –
that he should treat me so?"' Hostile reproach is stopped by one of
those moments of self-awareness recorded so steadily and imaginatively
in Dorothea. 'She began to hear herself, and was checked into

stillness.' The most amusingly and the most chillingly self-absorbed characters in the novels never hear themselves, and most of the sensitive souls don't manage it as often as Dorothea. Even with her, self-awareness doesn't come easily. It checks and silences, but silence is not followed by a quick recovery. Anger makes way for fatigue, bitterness, a jarringly lucid vision of her relation to her husband, contempt, and beginning of rejection:

> In the jar of her whole being, Pity was overthrown. Was it her fault that she had believed in him – had believed in his worthiness? – And what, exactly, was he? – She was able enough to estimate him – she who waited on his glances with trembling, and shut her best soul in prison, paying it only hidden visits, that she might be petty enough to please him. In such a crisis as this, some women begin to hate.

George Eliot's notation registers the motion and mixture of strong feeling through emotional personifications of a kind brilliantly but more commonly deployed by Fielding and Charlotte Brontë, and also through a vigorous *erlebte Rede* or free indirect style. The method is as mixed as the moods it records. George Eliot uses summary of feelings past and present, 'She had never deliberately allowed her resentment to govern her in this way before . . .'. She also provides generalization about the nature of the briefly ruling passion:

> Her anger said, as anger is apt to say, that God was with her – that all heaven, though it were crowded with spirits watching them, must be on her side.

This splendid indictment of a self-righteousness clothed in spiritual garments is followed by action. Tantripp brings Casaubon's message that he wants to dine alone, which spikes the guns of Dorothea's anger; and, like Isabel Archer, she sits in a motionless, meditative struggle:

> But the struggle changed continually, as that of a man who begins with a movement towards striking and ends with conquering his desire to strike. The energy that would animate a crime is not more than is wanted to inspire a resolved submission, when the noble habit of the soul reasserts itself. That thought with which Dorothea had gone out to meet her husband – her conviction that he had been asking about the possible arrest of all his work, and that the answer must have wrung his heart, could not be

long without rising beside the image of him, like a shadowy monitor looking at her anger with sad remonstrance. It cost her a litany of pictured sorrows and of silent cries that she might be the mercy for those sorrows – but the resolved submission did come. . . .

Not only does she go out and wait for him, but he responds uncharacteristically with 'gentle surprise' and 'kind quiet melancholy'.

The characters relate to each other's emotions, and are changed by the relation. The particularity achieved has three aspects: truth to the moment, truth to the relationship, and truth to the human being.

A subtlety in *Middlemarch* is George Eliot's presentation of feeling as an influence upon conduct. If at times this presentation is intense and elevated, she concedes that such influence is often transitory. Casaubon is not, as Dorothea nobly but still erroneously imagines, solely occupied with fear and sorrow; he is planning the moves of his dead hand. Those gentle kind feelings are surprised out of him. They make no difference to what he chooses to do and be in the little life that remains. They are a tribute to Dorothea's moral seductiveness.

The crucial scene with Rosamond in Chapter 81 is also marked by silent communication, touch, movement, and expression:

Looking like the lovely ghost of herself, her graceful slimness wrapped in her soft white shawl, the rounded infantine mouth and cheek inevitably suggesting mildness and innocence, Rosamond paused at three yards' distance from her visitor and bowed. But Dorothea, who had taken off her gloves, from an impulse which she could never resist when she wanted a sense of freedom, came forward, and with her face full of a sad yet sweet openness, put out her hand. Rosamond could not avoid meeting her glance, could not avoid putting her small hand into Dorothea's, which clasped it with gentle motherliness; and immediately a doubt of her own prepossessions began to stir within her. Rosamond's eye was quick for faces; she saw that Mrs Casaubon's face looked pale and changed since yesterday, yet gentle, and like the firm softness of her hand. But Dorothea had counted a little too much on her own strength: the clearness and intensity of her mental action this morning were the continuance of a nervous exaltation which made her frame as dangerously responsive as a bit of finest Venetian crystal, and in looking at Rosamond, she suddenly found her heart swelling, and was unable to speak – all her effort was required to keep back tears. She succeeded in that, and the emotion only passed over her face like the spirit of a sob; but it added to Rosamond's impression that Mrs Casaubon's state of mind must be something quite different from what she had imagined.

The cordial, pleading tones which seemed to flow with generous heedlessness above all the facts which had filled Rosamond's mind as grounds of obstruction and hatred between her and this woman, came as soothingly as a warm stream over her shrinking fears. Of course Mrs Casaubon had the facts in her mind, but she was not going to speak of anything connected with them. That relief was too great for Rosamond to feel much else at the moment.

Dorothea, completely swayed by the feeling that she was uttering, forgot everything but that she was speaking from out the heart of her own trial to Rosamond's. The emotion had wrought itself more and more into her utterance, till the tones might have gone to one's very marrow, like a low cry from some suffering creature in the darkness. And she had unconsciously laid her hand again on the little hand that she had pressed before.

Rosamond, with an overmastering pang, as if a wound within her had been probed, burst into hysterical crying as she had done the day before when she clung to her husband. Poor Dorothea was feeling a great wave of her own sorrow returning over her – her thought being drawn to the possible share that Will Ladislaw might have in Rosamond's mental tumult. She was beginning to fear that she should not be able to suppress herself enough to the end of this meeting, and while her hand was still resting on Rosamond's lap, though the hand underneath it was withdrawn, she was struggling against her own rising sobs. She tried to master herself with the thought that this might be a turning point in three lives – not in her own; no, there the irrevocable had happened, but – in those three lives which were touching hers with the solemn neighbourhood of danger and distress. The fragile creature who was crying close to her – there might still be time to rescue her from the misery of false incompatible bonds; and this moment was unlike any other: she and Rosamond could never be together again with the same thrilling consciousness of yesterday within them both. She felt the relation between them to be peculiar enough to give her a peculiar influence, though she had no conception that the way in which her own feelings were involved was fully known to Mrs Lydgate.

When Rosamond's convulsed throat was subsiding into calm, and she withdrew the handkerchief with which she had been hiding her face, her eyes met Dorothea's as helplessly as if they had been blue flowers. What was the use of thinking about behaviour after this crying? And Dorothea looked almost as childish, with the neglected trace of a silent tear. Pride was broken down between these two.

The sense of physical strain and of mutual recognition is finely rendered. Even when the women talk, the words make less immediate impact than the tones of their voices. The imagery is excellently sensitive to the physical communication: 'as nervously responsive as a bit of finest Venetian crystal', 'a warm stream', 'one's very marrow', 'As if a wound . . . had been probed.' The continually changing struggle of anger and pity recorded and dramatized in the Casaubon scene was an inner action; this communication of nervous strain, good will, warmth, control, hysteria, and sorrow takes place in the public world, in a conventional drawing-room visit. It shows insight into the workings of dialogue without words as well as insight into the ways in which people feel together. Such mutual strong sympathy is usually preserved for scenes between lovers, in George Eliot as in other Victorian novelists, but this scene is exceptional in many ways. Dorothea's powers reach into the world of action, moving Rosamond to tell the truth about Will's feelings, but Rosamond goes back to her habitual self; the basil-plant survives. The particularity of this moment not only registers the strengths of emotional influence, but also contributes to a medium of feeling in which character is less stable and simple than Victorian fiction sometimes makes it out to be.

Even in the less powerful scenes of passionate crisis, feeling is related to thought and action. The characters think, act, and relate in a complex drama of feeling, the passions rise in intensity and crisis from the narrative flow. Even the minor characters draw much of their substance from such flow. But *Middlemarch* has one additional contribution to make to the story of human passion. Self-conscious in so many ways, tending like much great art to be about itself, to register its author's creative experiences, to assimilate forms and turn them into themes, it has something to divulge about the shaping power of feeling. Ladislaw's character is the nearest thing in the novel to a portrait of the artist, and a Romantic artist at that. Dorothea's elevated play of passion is not quite untouched by irony, and Will's is subjected to strong criticism. In Chapter 47 the central character is Ladislaw, and the analysis of his love is instructive about feeling in the most dramatic fashion, since the lover learns through unlearning. What he unlearns is a simplification about the nature, place, and power of feeling.

Like Casaubon, Ladislaw has been educated in the passions by literature, not by the classical poets, but the English:

> What others might have called the futility of his passion, made an additional delight for his imagination: he was conscious of a generous movement, and of verifying in his own experience that higher love-poetry which had charmed his fancy. Dorothea, he said to himself, was for ever enthroned in his soul: no other woman could sit higher than her footstool; and if he could have written out in immortal syllables the effect she wrought within him, he might have boasted after the example of old Drayton, that –
> 'Queens hereafter might be glad to live
> Upon the alms of her superfluous praise.'

This episode raises two interesting problems concerning strong feeling: how far can one choose feelings? and to what extent does a passionate imagination help the knowledge and control of feeling? The second question is the more personal. George Eliot seems to be interested in showing how a highly imaginative and sensitive mind can be as wrong about anticipation and control as that of an ardent girl or a too inhibited pedant. I am not sure if she has mastered the problem she has set in this chapter, and it might be argued that the dramatic action carries more truth than the generalization and analysis. It is perhaps an episode which grows in subtlety in the writing. Certainly, the chapter's motto seems more confined in simplicities than what follows:

> Was never true love loved in vain,
> For truest love is highest gain.
> No art can make it: it must spring
> Where elements are fostering.
> So in heaven's spot and hour
> Springs the little native flower,
> Downward root and upward eye,
> Shapen by the earth and sky.

The motto applies in a general way to the story of Will and Dorothea, but is much more simple than the prose action.

Will is presented in a characteristic emotional complexity: he is, as usual, adoring, and, as often, irritable. His emotions are linked with the 'heat', irritability, and restlessness of his response to Lydgate in the preceding chapter. George Eliot shows the mixture finely, since the restless feelings continue in a desire to see Dorothea and find another

vent in plaguing Casaubon; the irritation with Lydgate hooks on to
Casaubon as a more appropriate object, and his adoration carries on,
steady, but sealed off from the world of action. Will's love has a certain
strength and a certain weakness in being insulated from the possibilities
of ordinary love:

> Was he not making a fool of himself? - and at a time when he was more than
> ever conscious of being something better than a fool? And for what end?
> Well, for no definite end. True, he had dreamy visions of possibilities:
> there is no human being who having both passions and thoughts does not
> think in consequence of his passions - does not find images rising in his mind
> which soothe the passion with hope or sting it with dread. But this, which
> happens to us all, happens to some with a wide difference; and Will was not
> one of those whose wit 'keeps the roadway': he had his bypaths where there
> were little joys of his own choosing, such as gentlemen cantering on the
> highroad might have thought rather idiotic. The way in which he made a
> sort of happiness for himself out of his feeling for Dorothea was an example
> of this. It may seem strange, but it is the fact, that the ordinary vulgar vision
> of which Mr Casaubon suspected him - namely, that Dorothea might
> become a widow, and that the interest he had established in her mind
> might turn into acceptance of him as a husband - had no tempting,
> arresting power over him; he did not live in the scenery of such an event,
> and follow it out, as we all do with that imagined 'otherwise' which is our
> practical heaven. It was not only that he was unwilling to entertain
> thoughts which could be accused of baseness, and was already uneasy in the
> sense that he had to justify himself from the charge of ingratitude - the
> latent consciousness of many other barriers between himself and Dorothea
> besides the existence of her husband, had helped to turn away his
> imagination from speculating on what might befall Mr Casaubon. And
> there were yet other reasons. Will, we know, could not bear the thought of
> any flaw appearing in his crystal: he was at once exasperated and delighted
> by the calm freedom with which Dorothea looked at him and spoke to him,
> and there was something so exquisite in thinking of her just as she was, that
> he could not long for a change which must somehow change her. Do we not
> shun the street version of a fine melody? - or shrink from the news that the
> rarity - some bit of chiselling or engraving perhaps - which we have dwelt
> on even with exultation in the trouble it has cost us to snatch glimpses of it,
> is really not an uncommon thing, and may be obtained as an everyday
> possession?

George Eliot's benevolence does not prevent her being cunning. She
permits the recognition that passions shape images, and a gentle irony,

easy to miss, explains how Will makes 'joys of his own choosing'. A luxury of passion, this choosing of joy. George Eliot herself seems to waver rather uncertainly between an approval of Will's freedom from 'the ordinary vulgar vision . . . that Dorothea might become a widow' and a recognition of the limits of adoration. She seems to have a real feeling for Will's sense that his adoration is rare and remote, endorsing his chivalric worshipping in the image of the street version of a fine melody. But more critically ironic is the comparison of his identification to the 'rarity – some bit of chiselling or engraving perhaps – which we have dwelt on with exultation in the trouble it has cost us to snatch glimpses of it' which we suddenly learn, shrinking, 'may be obtained as an everyday possession'. Both similes are followed by a statement of apparent approval: 'Our good depends on the quality and breadth of our emotion.' This didactic statement of value, made through the imagery of measurement, may make us feel uncertain, less because of the associations of the words than because of the claim made: is it in fact so easy to measure such quality and such breadth? George Eliot is a great analyst of the passions, but it would be foolish to claim that the analysis never falters into facility. Will is to obtain his love 'as an everyday possession'; worship, adoration, higher love-poetry, queens, and footstools are inappropriate images for love in the quotidian world of *Middlemarch*. In a way, George Eliot seems to know this, or at least to glimpse the deficiency of those troubadour images.

The chapter moves from Will's love – half-endorsed, half-criticized – to his enjoyment of jealousy and malice, in a morality play of Petty Objection and Sublime Inclination. The conquest of conscience cheers him up and makes him complacent, and George Eliot registers a rare passage of content, purchased, like much content, by fantasy rather than rational anticipation. It is a spiteful as well as a sweet intent; Will feels joyful not just because he is journeying sunnily towards his love, 'skirting the wood, where the sunlight fell broadly under the budding boughs. . . . Everything seemed to know that it was Sunday, and to approve of his going to Lowick Church,' but also because he is amused at the thought of annoying Casaubon. The spring idyll is not idyllically grounded in noble feeling.

Out of the day, the expectation, and the content, comes the one lyric of the novel, a fragile flight of feeling caught in the great prose narrative:

O me, O me, what frugal cheer
    My love doth feed upon!
A touch, a ray, that is not here,
    A shadow that is gone:

A dream of breath that might be near,
    An inly-echoed tone,
The thought that one may think me dear,
    The place where one was known,

The tremor of a banished fear,
    An ill that was not done –
O me, O me, what frugal cheer
    My love doth feed upon!

The lyric is the one proof of Will's creative powers and by no means a bad one. But its merits are less important than its function. It is immediately followed by the appropriate description of the 'delicate throat' of the singer, and of his springlike brilliance; 'he looked like an incarnation of the spring whose spirit filled the air – a bright creature, abundant in uncertain promises.' The hinge on which this chapter of the passions turns is the 'uncertain promise'. Will is residing in his passionate moment, framing and forming it through lyric, and George Eliot seems to question and define the nature of his poetic medium by placing it in the testing flow of narrative action.

She first contrasts its purity of feeling with the impure source in life. Lyric derives its power from isolating strong feeling, and the novelist provides the history from which lyric is usually happily cut off. The poem, which is 'not exactly a hymn' but which fits Will's 'Sunday experience', does so only by ignoring jealousy and malice and concentrating on longing and love. Will is no unimaginative selector from emotional experience, and has not lightly been compared with Shelley or allowed wisdom on the subject of poetry. In Chapter 22 he tells Dorothea: 'To be a poet is to have a soul so quick to discern that no shade of quality escapes it, and so quick to feel, that discernment is but a hand playing with finely ordered variety on the chords of emotion.' In that same chapter George Eliot qualifies her comments on Will's habits of amorous worship, remarking that while 'remote worship of a woman throned' plays an important part in men's lives, the 'worshipper longs for some queenly recognition', and she probably expects the reader to carry in his mind some recollection of the things she said and showed in Will's contradictory 'imaginative demands' in those scenes in Rome. The contrast in this later episode between lyric purity and the impure source still permits the poem to possess 'finely ordered variety'. Will's hymn-like lyric admits the undernourished state of remote worship; does sweetly if faintly lament frugality in 'O me, O me'; does show the delicious items in love's diet – 'a touch, a ray, a shadow, a dream of breath, a tone, a thought, a place', and the unpalatable ones – a tremor of fear, 'An ill that was not done.' This courtly worship is trying to imagine starvation as well as nourishment. But when the imagined future comes, it confounds the lyric poet.

For the lyric of love is not only given a past, which throws its purity into special relief; it is also given a future. Will gets that taste of frugal cheer which he has so sweetly sighed over in his poem, but its taste is simply sour. The sympathetic weather, the dream, tone, place of the lyric longing, all turn out to have held uncertain promises. The promises are broken as soon as Will arrives at Lowick church. All his expectations go awry. He has expected to sit with the curate's family, but the Tuckers have left Lowick; he has expected to enjoy the sight of Dorothea, but finds that he dares not look at her; he is surprised by discomfort, realizes that she may be upset, that he may have blundered, and that the expected amusement at Casaubon's expense is not forthcoming: 'It was no longer amusing to vex Mr Casaubon, who had the advantage probably of watching him and seeing that he dared not turn his head. Why had he not imagined this beforehand?'

Will's actual feelings make plain the simplifications of lyric purity, as the poet moves from the delightful indulgences of image-worship to the destructive extreme of self-contempt, hostility, and cynicism:

> There was no delivering himself from his cage, however; and Will found his places and looked at his book as if he had been a schoolmistress, feeling that the morning service had never been so immeasurably long before, that he was utterly ridiculous, out of temper, and miserable. This was what a man got by worshipping the sight of a woman!

In a novel which at least tries to deal plainly with unideal existence, this rejection of worship is an important strand in the pattern of feeling. It would be hard to argue, however, that George Eliot is thoroughly clear and full in analysing the descent of Will and Dorothea into the ordinary world. It is a descent implied in the Finale[2]

2. 'Dorothea herself had no dreams of being praised above other women' and 'Certainly those determining acts of her life were not ideally beautiful'.

of the novel, and touched on in this episode: but in the later passages describing their farewell and final union George Eliot still surrounds the lovers with a dazzling halo. There is no dazzle here. Will Ladislaw leaves Lowick, having to 'walk back sadly at mid-day along the same road which he had trodden hopefully in the morning. The lights were all changed for him both without and within.' He writes no more poems, and perhaps the reader knows why.

A novelist who also writes poetry is in a good position to appraise the dangers of lyric. Lyric isolates the moment of passion, cuts off the historical flow backwards and onwards in time, and thus enacts the timeless ritual of passion itself. There are lyrics (Donne's or Shakespeare's) that manage to convey both the intensity and the sense of its mortal bonds. *Middlemarch* conveys the intensity, but keeps it in time and place.

The Sunday morning itself confounds Wills's idyllic and selective expectations about Sunday mornings, dreams as idyllic and selective as those in the poem, though rendered in prose – 'I have always liked the quaintness of the church and congregation; besides, I know the Tuckers: I shall go into their pew.' George Eliot said early in the chapter that our anticipations are shaped by passion, that we 'find images' which 'soothe the passion with hope or sting it with dread', and she shows Will making his desirable, sympathetic, and selective background image of society and environment. Church, congregation, and curate all fall into place in his imaginary forecast; the church and congregation 'idyllic', the curate conveniently where he used to be. It turns out, however, that the congregation of Lowick is less pastorally stable than Will's image has expected: the Tuckers have moved on, instead of staying in their pew as handy minor characters, and there is a new face, 'Mr Rigg's frog-face . . . something alien and unaccountable'. 'The place where one was known' has not stood still. The 'group of rural faces' has changed slightly, and George Eliot insists on this change through Will's discomfited expectations, and through another spring image, tough in its implications, 'hardly with more change than we see in the boughs of a tree which breaks here and there with age, but yet has young shoots'. We are always aware of the passage of time in *Middlemarch*.

Things have changed, people have slightly shifted position even in Lowick 'at peace' in 1831, 'not more agitated by Reform than by the solemn tenor of the Sunday sermon'. But George Eliot is not just registering history as 'background'. Society's slow change mirrors

Will's anachronistic and literary habits of worship. It is out of the feudal sense of place and hierarchy that 'the three generations of decent cottagers came . . . with a sense of duty to their betters generally – the smaller children regarding Mr Casaubon, who wore the black gown and mounted to the highest box, as probably the chief of all betters, and the one most awful if offended.' The implications of this comic version of deference are various: Casaubon is powerful and is offended, and nearly keeps Dorothea and Will apart for good. More important in the union of social chronicle and drama of passion is George Eliot's display of the community of socially determined attitudes and feelings, where they emerge in deference to squire, vicar, or throned queen. The feminist impatience, which runs through the novel, pervades the analysis of adoration, but it is enlarged to take in other versions of misplaced deference.

Will's lyric is not only unaware of the social links between its passionate moment and lower forms or lesser variants, it is also unaware of the thickly peopled world. In this inveterately social novel, we are perpetually reminded of the community. George Eliot insists[3] on placing her drama of personal passion in the peopled environment. The 'quaint' congregation has its point of view, too. It is composed of people who also tend, like Will, to look up, and who are also all making up their experience with self-flattering bias and selection. A comic displacement urges this multiple viewpoint as a social and psychological truth, amusing but serious:

> The congregation had been used to seeing Will at church in former days, and no one took much note of him except the quire, who expected him to make a figure in the singing.

> The clerk observed with surprise that Mr Ladislaw did not join in the tune of Hanover, and reflected that he might have a cold.

The clerk and members of the congregation are not rustic fools designed to frame fine intensities, but human reminders that passion occurs, as Auden says, 'While someone else is eating or opening a window or just walking dully along.'[4] It is probably more precise and more faithfully attentive to the art of George Eliot to say that one

---

3. As Dickens did too, for instance, in the brilliant psychological analysis of the professional and social shaping of Bradley Headstone in *Our Mutual Friend*.
4. 'Musée des Beaux Arts'.

passion is seen to occur in the world of everyone else's passion. To the choir and the clerk, Will is someone who will figure in the music. If he is silent, it is because he must have a cold. Such density and candour go to make the richness and reality of *Middlemarch*, registering the problems of passion in that world of ordinary experience which was George Eliot's province.

1971; published 1975

6
Middlemarch: Public and Private Worlds

When we make use of the crude, common, convenient term 'world' in order to say something about the work of a novelist, we probably have in mind one or more of these meanings: the refraction of social and personal experience, from which we may inferentially reconstruct a source 'world', rather as Humphry House does in *The Dickens World*; the uniquely typical life of the novel's imaginary and consistent history, geography, population, ethos, sociology, metaphysics; and the total *œuvre* which bears the imprint of its novelist-god. We bring to the response and analysis of all or any of these worlds that private and public world which we ourselves inhabit, making our inferences and reconstructions according to our time, place, personal experience, belief and life-style. The world of George Eliot and the world of *Middlemarch* is remade for each reader and at each reading. As someone remarked at one of the three *Middlemarch* conferences in 1971-2, 'Why did *we* write *these* papers?' The answers were too complex, private and inaccessible to be appended.

If as critics of fiction we take our bearings not only from each other but from what our novelist perceives about the nature of fiction, we find that George Eliot discourages us from using the term 'world' unreflectively. One of the things *Middlemarch* has to show, explicitly and implicitly, is the plurality of personal worlds. We learn to handle the metaphor as a metaphor, provisionally and ironically, both when reading novels and when reflecting on those worlds outside novels which are made up of many kinds of experience, including that of reading novels.

104

The word 'world' occurs in *Middlemarch* in the final sentence, as late and as memorably as possible. By the time she gets there George Eliot has earned the right both to vagueness and to melioristic suggestion in words which could not be taken from a first sentence in any of her novels: 'the growing good of the world is partly dependent on unhistoric acts'. This open and extensive use of the word includes past and future, is morally and socially undefined, and derives meaning from everything that has come before it in the novel. The first use of 'world' is a very closed, precise and relativist one, which makes it plain that George Eliot sees the individuality of such acts of construction. She tells us in Chapter 1 that Dorothea's mind 'was theoretic, and yearned by its nature after some lofty conception of the world which might frankly include the parish of Tipton and her own rule of conduct there'. The imagery of yearning and height emphasizes the activity of construction, Dorothea's characteristic range from near to far, her refusal to be either abstract or parochial, her beginning with self and Tipton, and her aspirations beyond into the larger 'world'.

The next emphatic appearance of the word[1] comes when Casaubon introduces his 'world' in Chapter 2, at the dinner party in Tipton Grange where he and Dorothea first meet. His use of the word is in one sense large, but is essentially restricted both in time and personal style: 'My mind is something like the ghost of an ancient, wandering about the world and trying mentally to construct it as it used to be, in spite of ruin and confusing changes.' Dorothea immediately picks up and reinterprets his ideal of construction in the light of her own, judging and deprecating her loftiness in comparison with what seems to be the new Casaubon scale:

> To reconstruct a past world, doubtless with a view to the highest purposes of truth – what a work to be in any way present at, to assist in, though only as a lamp-holder!

The reconstruction continues in the next chapter, and after an evening, a day, and the part of a morning spent in his company, she concludes:

> 'He thinks with me,' said Dorothea to herself, 'or rather, he thinks a whole world of which my thought is but a poor twopenny mirror. And his feelings too, his whole experience – what a lake compared with my little pool!'

1. There are more casual or casual-seeming appearances between the two.

After Casaubon drives off to Lowick at three o'clock on the 'beautiful breezy autumn day', Dorothea walks in the wood, thinking intensely about her need for Casaubon as a guide to the past. Casaubon has been introduced to the reader as a historian,[2] and George Eliot emphasizes Dorothea's historical consciousness, her sense of the past, and its relation to her needs in the present, and for the future. Walking along the bridle path, she longs for a guide 'who would take her along the grandest path'. The literal and metaphorical imagery of paths insists that she has failed to read the significance of Casaubon's introductory images; all too accurately he describes himself as like a ghost – but of an ancient, capable only of 'wandering . . . and trying' rather than firmly guiding. He is a historian who ignores the evidence of history, 'trying mentally to construct it as it used to be, in spite of ruin and confusing changes'. Compare Dorothea's very different sense of futurity:

'There would be nothing trivial about our lives. Everyday-things with us would mean the greatest things. It would be like marrying Pascal. I should learn to see the truth by the same light as great men have seen it by. And then I should know what to do, when I got older: I should see how it was possible to lead a grand life here – now – in England.' (Chapter 3)

She inserts into her view of Casaubon's world view her own moral purpose of practical and immediate construction, and her emphasis on the here-and-now and England strongly contrasts with his backward, evidence-ignoring, time-leaping look, just as her careful but innocent gloss 'doubtless for the highest purposes of truth' draws attention to his entire neglect of moral end. Perhaps the greatest contrast is between the intensity and vigour of her language, feelings and movement, and his total languor and flatness. The speech about the ghost of an ancient is a non-answer to Brooke's questions about Southey (Casaubon having pardonably failed in 'keeping pace with Mr Brooke's impetuous reason') and it is also expressively delivered, 'with precision, as if he had been called upon to make a public statement' and in a 'balanced sing-song neatness'.

Casaubon's images for the historical sense are dead and unself-consciously archaic, Dorothea's are alive and self-reflectively modern.

2. '. . . understood for many years to be engaged on a great work concerning religious history' (Chapter 1).

Casaubon recognizes the existence of change, and has after all written his 'timely' pamphlet on the Catholic question; but he finds the evidence of historical change an obstacle to his static research as he tries to reconstruct the far past without taking account of the processes of history. Dorothea's viewpoint is not only self-reflectively modern, but very close to the most influential self-conscious reflections on the nature of history which were available to George Eliot, at the time of writing *Middlemarch* (1869–71) as well as the time of the novel's action (1829 to 1831). Carlyle wrote two essays in *Fraser's Magazine* (in 1830 and 1833) which insisted on the participation of the present in the consciousness of history and which described history, in an image which needs no underlining, as 'a web'[3] composed of unrecorded acts, as inclusive of the present, as including the moderns both as actors and as relators. Here are two extracts from Carlyle's essay 'On History Again' (1833):

> Only he who understands what has been, can know what should be and will be. It is of the last importance that the individual have ascertained his relation to the whole; 'an individual helps not,' it has been written: 'only he who unites with many at the proper hour'. How easy, in a sense, for your all-instructed Nanac [Nanac Shah too, we remember, steeped himself three days in some sacred Well; and there learnt enough] to work without waste or force (or what we call fault); and, in practice, act new History, as perfectly as, in theory he knew the old! Comprehending what the given world was, and what it had and what it wanted, how might his clear effort strike in at the right time and the right point; wholly increasing the true current and tendency, nowhere cancelling itself in opposition thereto! Unhappily, such smooth-running, ever-accelerated course is nowise the one appointed us. . . .

> To use a ready-made similitude, we might liken Universal History to a magic web; and consider with astonishment how, by philosophic insight and indolent neglect, the ever-growing fabric wove itself forward, out of that ravelled immeasurable mass of threads and thrums (which we name *Memoirs*); nay, at each new lengthening, (at each new *epoch*), changed its whole proportions, its hue and structure to the very origin. Thus, do not the records of a Tacitus acquire new meaning, after seventeen hundred years, in the hands of a Montesquieu? Niebuhr has to reinterpret for us, at a still greater distance, the writings of a Titus Livius: nay, the religious archaic

---

3. I think it likely that George Eliot's fondness for 'web', 'current' and 'epoch' derived from Carlyle.

chronicles of a Hebrew Prophet and Lawgiver escape not the like fortune; and many a ponderous Eichhorn scans, with new-ground philosophic spectacles, the revelation of a Moses, and strives to reproduce for this century what, thirty centuries ago, was of plainly infinite significance to all. Consider History with the beginnings of it stretching dimly into the remote Time; emerging darkly out of the mysterious Eternity: the ends of it enveloping *us* at this hour, whereof we at this hour, both as actors and relators, form part!

Middlemarch is the first English novel to analyse the psychology of historical consciousness. Its analysis involves seeing the relation of public and private worlds, recognizing that private experience shapes the sense of the public, just as the 'larger public life' shapes the private world.

In *The Historical Novel* Lukacs is concerned with the ways in which novelists reflect and analyse historic events and historic causality. It is true, as he says, that the necessary condition for the growth of the historical novel was the development of historical and global consciousness at the beginning of the nineteenth century. It is also true, as he knew, that the new genre of historical novel led to sharper reflections on the historical consciousness which fed back again into the social novel, enriching its presentation of the private and public life. George Eliot provides us with an instance which falls outside the categories of Lukacs. *Middlemarch* is not only an instance of History by Indirection, as Jerome Beaty has shown,[4] and an exploration of History as Analogy, as David Carroll argued soon after Beaty,[5] but is a very precocious novel about the sense of history. It describes as a part of a psychological, moral and social complex, what it feels like to have and to use the sense of history. Dorothea knows that she relates to the immediate and distant past, she is fully conscious of the Carlylean continuity in which yesterday continues history into today, and in which tomorrow needs to be aware of last week, last year, and last century. This awareness is examined not only in Dorothea but throughout *Middlemarch*. It is shown in many variant forms, negative and positive. It is evaluated in presences, absences and displacements. Its analysis proffers one of the most original insights in *Middlemarch*.

The insight is highly characteristic of George Eliot, who as a novelist

4. Jerome Beaty, 'History by Indirection: The Era of Reform in *Middlemarch*' (*Victorian Studies*, I, 1957, pp. 973-9).
5. David R. Carroll, 'Unity Through Analogy: An Interpretation of *Middlemarch*' (*Victorian Studies*, II, 1959, pp. 305-16).

seems to have incorporated into her art most swiftly and subtly her creative experiences as well as those from life. Perhaps all great works of art are about themselves, and in order fully to see this self-preoccupation in *Middlemarch* we too have to look back into the history of her other novels. Into each novel goes what has been learnt from the previous ones, not only as the craft matures but as her experience as a novelist instructs her in the themes of imagination and narration. In and through writing she learnt more about imagination and love, about the ways in which we shape our sense of the world inside and outside novels. For instance, her interest in the life-narrations which loom large in all experience was fairly rudimentary in *Scenes of Clerical Life*, but it became a prominent aspect of fictional psychology in *Adam Bede* and *The Mill on the Floss*, which took their author's experience of story-telling into their content and argument, as well as into their form. One could say the same about her interest in imagistic and dramatic modes. Her experience of metaphor is incorporated in her handling of Casaubon's and Featherstone's imagination, in her analysis of the way their thinking gets entangled in metaphor; and her experience of the lyrical intensities and limits of poetry gets into the presentation of Ladislaw. The experience of studying and imagining the past, familiar to the author of all these retrospective novels, was of course most intense in the writing of *Romola*, her only conventional historical novel. But the other fiction is instructive too.

George Eliot's way of connecting outer and inner, public and private, historic and unhistoric, is to locate and understand the link within the individual consciousness. She does not historicize the life of the individual, perhaps having learnt from *Romola*. Nor does she dehistoricize experience by showing the gulf between the private and the public life as she did in *Scenes of Clerical Life*, where she stressed the historical colour, and emphasized the date of customs and costumes, while exclaiming about the past's innocence of its future, through sudden shifts of perspective in which characters and passions were high-lighted against history. In 'Mr Gilfil's Love Story', for instance, the narrator makes a bid for pathos by switching from personal foreground to public background rather artificially, using the historical perspective to 'mark the time' and to act as an intensifier of the heroine's small helplessness:

> While this poor little heart was being bruised with a weight too heavy for it,
> Nature was holding on her calm inexorable way, in unmoved and terrible

beauty. The stars were rushing in their eternal courses; the tides swelled to the level of the last expectant weed; the sun was making brilliant day to busy nations on the other side of the swift earth. The stream of human thought and deed was hurrying and broadening onward. The astronomer was at his telescope; the great ships were labouring over the waves; the toiling eagerness of commerce, the fierce spirit of revolution, were only ebbing in brief rest; and sleepless statesmen were dreading the possible crisis of the morrow. What were our little Tina and her trouble in this mighty torrent, rushing from one awful unknown to another? Lighter than the smallest centre of quivering life in the water-drop, hidden and uncared for as the pulse of anguish in the breast of the tiniest bird that has fluttered down to its nest with the long-sought food, and has found the nest torn and empty. (Chapter 5)

This transition marks a parallel, instead of a contrast, between private and public passions:

The last chapter has given the discerning reader sufficient insight into the state of things at Cheverel Manor in the summer of 1788. In that summer, we know, the great nation of France was agitated by conflicting thoughts and passions, which were but the beginnings of sorrows. And in our Caterina's little breast, too, there were terrible struggles. (Chapter 3)

These are crude and arbitrary uses of historical reference, and although she was to continue to use history as background and analogy in *Daniel Deronda*, the image of historical perspective reappears there in a newly functional form, registering in portentous questions the sense of history inside Gwendolen's mind. George Eliot has several times remarked Gwendolen's lack of any historical sense by the comparison with the grand march of events, and at the end of the novel forces her to feel the powerful pressure of the public world:

'What are you going to do?' she asked, at last, very timidly. 'Can I understand the ideas, or am I too ignorant?'
    'I am going to the East to become better acquainted with the condition of my race in various countries there,' said Deronda, gently – anxious to be as explanatory as he could on what was the impersonal part of their separateness from each other. 'The idea that I am possessed with is that of restoring a political existence to my people, making them a nation again, giving them a national centre, such as the English have, though they too are scattered over the face of the globe. That is a task which presents itself to me as a duty: I am resolved to begin it, however feebly. I am resolved to devote

my life to it. At the least, I may awaken a movement in other minds, such as has been awakened in my own.'

There was a long silence between them. The world seemed getting larger round poor Gwendolen, and she more solitary and helpless in the midst. The thought that he might come back after going to the East, sank before the bewildering vision of these wide-stretching purposes in which she felt herself reduced to a mere speck. There comes a terrible moment to many souls when the great movements of the world, the larger destinies of mankind, which have lain aloof in newspapers and other neglected reading, enter like an earthquake into their own lives – when the slow urgency of growing generations turns into the tread of an invading army or the dire clash of civil war, and grey fathers know nothing to seek for but the corpses of their blooming sons, and girls forget all vanity to make lint and bandages which may serve for the shattered limbs of their betrothed husbands. (Chapter 69)

It is the experience of writing *Middlemarch* which has transformed the image. There is some sense now in making a to-do about the gap between the public and the private event and passion, because the novelist has come to see the moral implications of wondering and caring about the great world. The characters in *Scenes of Clerical Life* and *Adam Bede* were innocents. Maggie Tulliver asked many questions about the nature, use and relevance of logic, literature, and geometry, but the acknowledgment of her historical identity is made by the author's commentary, outside the character. We see that Maggie is representative of certain restrictions and limitations, in sex, family, occupation, society, and ethos, but we also see her ignorance of the historical conditions. *Romola* is an historical novel, which reconstructs major events and historical characters and also attempts, in Thackerayan fashion, to show the quotidian and familiar inhabitants of a past time. The effort to imagine and to research for *Romola* must have made George Eliot sharply conscious of the historian's activity and may have led her, in *Middlemarch*, to put the historical action inside the mind; this psychological analysis of historical thinking was probably helped also by the writing of *Felix Holt*, a more external novel about the 1832 Reform Act which left her freer to explore what Carlyle saw as the historical significance of the unhistoric life. *Felix Holt* exhausted the desire to show political reaction and characters, and she was free in *Middlemarch* to locate the consciousness of history within her characters. But *Romola* provided the crucial experience, for in writing it she had to think about the relation of cultural and social history, the nature of historical consciousness, and the purpose and reception of a novel written for the present age about the past. Perhaps the greatest achievement of *Romola* was to make *Middlemarch* possible.

Middlemarch is a novel about good and bad historians. It is also about people, good and bad, who have no sense of history. In *Daniel Deronda* George Eliot is writing from the moral base delicately but firmly created by Jane Austen in *Mansfield Park*, where she relates Fanny Price's awareness of the larger world – 'Did you not hear me question him about the slave-trade?' – to her capacity for rhapsody, wonder, veneration, sympathy, and knowledge. In *Daniel Deronda*, as in *Mansfield Park*, virtue is forced out of its fugitive cloisters into a sense of the world, but in *Middlemarch* George Eliot shows a realist tolerance of decent people without much sense of history. Less like a fable than any of her other novels, *Middlemarch* has a moral spectrum of many shades. History is projected indirectly, as Jerome Beaty has said, sometimes off-centre, sometimes muted, sometimes statically but vividly imaged, as in Rome, the city of visible history. George Eliot's concern with the historical consciousness in *Middlemarch* is not simply a moral one, for she observes the co-existence of a public sense with moral responsibility or moral inactivity, and the co-existence of public ignorance with a lack of moral sense or with moral decency.

Rosamond Vincy has no historical sense, and rests unperturbed, while her father, whose historical sense is strong in those connections and causes that affect his trade, tells her with bluntness that she wasn't educated to marry a poor man and that this is a bad time to do so, 'with this disappointment about Fred, and Parliament going to be dissolved, and machine-breaking everywhere, and an election coming':

> 'Dear papa! what can that have to do with my marriage?'
> 'A pretty deal to do with it! We may all be ruined for what I know – the country's in that state! Some say it's the end of the world, and be hanged if I don't think it looks like it! Anyhow, it's not a time for me to be drawing money out of my business, and I should wish Lydgate to know that.'
> 'I am sure he expects nothing, papa. And he has such very high connections: he is sure to rise in one way or another. He is engaged in making scientific discoveries.' (Chapter 36)

Vincy's sense of the world is worldly-wise, Rosamond's worldly and ignorant, insufficient for an appraisal of her lot, frighteningly sufficient for persuasion. She silences her father by a superficially impressive mention of 'scientific discoveries', and he cuts no ice with his quick run-through of topical disasters, private and public. Their dialogue makes no simple correlation of virtue and knowledge; Vincy's narrow sense of the larger world is created and bounded by self-interest, innocent both of scientific discoveries and their possible relation to 'rising in one way or another'. (The last phrase is a tiny example of George Eliot's apparently effortless wringing of irony from the common phrase.) Rosamond runs randomly through various facts about Lydgate, 'See how he has been called in by the Chettams and Casaubons'; 'And he has such very high connections: he is sure to rise in one way or another. He is engaged in making scientific discoveries'; 'Mr Lydgate is a gentleman'. Her sense of social causality is dangerously obtuse; these two materialists, father and daughter, the warm-hearted and the cold, have a worldly sense but no imaginative knowledge of the public world.

There is a famous instance of displacement quoted by Gordon Haight[6] and Jerome Beaty,[7] when at the end of the novel various Middlemarch Tories are gathered together at Freshitt Hall, in October 1831, discussing the defeat of the Reform Bill. Because of the Bill 'Mr Cadwallader came to be walking on the slope of the lawn near the great conservatory at Freshitt Hall, holding the "Times" in his hands behind him, while he talked with a trout-fisher's dispassionate-ness about the prospects of the country to Sir James Chettam.' Not only the men but 'The ladies also talked politics, though more fitfully'. From this fitful feminine talk the political facts filter through. Gossip is sifted through the response of various private passions and humours: Mrs Cadwallader, representing birth and breeding, 'was strong on the intended creation of peers' which she has learnt about from her aristocratic cousin; Lady Chettam is dim, decorous and irrelevant, Celia dotingly maternal, 'It would be very nice, though, if he were a Viscount'. When Mr Brooke arrives the others naturally interpret his gloom as political, only to find that it is his response to Dorothea's intended marriage and not to the Lords' rejection of the Bill. So the personal event immediately takes over from the crisis in the public world, not only for Brooke, but for the whole party. George Eliot is displacing history not simply to present it with subtlety but to insist that private relationships and interest drive out the larger happening.

One of her most interesting scenes of displacement comes in Chapter

6. Introduction to Riverside edition of *Middlemarch* (Boston, 1956).
7. 'History by Indirection: The Era of Reform in *Middlemarch*', loc. cit.

56, where the public world is elaborately and prominently analysed. It
opens quietly, marking the connection between the construction of the
railways and Caleb Garth's newly undertaken management of the
farms and tenements attached to Lowick Manor. Although George
Eliot insists that in praising Dorothea's 'head for business', Caleb had
in mind not money but the skilful application of labour, he is plainly
said to have a bias 'towards getting the best possible terms from
railway companies'. He undertakes a survey with the railway's agents,
and it is interrupted by 'six or seven' labourers attacking with their
hay-forks. George Eliot has more elaborate treatment of historical
events in this chapter than anywhere else in the novel, and its
displacement is the more pointed. The introductory exposition is
built up with careful attention to steps and stages, in a long, witty,
dramatized exposition on the views of the women who swear that
nothing will bring them to travel by rail, and the proprietors who
intend to get the highest possible price 'for permission to injure
mankind'. The slow understanding of Solomon Featherstone, the road
overseer, is then unfolded for comedy and social respresentation. He
isn't exactly a fool: 'Well, there's this to be said, Jane . . . the more
spokes we put in their wheel, the more they'll pay us to let 'em go on, if
they must come whether or not.' There follows the careful analysis of
Solomon's by no means unsubtle and ineffective provocations, and the
revolt of the Frick labourers, bored, suspicious, conservative, anti-
urban, and all for a bit of 'good foon'. In spite of its rather
condescending humour about the rustic rebels, this scene is one in
which George Eliot raises a central political question, one which she
finds and leaves unanswerable. 'Nettle-seed needs no digging', but the
one labourer who stands outside the attack, old Timothy Cooper, 'who
had stayed behind turning his hay while the others had been gone on
their spree', with the full authority of intelligence, experience, and
non-violence, accuses Caleb Garth of being exactly what he is, a
master's man. Caleb has been speaking soothingly, his author
approving of his artless pauses and images:

> 'But come, you didn't mean any harm. Somebody told you the railroad
> was a bad thing. That was a lie. It may do a bit of harm here and there, to
> this and to that; and so does the sun in heaven. But the railway's a good
> thing.'
> 'Aw! good for the big folks to make money out on,' said old Timothy
> Cooper, who had stayed behind turning his hay while the others had been

gone on their spree; – 'I'n seen lots o' things turn up sin' I war a young un – the war an' the peace, and the canells, an' the oald King George, an the Regen', an' the new King George, an' the new un as has got a new ne-ame – an' it's been all aloike to the poor mon. What's the canells been t'him? They'n brought him neyther me-at nor be-acon, nor wage to lay by, if he didn't save it wi' clemmin' his own inside. Times ha' got wusser for him sin' I war a young un. An' so it'll be wi' the railroads. They'll on'y leave the poor mon furder behind. But them are fools as meddle, and so I told the chaps here. This is the big folks's world, this is. But yo're for the big folks, Muster Garth, yo are.'

It is a powerful moment, and rises to an even higher peak when George Eliot has the sense and candour to admit not only that Caleb has no reply, but that there is no reply:

Timothy was a wiry old labourer, of a type lingering in those times – who had his savings in a stocking-foot, lived in a lone cottage, and was not to be wrought on by any oratory, having as little of the feudal spirit, and believing as little, as if he had not been totally unacquainted with the Age of Reason and the Rights of Man. Caleb was in a difficulty known to any person attempting in dark times and unassisted by miracle to reason with rustics who are in possession of an undeniable truth which they know through a hard process of feeling, and can let it fall like a giant's club on your neatly carved argument for a social benefit which they do *not* feel.

Timothy completes the drama and shatters the argument, and his role and function are specially satisfying when one compares him with Dickens's Stephen Blackpool: Timothy's wise and consistent detachment does not criticize his fellow-labourers, but speaks from his hay-turning, and to the point. The scene is thorough in analysis and self-contained in drama, depending on striking nonce-characters and real political debate. All the more startling, then, to find this political impact abruptly displaced. For the coming of the railway is not there in its own right but is used instrumentally to discover Fred Vincy's moment of vocation. What was shown as a vital and unresolved clash between socially representative forces comes to be described as an accident:

For the effective accident is but the touch of fire where there is oil and tow; and it always appeared to Fred that the railway brought the needed touch.

Fred is not lowered by his self-interest and lack of social imagination, but George Eliot seems to bring her own social imagination into unusually full play, in order most calmly to turn its direction. What had seemed of central interest was not, after all, the point of the scene, and the large historical events of the railway and revolt recede in interest, like a Holy Family inconspicuous in a corner of a Breughel, and truly enough, since for Caleb and Fred the personal life is what matters. It is a crisis of some social moment in the personal life, too, but the sense of a diversion from history is still impressive. For Caleb and Fred the railway was only the precipitating accident, and when Caleb tells his wife the story of the day George Eliot repeats the displacement by devoting a mere summarizing half-sentence to the labourers' attack, and over a page to the personal crisis: 'He had already narrated the adventure which had brought about Fred's sharing in his work, but had kept back the further result'. In the story of love, vocation, and parenthood, the historical moment is subordinate, so it is fore-shortened, diminished and dismissed.

Here George Eliot has her history and reduces it to the appropriate proportions, as she may have learnt to do from *Romola*, where she had not managed things quite so well. It was her 1829, and it was her reader's 1829, from their perspective of 1871–2; but for Caleb and Fred it was the innocent present tense, and the historical significance of their date and their adventure lay in the future.

For Dorothea, the present is not historically innocent. To go back to the beginning, in that first big social scene in Chapter 2, where Casaubon and Chettam dine with Brooke and his two nieces in a promisingly mixed and unmarried party, the characters present the public world through private passions, tastes and concerns. The historical sense is dramatized as an interest naturally, waywardly, and unpredictably correlated with conscience. Like Jane Austen in *Mansfield Park*, George Eliot is writing about social conscience and social consciousness, and the dinner-party acts like many of Jane Austen's group scenes to show the snatch-and-grab action of social converse, and the personal impetus behind our sense of the public world. We make up our private and public worlds at the same time, and the relation between the two is complex. Chapter 2 establishes time, place and culture in a desultory but continuous conversation, its slivers of talk brilliantly suiting the small dinner-party of intimates, acquaintances, and strangers. The talk turns round, and each turn is public in theme, private in motive and address. The chapter-motto is

Don Quixote's transformation of the basin into the Helmet of Mambrino, the emblem standing for Dorothea's aspiration, nobility, madness, delusion, anachronism and appositely prefacing a scene of multiple illusion where the characters clandestinely and mistakenly solicit each other. Brooke soliloquizes erratically, fixed by one of George Eliot's sharp alliterative shafts, as 'these motes from the mass of a magistrate's mind' shame Dorothea, conscious chiefly of the Locke-like Casaubon; Chettam, 'excellent baronet', hopefully woos Dorothea with Davy's Agricultural Chemistry; Casaubon is alerted by Dorothea's energetic and high-principled speech; Dorothea is entangled by modest self-abnegatory boasts; Celia finds Casaubon's moles repugnant and pities Sir James's delusions; Casaubon makes his revealing speech about living with the dead. The public world is rapidly sketched in this private drama, where the counters are Wordsworth, Humphry Davy, Cambridge, agricultural experiments, electricity, Adam Smith, political economy, the limitations of young ladies, Southey, hunting, rural housing, and Wilberforce. As the hard facts of history are blown about like bubbles, the public is there for the readers because it is there for the characters. George Eliot fixes the ways in which people create their fictions of each other, shows how the private fiction merges with the public, and begins to measure the weight of the individual public consciences.

The novel distinguishes two dimensions, the public and the personal, or the historic and the unhistoric. It was not wrong for Fred and Caleb to fail to observe how their personal interests were minor events, compared with the coming of the railway or Timothy's unanswerable argument. But for Mr Brooke, philanthropist and would-be politician, or Casaubon, cleric and would-be historian, there is a moral failure. What they attempt is life in the public world, so their failures in public consciousness *are* failures. It is as a religious historian that Casaubon is first introduced, and it is as a historian that he first speaks of himself. What he says is highly significant, and we are required not only to attend to the words but also to Dorothea's swift quixotic interpretation:

'I feed too much on the inward sources; I live too much with the dead. My mind is something like the ghost of an ancient, wandering about the world and trying mentally to construct it as it used to be, in spite of ruin and confusing changes.'

Romola too contains the ghost of an ancient, and in it George Eliot learnt the difficulties and sterilities of trying to reconstruct a past world, of going back, like Casaubon, over irksome intervening timemarks. Casaubon's researches were shaped by his author's, and in her presentation of his historical scholarship, the debt to *Romola* is almost too painfully plain. Sartre's Roquentin gave up history for fiction because history lacked particulars; Casaubon is certainly the kind of historian who lacks a sense of particulars as he also lacks Carlyle's sense that history must include the present. Casaubon as historian is doubly dead, not only the ghost but the ghost of an ancient, and one who tried to reconstruct the past 'in spite of ruin and confusing changes' as if process could be ignored. Casaubon is the negation of the historical consciousness, and Dorothea (Fanny Price's successor) is its active exemplar. Her concern is conspicuously aware of the present, and she is unable to ignore ruin and confusing changes. She is not the only character in search of historical meaning, but the most urgent and ingenuous seeker. When we first see her she interprets Casaubon's too revealing self-description according to her own needs to reconstruct the past for an epistemological purpose: 'To reconstruct a past world, doubtless with a view to the highest purposes of truth – what a work to be in any way present at, to assist in, though only as a lampholder!' The highest purposes of truth are vague, but George Eliot's point about Dorothea's meliorism (perhaps about religion in general) is that it is vague, admiring glorious things in a blind sort of way, as Dorothea tells Will, widening the skirts of light. Still, there is precision as well as vagueness in Dorothea's inner narrative, and as she revises her vision, in that fluent reworking of memory and fantasy which composes consciousness, she becomes decidedly less vague. She wants to reconstruct the past in order to know how to live in the present: 'The thing which seemed to her best, she wanted to justify by the completest knowledge; and not to live in a pretended admission of rules which were never acted on.' This becomes more concrete as her fantasy of instructive marriage weaves its web:

> There would be nothing trivial about our lives. Everyday-things with us would mean the greatest things. It would be like marrying Pascal. I should learn to see the truth by the same light as great men have seen it by. And then I should know what to do, when I got older: I should see how it was possible to lead a grand life here – now – in England. (Chapter 3)

It seems possible that T. S. Eliot, who admired George Eliot, may have found his namesake's words echoing somewhere in the mind when in *Little Gidding*, also concerned with pressures of past on the present and needs for tradition, he wrote, 'Now and in England,' and 'History is now and England'. Dorothea's need for history is not unlike T. S. Eliot's.

She is badly in need of the 'guide who would take her along the grandest path' when she goes from England on her wedding journey to Rome. We first see her there, usefully and appropriately, through the eyes of two other historians, Naumann and Will Ladislaw. Naumann is a key figure, who as a Nazarene painter has his own interest in going back in time. He calls Will to come and admire his 'fine bit of antithesis':

> 'There lies antique beauty, not corpse-like even in death, but arrested in the complete contentment of its sensuous perfection: and here stands beauty in its breathing life, with the consciousness of Christian centuries in its bosom.' (Chapter 19)

and a little later:

> 'If you were an artist, you would think of Mistress Second-Cousin as antique form animated by Christian sentiment – a sort of Christian Antigone – sensuous force controlled by spiritual passion.' (Chapter 19)

Will explains the theory that lies behind this conscious interest in historical compression through symbol, when he tells Casaubon later on that his friend is one 'of the chief renovators of Christian art, one of those who had not only revived but expanded that grand conception of supreme events as mysteries at which the successive ages were spectators, and in relation to which the great souls of all periods became as it were contemporaries' (Chapter 22). He dazzlingly flatters Casaubon and amuses Dorothea by the account of his mimicry of Naumann's 'breadth of intention' by painting Tamburlaine in his chariot representing 'the tremendous course of the world's physical history lashing on the harnessed dynasties'. Dorothea, a little less humourless than she has been made out, sees the joke:

> 'Do you intend Tamburlaine to represent earthquakes and volcanoes?'
> 'Oh yes,' said Will, laughing, 'and migrations of races and clearings of forests – and America and the steam-engine. Everything you can imagine!'

'What a difficult kind of shorthand!' said Dorothea, smiling towards her
husband. 'It would require all your knowledge to be able to read it.'
(Chapter 22)

George Eliot's conversational small-change can be as resonant as her
imagery: 'everything you can imagine' and 'it would require all your
knowledge' are to reveal their density: to understand the course of the
world's history indeed requires everything that Dorothea can imagine
and more than all Casaubon's knowledge.

Her imagination does rather better than his knowledge, when she
asks him about another mythical image, Raphael's[8] 'Cupid and
Psyche'. Dorothea asks a personal and passionate question, about
personal feeling, 'But do you care about them?' when he has
impersonally and coldly commended the frescoes because 'most
persons think it worth-while' to visit them. He turns away Dorothea's
'But do you care' to reply in the passive voice, 'They are, I believe,
highly esteemed', and speaks from a pedant's knowledge and
judgment, having nothing else:

> 'They are, I believe, highly esteemed. Some of them represent the fable of
> Cupid and Psyche, which is probably the romantic invention of a literary
> period, and cannot, I think, be reckoned as a genuine mythical product.
> But if you like these wall-paintings we can easily drive thither; and you will
> then, I think, have seen the chief works of Raphael, any of which it were a
> pity to omit in a visit to Rome. He is the painter who has been held to
> combine the most complete grace of form with sublimity of expression.
> Such at least I have gathered to be the opinion of conoscenti.'
>
> This kind of answer given in a measured official tone, as of a clergyman
> reading according to the rubric, did not help to justify the glories of the
> Eternal City, or to give her the hope that if she knew more about them the
> world would be joyously illuminated for her. (Chapter 20)

Sexual passion, nerve, beauty, light,[9] loss – he is blind to these, even on
his wedding journey in Rome. His is the dulled scholar's inability to

---

8. George Eliot's knowledge and scrupulousness are beautifully filtered through
Casaubon's pedantry when he accurately describes the frescoes as 'designed or painted
by Raphael'. The frescoes are now known to have been designed but not painted by
Raphael.
9. When I made this comment I had not seen the Cupid and Psyche frescoes in the Villa
Farnesina in Rome, and assumed that they would include what most of us will think of as
the heart of the myth – the dangerous light which Psyche holds up to Cupid. However,
the frescoes were never completed, and what Dorothea and Casaubon would have seen

speak personally, passionately, even aesthetically to the eager student of culture who demands personal response, but finds only arid scholarship, and conventional judgment.

Dorothea is also attempting a personal response to Rome's bewildering cultural mixture, which confounds her by its sensuality, its aestheticism, and its 'ruin and confusing changes'. It is perfectly in keeping with Casaubon's lack of passion that he should fail to respond to 'Cupid and Psyche' and to the romantic period, but equally important and less conspicuous is the total failure of his historical sense. The demand that he should relate past to present is implicit in her 'do you care?' What Naumann so confidently sees and renders in visual symbols of Christian art, through an ethical aesthetic mediaevalism that can condense, assimilate, and reconstruct, and what Will so brilliantly parodies in his claim that Rome's very miscellaneousness 'made the mind flexible with constant comparison, and saved you from seeing the world's ages as a set of box-like partitions without vital connection', is precisely the complex record of history and culture that startles and troubles Dorothea. It is no simple case of culture-shock; her struggles in England are also struggles to understand the environment, to relate the manor house and the tenant's pig-sty cottage, the politics and neglected fences, the smirking Correggiosities in Tipton Manor and the poverty outside, theory and practice, art and nature. Rome, where Dorothea's strength is low, and her susceptibility strained, is not only a superb symbol of the history of politics, religion and art, but a correlative for the shocks and revulsions of the wedding journey:

> . . . after the brief narrow experience of her girlhood she was beholding Rome, the city of visible history, where the past of a whole hemisphere seems moving in funeral procession with strange ancestral images and trophies gathered from afar.
>
> But this stupendous fragmentariness heightened the dream-like strangeness of her bridal life. Dorothea had now been five weeks in Rome, and in the kindly mornings when autumn and winter seemed to go hand in hand like a happy aged couple one of whom would presently survive in chiller loneliness, she had driven about at first with Mr Casaubon, but of late

---

was not Psyche's lamp but a series showing the labours of Psyche and the final magnificent wedding celebration. There is, I believe, a complex irony in this reference, but it is not the one which most readers have assumed.

In the Open University film *A View of Middlemarch*, which I made with John Gilbert, we inadvertently distorted the emphasis by using a sculpture of Cupid and Psyche from Arbury Hall which shows the conventional episode.

chiefly with Tantripp and their experienced courier. She had been led through the best galleries, had been taken to the chief points of view, had been shown the grandest ruins and the most glorious churches, and she had ended by oftenest choosing to drive out to the Campagna where she could feel alone with the earth and sky, away from the oppressive masquerade of ages, in which her own life too seemed to become a masque with enigmatical costumes.

To those who have looked at Rome with the quickening power of a knowledge which breathes a growing soul into all historic shapes, and traces out the suppressed transitions which unite all contrasts, Rome may still be the spiritual centre and interpreter of the world. But let them conceive one more historical contrast: the gigantic broken revelations of that Imperial and Papal city thrust abruptly on the notions of a girl who had been brought up in English and Swiss Puritanism, fed on meagre Protestant histories and on art chiefly of the hand-screen sort; a girl whose ardent nature turned all her small allowance of knowledge into principles, fusing her actions into their mould, and whose quick emotions gave the most abstract things the quality of a pleasure or a pain; a girl who had lately become a wife, and from the enthusiastic acceptance of untried duty found herself plunged in tumultuous preoccupation with her personal lot. The weight of unintelligible Rome might lie easily on bright nymphs to whom it formed a background for the brilliant picnic of Anglo-foreign society; but Dorothea had no such defence against deep impressions. Ruins and basilicas, palaces and colossi, set in the midst of a sordid present, where all that was living and warm-blooded seemed sunk in the deep degeneracy of a superstition divorced from reverence; the dimmer but yet eager Titanic life gazing and struggling on walls and ceilings; the long vistas of white forms whose marble eyes seemed to hold the monotonous light of an alien world: all this vast wreck of ambitious ideals, sensuous and spiritual, mixed confusedly with the signs of breathing forgetfulness and degradation, at first jarred her as with an electric shock, and then urged themselves on her with that ache belonging to a glut of confused ideas which check the flow of emotion. (Chapter 20)

Dorothea's sense of history does not make sense of Rome. The debate with Will is broken off by Casaubon's illness and never taken up again during the novel; for Will ceases to represent Shelleyan romanticism and Nazarene discipleship, and moves into politics. He retains his ability to make connections as we see when he rebukes Brooke for trying to box off his philanthropy from Reform. Dorothea never receives the answer about the present from the past, but George Eliot sees, from the perspective of forty years later, what Dorothea needed to question in 1829.

Dorothea hasn't enough money to drain her piece of land and found her ideal community; she is far too late to be a Saint Theresa; she cannot even internalize her author's sharply feminist[10] consciousness. Ideas about reform, vocation, culture, money, marriage, religion, meliorism, are all generalized and also internalized, refracted through the consciousness of Dorothea and others. Dorothea asks questions about history, not the young ladies' 'toybox' history of the world which she was taught in that education 'at once narrow and promiscuous', but a history which she both exemplifies and demands, a history that will make the past relevant to the present 'here – now – in England'. It is also a demand for a history which makes sense to an ordinary woman.

Ordinary in achievement but not in endowment, because she is endowed with George Eliot's historical imagination which tries to extend its personal experience through a knowledge of the public world, as truthfully and as feelingly as possible. Dorothea's strength lies in aspiration, not in action or creation. To call her creative efforts attempts at loving, like those of Little Dorrit, will not quite do, because her search is for culture, history, and economic information which she can use and relate to herself, her immediate environment, and her present. Dorothea asks for knowledge to be relevant, a hundred years before the demand created the household word, and her questioning is in the most radical spirit of challenge:

> To poor Dorothea these severe classical nudities and smirking Renaissance-Correggiosities were painfully inexplicable, staring into the midst of her Puritanic conceptions: she had never been taught how she could bring them into any sort of relevance with her life. (Chapter 9)

If the novel's last sentence speaks of the unhistoric act, its first sentence speaks of history, in the largest sense of 'the history of man'. On several occasions George Eliot, quoting Fielding as a revered precedent, speaks of herself as a historian: she is writing the kind of novel which is not only better history than the conventional historical novel, but better history than is written by some historians. The novelist, unlike the historian, can create the innumerable biographies of individuals, and set her action in a remote valley, or a remote

---

10. Feminism is the one theme of the novel not to be so internalized, showing the novelist's care to avoid anachronisms in political consciousness.

provincial society. Carlyle's first *Essay on History* (1830) is not only contemporaneous with the action of *Middlemarch*, but gives a fair picture of its mode of history:

> Social Life is the aggregate of all the individual men's Lives who constitute society; History is the essence of innumerable Biographies. But if one Biography, nay, our own Biography, study and recapitulate it as we may, remains in so many points unintelligible to us; how much more must these millions, the very facts of which, to say nothing of the purport of them, we know not, and cannot know!

and also:

> Of this Historian himself, moreover, in his own special department, new and higher things are beginning to be expected. From of old, it was too often to be reproachfully observed of him, that he dwelt with disproportionate fondness in Senate-houses, in Battle-fields, nay, even in Kings' Antechambers; forgetting, that far away from such scenes, the mighty tide of Thought and Action was still rolling on its wondrous course, in gloom and brightness; and in its thousand remote valleys, a whole world of Existence, with or without an earthly sun of Happiness to warm it, with or without a heavenly sun of Holiness to purify and sanctify it, was blossoming and fading, whether the 'famous victory' were won or lost.

George Eliot's novel illustrates and explains Carlyle, creating a kind of historical fiction not to be found in Lukacs. The innumerable biographies make up history; the novelist can show not only the social and political pressures on ordinary lives, but also the pressures on remarkable people held back from remarkable achievements, denied biographers, having led only very private lives, resting 'in unvisited tombs'. An essential part of this portrayal of frustration and aspiration (in others beside Dorothea) is the action of historical consciousness. It is the convincing medium of quest and confusion, as well as the internalized version of the novel's own feat. In such ways *Middlemarch* earns its right to be vague in its last sentence, after so much precision and particularity:

> . . . the growing good of the world is partly dependent on unhistoric acts. . . .

If Middlemarch is the most remarkable example before *Ulysses* of a novel about past and present, it is partly so by virtue of a consciousness of history which is shared by its heroine and its author. The consciousness led Dorothea to her unhistoric acts, but led George Eliot (whose tomb *is* visited) to the historic act of writing *Middlemarch*.

1972; published 1976

7

The Reticent Narrator

George Eliot's chief narrating characters can scarcely be thought of as characters at all. They are disembodied, not activated by the tension and continuity of plot. When we describe or define them, we conceive of them as voices rather than fictitious persons. The voices speak in various tones, which come to seem characteristic and even unified, both within novels and across her *oeuvre*. The voices express ideas, opinions, and emotions, which give them colour, substance and continuity. They tell completely – or almost completely – and omnisciently – or almost omnisciently – the stories of many characters, but never their own. When they provide anecdotal glimpses of autobiographical history, those glimpses are brief and elusive. Whether we think of George Eliot's narrating voices as singular or plural, they are intimate, but reticent.

The tones of George Eliot's authorial voices are various, but there is enough unity and continuity for us to think of them as emanating from one source, and making up one coherent narrating character. From the early essays to *Theophrastus Such*, and from her first tales to *Daniel Deronda*, her voices develop a flexible language for rumination, judgment, reminiscence, humour, satire, irony, and sympathy. In non-fiction and in fiction, her affective and analytic medium has a broad range. Before George Eliot ever adopted that pseudonym to which we now familiarly assimilate our total sense of the person, she created the light and shade of temperament and mood, but withheld the particulars of character, plot, and extended relationship. She created a story-teller who tells everything except a personal life-story.

She wrote her essays and novels within historically defined customs and conventions, but her use of the omniscient author's commentary, while in some ways resembling that of Thackeray or Dickens,[1] has distinctive features of its own.

She was a woman who chose to use a man's pseudonym.[2] Rejecting Jane Austen's way, which was to write anonymously, and Charlotte Brontë's way, which was to use an androgynous pseudonym, Currer Bell, she adopted 'George' because it was George Henry Lewes's name, and 'Eliot' because it was 'a good mouth-filling, easily-pronounced word'.[3] She was following convention, like these women writers, and also like young Dickens and Thackeray, in choosing not to write in her own name, but her attitude to her own name was complicated. She was born Mary Ann Evans, came to prefer the form Mary Anne, was variously called Marian, Pollian, and Polly, used the name of Mrs Lewes to which she had no legal right, and eventually that of Mrs John Cross, to which she was entitled. She could not always write her chosen name easily. When she first wrote the equivocal letter[4] telling her brother Isaac that she had 'changed' her name, she signed herself 'Marian Lewes', and she was already used to telling those friends who knew she was not married to Lewes that she must be addressed as 'Mrs Lewes', not 'Miss Evans'. The sense of naming and the sense of identity were more than literary questions.

1. Thackeray deliberately confuses and undermines the sense of authorial continuity, while Dickens resembles George Eliot in the withdrawal of detail, but is also much less free with moral and psychological generalities.
2. *Letters*, II, p. 292.
3. J. W. Cross, *George Eliot's Life as Related in her Letters and Journals* (Edinburgh and London, 1885), I, p. 431.
4. *Letters*, II, pp. 331-2:

My dear Brother

You will be surprized, I dare say, but I hope not sorry, to learn that I have changed my name, and have someone to take care of me in the world. The event is not at all a sudden one, though it may appear sudden in its announcement to you. My husband has been known to me for several years, and I am well acquainted with his mind and character. He is occupied entirely with scientific and learned pursuits, is several years older than myself, and has three boys, two of whom are at school in Switzerland, and one in England.

We shall remain at the coast here, or in Brittany for some months, on account of my health, which has for some time been very frail, and which is benefited by the sea air. The winter we shall probably spend in Germany. But any inconvenience about money payments to me may, I suppose, be avoided if you will be kind enough to pay my income to the account of Mr. G. H. Lewes, into the Union Bank of London, Charing Cross Branch, 4, Pall Mall East, Mr. Lewes having an account there. . . . I remain, dear Isaac.

Your affectionate Sister
Marian Lewes.

We tend to attach the clearly masculine references which occur in some of her novels, and the androgynous-seeming references in others, to the assumed name of George Eliot. But this was not thought of until she had been writing anonymous journalism for more than a decade, and had begun to publish *Scenes of Clerical Life* as a serial in 1857. The pseudonym appeared in the two-volume edition of *Scenes of Clerical Life* in 1858, but Marian Evans, or Marian Lewes, was already committed to telling her stories as a man addressing men and women, and masculine allusion had already coloured her narrator's voice. Even after the appearance of the fictitious name, there is obviously no simple derivation of narrator from author, though since the narrator often speaks with authorial self-consciousness, it is understandable that the two are often associated or conflated. As we trace the movement of the narrator's voice, in these central authorial appearances throughout the stories and novels, two developments are noticeable. There is a gradual diminution of autobiographical anecdote; it becomes generalized and eventually vanishes. There is also a gradual disappearance of the masculine allusions which identify the early narrators; they drop from explicit detail into implication, into a form of androgynous address, with occasional female markings, and finally into an attempt to speak carefully and comprehensively not for men or for women, but for human nature.

The masculine narrator first appears in Mary Ann Evans's first published prose, 'Poetry and Prose, from the Notebook of an Eccentric', which came out in the *Coventry Herald and Observer* in December 1846, and in January and February 1847. There are two narrators in these sketches and essays, one being the traditional editor of unpublished manuscripts, the other, Macarthy, a failed author and thwarted idealist whose work is posthumously published by his best friend. The fiction of masculine identity continues through the early anonymous journalism, especially interesting when the subject is Woman, as in the essay 'Woman in France: Madame de Sablé',[5] and it was adopted for *Scenes of Clerical Life*. The narrator of *Scenes of Clerical Life* uses a many-toned voice, whose range includes arch jokes, solemn analysis, pondered judgment, and intensive apostrophe. The sex of the narrator is established very plainly in the second chapter of 'Amos Barton', where we have the first appearance of masculine identification. After an earnest, generalized appeal, there follows the heavy joke,

5. *Westminster Review*, LXII, October 1854, pp. 448–73; reprinted in *Essays of George Eliot* (ed. Thomas Pinney, London, 1963), pp. 52–81.

'Let me discover that the lovely Phoebe thinks my squint intolerable, and I shall never be able to fix her blandly with my disengaged eye again', which suggests the narrator's sex, somewhat crudely, in a sentence. In the next chapter there is another masculine comment, selectively addressed to readers of a single sex, in the comic manner of Sterne or Thackeray:

> You and I, too, reader, have our weakness, have we not? which makes us think foolish things now and then. Perhaps it may lie in an excessive admiration for small hands and feet, a tall lithe figure, large dark eyes, and dark silken braided hair.

The masculinity is that of an explicitly fictionalized author who describes his craft and intentions straightforwardly, especially when making transitions from one group of characters to another, as in the last sentence of Chapter 2:

> And just now I am bent on introducing you to Mr Bridmain and the Countess Czerlaski, with whom Mr and Mrs Barton are invited to dine to-morrow.

(Such technical self-consciousness is still used to handle the description and introduction of characters in *Adam Bede*, *The Mill on the Floss* and *Middlemarch*.) The dominant tone is that of personal reminiscence. The autobiographical anecdotes rise out of a nostalgic medium, which allows for historical and personal contrasts between the time of writing (and reading) and that of the action, valuably establishing dates and allowing for elegiac exclamations of regret and longing. In the first chapter the anecdotes give us glimpses of episodes in the narrator's childhood, infantile and sexually undifferentiated:

> Then inside, what dear old quaintnesses! which I began to look at with delight, even when I was so crude a member of the congregation, that my nurse found it necessary to provide for the reinforcement of my devotional patience by smuggling bread-and-butter into the sacred edifice.

and

> There were inscriptions on the panels of the singing-gallery, telling of benefactions to the poor of Shepperton, with an involuted elegance of capitals and final flourishes, which my alphabetic erudition traced with ever-new delight.

and

tall dark panels, under whose shadow I sank with a sense of retirement
through the Litany, only to feel with more intensity my burst into the
conspicuousness of public life when I was made to stand up on the seat
during the psalms or the singing.

All the anecdotes in 'Amos Barton' are compressed into this one early
paragraph. The absence of masculine reference at the beginning may
have satisfied the author's scrupulous fidelity to early memories, and
the narrative may have fulfilled some function of conflating fact with
fiction. The second story, 'Mr Gilfil's Love Story', is set too far back to
draw on personal memories, its end beginning 'thirty years ago', and
the earliest date in its elaborate retrospective structure, 1773, fixing the
time when Sir Christopher and Lady Cheverel find Caterina in Milan.
George Eliot had obviously decided on a continuity of narrator, so this
story contains no personal reminiscence or anecdote, but it is linked to
the previous story through the narration of Mrs Patten, a character
whose memory can go back thirty years, and whose recollections
in 'Amos Barton' anticipated 'Mr Gilfil'. She is a useful choric
character in both stories, and in 'Mr Gilfil' it is through her expansive
reminiscence that we move back from the time of Gilfil's death to the
time when he brought his bride to Shepperton. There are a few
personal comments about Gilfil's later years, which are within the
range of the narrator's and George Eliot's own memory. In the first
chapter the narrator authenticates Gilfil's brisk way with spiritual
functions, 'the utmost I can say for him in this respect is, that he
performed those functions with undeviating attention to brevity and
despatch,' and speaks for Mrs Patten's response to his preaching, 'I am
not aware that she ever appeared to be much struck by the sermon on
anger.' The first-person authorial narrator is distinguished by a
straightforward businesslike tone, especially in the major modulation
from Mrs Patten's narrative ('thirty years ago') to the point at which
the central narrative begins ('It is the evening of the 21st of June 1788'):

It was clear that the communicative old lady had nothing to tell of Mrs
Gilfil's history previous to her arrival in Shepperton, and that she was
unacquainted with Mr Gilfil's love-story.
But I, dear reader, am quite as communicative as Mrs Patten, and much
better informed; so that, if you care to know more about the Vicar's

courtship and marriage, you need only carry your imagination back to the latter end of the last century, and your attention forward into the next chapter.

In 'Janet's Repentance' we come back to the narrator's remembered past. It has advanced from early childhood to adolescence, there is no nostalgia, and a line of comic anecdotal detail fixes the masculine identity:

> I remember blushing very much, and thinking Miss Landor was laughing at me, because I was appearing in coat-tails for the first time, when I saw her look down slyly towards where I sat, and then turn with a titter to handsome Mr Bob Lowme, who had such beautiful whiskers meeting under his chin. But perhaps she was not thinking of me, after all; for our pew was near the pulpit, and there was almost always something funny about old Mr Crewe. His brown wig was hardly ever put on quite right, and he had a way of raising his voice for three or four words, and lowering it again to a mumble, so that we could scarcely make out a word he said; though, as my mother observed, that was of no consequence in the prayers, since every one had a prayer-book; and as for the sermon, she continued with some causticity, we all of us heard more of it than we could remember when we got home. (Chapter 2)

and

> I know, Ned Phipps, who knelt against me, and I am sure made me behave much worse than I should have done without him, whispered that he thought the Bishop was a 'guy', and I certainly remember thinking that Mr Prendergast looked much more dignified with his plain white surplice and black hair. He was a tall commanding man, and read the Liturgy in a strikingly sonorous and uniform voice, which I tried to imitate the next Sunday at home, until my little sister began to cry, and said I was 'yoaring at her'. (Chapter 6)

As the narrator grows up, he is given the solidity of specified mother, little sister, friends and acquaintances. George Eliot is becoming more confident in her use of such detail, and the fictionalized recollection of brother and sister may draw on actual memory,[6] and certainly

6. Gordon Haight informs us that there is no record of George Eliot's confirmation, and refers us to a record of a confirmation at Nuneaton by Bishop Ryder (14 August, 1829) of 606 people (*George Eliot*, p.21). It is possible that either Robert (b. 1802) or even Isaac (b. 1816) was confirmed on this occasion.

introduces for the first time a significant personal theme of her fiction. As in 'Amos Barton', the masculine identity is also present in the address to the reader:

> Poor women's hearts! Heaven forbid that I should laugh at you, and make cheap jests on your susceptibility towards the clerical sex . . . (Chapter 3)

But the same chapter contains sardonic sentences that may strike us as imperfectly sustaining the masculine fiction:

> When a man is happy enough to win the affections of a sweet girl, who can soothe his cares with crochet, and respond to all his most cherished ideas with beaded urn-rugs and chair-covers in German wool, he has, at least, a guarantee of domestic comfort, whatever trials may await him out of doors.

In *Adam Bede* the masculine identification is present in two details. In Chapter 17 there is a conversation between the narrator and a very minor character called Gedge, who addresses his remarks to 'Sir'; and there is a high-toned adulation of women in Chapter 33, which explicitly voices masculine experience and goes beyond the pitying intensities of 'Janet's Repentance':

> Beauty has an expression beyond and far above the one woman's soul that it clothes, as the words of genius have a wider meaning than the thought that prompted them: it is more than a woman's love that moves us in a woman's eyes - it seems to be a far-off mighty love that has come near to us, and made speech for itself there; the rounded neck, the dimpled arm, move us by something more than their prettiness - by their close kinship with all we have known of tenderness and peace.

For the most part, however, the generalizations in *Adam Bede*, even when concerned, as they frequently are, with marriage, beauty, and the relations of men and women, tend to be equivocally phrased, and transcend sexual differentiations. The narrator's exchange with Gedge occurs in the same chapter as that of another conversation, with Adam Bede in old age; both show the thinning down of authorial anecdote. Neither episode is fully anecdotal, but is a narration of talk, in which the narrator appears only as a listener, with no characterizing detail of person or action. There is also an extended use of the free indirect style, begun in 'Janet's Repentance', which merges authorial narration with the idiolect of characters, permitting a convenient transference of sexual identification:

No man can escape this vitiating effect of an offence against his own sentiment of right, and the effect was the stronger in Arthur because of that very need of self-respect which, while his conscience was still at ease, was one of his best safeguards. Self-accusation was too painful to him - he could not face it. He must persuade himself that he had not been very much to blame; he began even to pity himself for the necessity he was under of deceiving Adam: it was a course so opposed to the honesty of his own nature. But then, it was the only right thing to do. (Chapter 29)

The Mill on the Floss continues the subdued masculine details in narration, and the diminution of anecdote. The novel begins with one of George Eliot's most elaborate and concentrated chapters of authorial introduction. It is given up to self-consciousness, emotional and technical. Lyrical and visual expansiveness are combined with narrative reticence; the riverscape is the occasion for nostalgic brooding, but emotion is entirely dissociated from personal action and event:

How lovely the little river is, with its dark, changing wavelets! It seems to me like a living companion while I wander along the bank and listen to its low placid voice, as to the voice of one who is deaf and loving. I remember those large dipping willows. I remember the stone bridge.

It is an entirely affective and sensuous language:

As I look at the full stream, the vivid grass, the delicate bright-green powder softening the outline of great trunks and branches that gleam from under the bare purple boughs, I am in love with moistness. . . .

This is unlike the nostalgic harking back to childhood and church-going in *Scenes of Clerical Life*; it marks memory not through observing change, but through noting unchanging things, in its loving address to the inhuman phenomenal world. What is praised and evoked is the vividness of vegetation and animal life. Apostrophe and personification make an intense address, but to the scene, not the reader. What is particularized is the impersonal motion of the senses. Even memories are confined to sensation and the effect is one of inward-looking, implicit recollection. The authorial presence is strong in some ways, muted in others.

At the end of the introductory chapter, the landscape becomes peopled with the characters of fiction. They are not introduced suddenly, but through a careful modulation from nature to the working life of the mill, to the horses and waggoner. 'The little girl' is introduced as a fellow-watcher, on the same stone bridge; with the narrator's solicitude – 'it is time the little playfellow went in' – comes the thought of another departure – 'It is time, too, for me to leave off resting my arms on the cold stone of this bridge', and with the sensation of touch comes the waking. Dream has blurred with memory and invention, as the waking tells us, moving from the fiction of inwardness to that of authorial direction:

> I have been pressing my elbows on the arms of my chair, and dreaming that I was standing on the bridge in front of Dorlcote Mill, as it looked one February afternoon many years ago. Before I dozed off, I was going to tell you what Mr and Mrs Tulliver were talking about, as they sat by the bright fire in the left-hand parlour, on that very afternoon I have been dreaming of.

In this most personal novel, closer than any other to the events of Mary Ann Evans's childhood and adolescence, and motivated strongly by love, isolation, nostalgia, and defensiveness, the narrator has cut away the autobiographical suggestions of anecdote, to release visual memory, working under great pressure to produce pictures of a hallucinatory sharpness. The use of the present tense is right for dream, right for nostalgic conjuration, right for an introduction. (It may remind us of the use of the present tense for the beginnings of Dickens's *Bleak House* and *Edwin Drood*.) And its repetitions are incantatory, also right for the dream and the intensities of recollection. The management of the awakening is skilful, and its descent to the details of armchair chat is deliberated anti-climax. We are reminded that dreams, memory, and imagination are inextricably interwoven, and the reminder introduces the story.

The Mill on the Floss contains one generalized passage which is clearly masculine in reference:

> Is there any one who can recover the experience of his childhood, not merely with a memory of what he did and what happened to him, of what he liked and disliked when he was in frock and trousers, but with an intimate penetration, a revived consciousness of what he felt then – when it was so long from one Midsummer to another? what he felt when his schoolfellows shut him out of their game because he would pitch the ball wrong out of mere wilfulness; or on a rainy day in the holidays, when he

didn't know how to amuse himself, and fell from idleness into mischief, from mischief into defiance, and from defiance into sulkiness; or when his mother absolutely refused to let him have a tailed coat that 'half', although every other boy of his age had gone into tails already? (Book One, Chapter 7)

The narrator's generalization fixes masculine detail, which emerges easily but unmistakably in the context of Tom's schooling. It is distinguished by being the last of its kind. After this novel, the masculine identifications stop. *The Mill on the Floss* also contains one generalized address to the reader which seems to have the ring of personal female experience. The tone is significantly strident:

Gentlemen, you are aware, are apt to impart these imprudent confidences to ladies concerning their unfavourable opinion of sister fair ones. That is why so many women have the advantage of knowing that they are secretly repulsive to men who have self-denyingly made ardent love to them. (Book Six, Chapter 2)

In *Silas Marner*, there is the last full anecdote:

'Is there anything you can fancy that you would like to eat?' I once said to an old labouring man, who was in his last illness, and who had refused all the food his wife had offered him. 'No,' he answered, 'I've never been used to nothing but common victual, and I can't eat that.' Experience had bred no fancies in him that could raise the phantasm of appetite. (Chapter 1)

This is a clear anecdote which proposes no masculine identification. Rather, it may suggest the social experience of womanly cottage-visiting. George Eliot is using this form of first-person anecdote for the last time, and it is interesting that it should have so unmistakably freed itself from masculinity. In the novels that follow, we may speculate about masculine or feminine suggestions, but none are explicit or definite. The authorial narrative takes up again the concentrated use of affective and generalized tones and terms present from the beginning.

Silas Marner was written after George Eliot had begun to work on *Romola*, which may have been significant, since the historical dating of *Romola* gave no scope for authorial reminiscence. If 'Mr Gilfil' was to inhibit the authorial narrative by its late eighteenth-century setting, the fifteenth-century *Romola* clearly made no room for the personal voice. Most of the first-person narrative in *Romola* is in the plural, and much of it is rapidly concentrated in the Proem, before handing over the surview of impersonalized pity and irony to the Florentine Spirit, a time-traveller from the fifteenth century. There is the occasional 'we' in the text – 'We are made so, almost all of us, that the false seeming which we have thought of with painful shrinking . . .' (Chapter 65) – and there is also the occasional interpolated address to the Victorian reader – 'It was a human foible at that period (incredible as it may seem)' (Chapter 7); but the bulk of generalized moral and psychological comment takes an impersonal third-person form:

> It is not force of intellect which causes ready repulsion from the aberration and eccentricities of greatness, any more than it is force of vision that causes the eye to explore the warts on a face bright with human expression; it is simply the negation of high sensibilities. (Chapter 44)

and

> After all has been said that can be said about the widening influence of ideas, it remains true that they would hardly be such strong agents unless they were taken in a solvent of feeling. (Chapter 52)

A rare authorial illustration uses embryonic narrative and expanded image, and is clearly impersonal and uncommitted to period:

> . . . it was only that possibility which clings to every idea that has taken complete possession of the mind: the sort of possibility that makes a woman watch on a headland for the ship which held something dear, though all her neighbours are certain that the ship was a wreck long years ago. (Chapter 67)

Felix Holt has no clearly masculine reference in its narrative commentary, and there are two inset and subdued narratives, which show a development of authorial rhetoric. One of these goes back to the autobiographically nostalgic anecdotes of childhood in *Scenes of Clerical Life*. It uses the first-person plural in the interests of a generalized narrative suggestiveness, unattached to masculine or feminine character:

> . . . many of us know how, even in our childhood, some blank discontented face on the background of our home has marred our summer mornings.

Why was it, when the birds were singing, when the fields were a garden, and when we were clasping another little hand just larger than our own, there was somebody who found it hard to smile? (Chapter 49)

This passage plays its part in the expanding drama of Esther Lyon's imagination as she exchanges luxurious fantasy for 'strong vision'. There is a gradual expansion of inner and outer action in this scene: Esther's inner transformation begins with the magnetic portrait of young Mrs Transome, which has made disenchanted and disenchanting associations, moves into the mythological example of Eve embittered in Paradise by Adam's reproach, and culminates in the generalized recollection of childhood. The three images are joined to move out of the novel's particularity into the appeal to common experience. Through the generalization of 'many of us', personal memory is intensely felt, revealing and reticent.

The other example occurs later in the same chapter, perhaps generated by the infectiousness of memory and the evocation of spoilt pastoral, though also encouraged by the scene of extended inner conflict and crisis. Esther's 'revolutionary struggle', as it is called, is nearly at an end. She is drawn by the strong vision of Felix Holt's idealism, and repelled by the disenchanted airs of Transome Court:

There was something which she now felt profoundly to be the best thing that life could give her. But – if it was to be had at all – it was not to be had without paying a heavy price for it, such as we must pay for all that is greatly good. A supreme love, a motive that gives a sublime rhythm to a woman's life, and exalts habit into partnership with the soul's highest needs, is not to be had where and how she wills: to know that high initiation, she must often tread where it is hard to tread, and feel the chill air, and watch through darkness. It is not true that love makes all things easy: it makes us choose what is difficult. (Chapter 49)

This is unlike the other generalized references of buried narrative, in offering a less commonplace allusiveness. Like the others, it invokes and images a moral universal, animated by feeling. The particulars of narration are subdued; structure and action are typified. There is a compressed allegory of initiation: through a hard journey, cold, dark, love, and difficult choice. The exaltation may take its vibrancy from George Eliot's autobiographical experience. There is no sexual differentiation; when she speaks of Esther, she uses images or illustrations which often allude to women, but which express nothing

exclusively male or female. There is a tendency to move into the appeal
to general human experience.

When we come to consider *Middlemarch*, her most feminist novel,
there is another difference. When the narrator, in one of many small
glancing asides, speaks of Rosamond's creative vanity having 'a
woman's whole day and mind to work in' (Chapter 43), the
observation could be made by a man or a woman, but it emerges from
a socially sensitive scrutiny of the conditions which create a woman's
imaginative constructions. The remark is too specialized in interest to
be called a commonplace. At least one large conspicuous passage of
feminist authorial commentary strikes us even more strongly, and
cannot easily be taken as androgynous. It is a cunning piece of free
indirect style, in which the rhetoric moves in and out of the character's
mind, and the narrator takes us on a swerving course of sympathy and
satire:

> He was made of excellent human dough, and had the rare merit of knowing
> that his talents, even if let loose, would not set the smallest stream in the
> county on fire: hence he liked the prospect of a wife to whom he could say,
> 'What shall we do?' about this or that; who could help her husband out
> with reasons, and would also have the property qualification for doing so.
> As to the excessive religiousness alleged against Miss Brooke, he had a very
> indefinite notion of what it consisted in, and thought that it would die out
> with marriage. In short, he felt himself to be in love in the right place, and
> was ready to endure a great deal of predominance, which, after all, a man
> could always put down when he liked. Sir James had no idea that he should
> ever like to put down the predominance of this handsome girl, in whose
> cleverness he delighted. Why not? A man's mind - what there is of it - has
> always the advantage of being masculine, - as the smallest birch-tree is of a
> higher kind than the most soaring palm, - and even his ignorance is of a
> sounder quality. (Chapter 2)

It is hard to imagine anyone but a woman writing this sardonic piece of
feminist commentary. Far from seeming out of control, however, it is
beautifully in keeping with the double time-sense of the novel, in which
all the topics articulated by the characters are attributable to the
historical consciousness of the late 1820s and early 1830s, while the
feminist topic which belonged to the historical consciousness of the
period of writing (late 1860s and early 1870s) is not internalized but
articulated only by the authorial voice.[7]

7. As I have argued more fully in Chapter 6.

In *Middlemarch* there is no narrator's anecdote, but George Eliot continues the subdued narrations she used in Chapter 49 of *Felix Holt*. When Lydgate's infatuation with Laure is being retrospectively narrated, the narrator interrupts with this sharply imaged and dynamic generalization:

> Strange, that some of us, with quick alternate vision, see beyond our infatuations, and even while we rave on the heights, behold the wide plain where our persistent self pauses and awaits us. (Chapter 15)

The sentence hovers between the commonplace and something more personal and specific. The discriminating 'some of us' echoes the 'many of us' of *Felix Holt*; through its scrupulous selection the narrator makes a limited identification with Lydgate, not claiming that his experience is universal, but confessing in wryly sympathetic tones that it is not singular. The analysis of emotion is finely condensed in three words: 'quick alternate vision' identifies 'vision' and describes its speed and structure. The imagery of height and wide plain is active, growing out of the dead metaphor 'see beyond' into an emblematic landscape. It is a peopled scene: irrational desire and rational understanding are dramatized as the infatuated self raving on the heights and the *alter ego* whose patience is clarified by the complex word 'persistent'. A persistent self knows that infatuation is transient, that it has only to wait, in the plain where width and flatness acknowledge the nature of quotidian obligation. The miniature allegory transcends divisions into men and women.

In *Felix Holt* and *Middlemarch* George Eliot discovers modes of condensed narration which brim with the pressure of personal experience,[8] but insist on reticence. Brevity and generality make effective understatements. Some work through allegory, some through a reduced vignette which is less than anecdotal, as in these two from *Daniel Deronda*:

> While Gwendolen . . . was hoping that Grandcourt in his march up and down was not going to pause near her, not going to look at her or speak to her, some woman under a smoky sky, obliged to consider the price of eggs in arranging her dinner, was listening for the music of a footstep that would remove all risk from her foretaste of joy; some couple, bending, cheek by cheek, over a bit of work done by the one and delighted in by the other,

---

8. Tolstoy is the only novelist I know of who is comparable to George Eliot in this reticent voicing of experience.

were reckoning the earnings that would make them rich enough for a
holiday among the furze and heather. (Chapter 54)

Though less intense than the *Middlemarch* example, they resemble it in
creating an affective pressure through reticence. (We do not have to
relate either example to the relationship of George Eliot and George
Henry Lewes to recognize the tribute to loving companionship.) These
profiles of feeling are related with feeling; affection and happiness are
celebrated affectionately and happily. The twinned sketches *are*
examples; they act as ironic and critical contrasts with the narrative's
main subject, the hateful separateness of Gwendolen and Grandcourt,
but they are not merely illustrative. George Eliot's miniature narratives
are like good metaphors, in which vehicle is not merely subdued to
tenor, but asserts a vitality of its own. It is this animation which
strongly and quietly diffuses the narrator's presence through the action
and discourse of the novel.

Such examples are rare, but the more striking for their rarity. They
seem to develop out of the expansive narrator's anecdote of the early
stories, and also out of the briefly animated examples which particularize some of the long passages of generalized commentary, as in this
analysis of Arthur Donnithorne from Chapter 12 of *Adam Bede*:

> . . . we don't inquire too closely into character in the case of a handsome
> generous young fellow, who will have property enough to support
> numerous peccadilloes – who, if he should unfortunately break a man's legs
> in his rash driving, will be able to pension him handsomely; or if he should
> happen to spoil a woman's existence for her, will make it up to her with
> expensive *bons-bons*, packed up and directed by his own hand.

In the narration of the last four novels there is an insistence on
undifferentiated humanity, on man and woman. Clearly, the modern
reader's sense of gender will be affected by the knowledge that George
Eliot was a woman, but this was also known by many of her
contemporaries, after the publication of *Adam Bede*. She went on using
the pseudonym[9] in the knowledge that her identity was a gradually
opening secret, and this awareness may have persuaded her to cut
down and cut out the masculine references. But it is not until *Daniel*

9. It was not used for *Romola* in its serial publication (*The Cornhill Magazine*, July
1862–August 1863), or for 'The Lifted Veil' (*Blackwood's Edinburgh Magazine*, July 1859),
or 'Brother Jacob' (*Cornhill*, July 1864).

Deronda that we find several references which carefully disclaim masculinity and femininity, and explicitly link men with women. In Chapter 24, the narrator makes one of several appeals on behalf of Gwendolen's pitiable 'world-nausea':

> And poor Gwendolen had never dissociated happiness from personal pre-eminence and *éclat*. That where these threatened to forsake her, she should take life to be hardly worth the having, cannot make her so unlike the rest of us, men or women, that we should cast her out of our compassion. . . .

In Chapter 36 the narrator speaks of Deronda's susceptibility to Gwendolen's 'peculiar' manner, saying, 'I suppose neither man nor woman would be the better for an utter insensibility to such appeals.' In Chapter 35 we are told that Deronda 'had discerned in her more of that tender appealing charm which we call womanly'. In Chapter 38 Mordecai's conception of the second self is compared to 'the boy's or girl's picturing of the future beloved'. And in Chapter 50, after speaking carefully of 'a feeling distinct from that exclusive passionate love of which some men and women (by no means all)[10] are capable, which yet is not the same with friendship, nor with a merely benevolent regard, whether admiring or compassionate', the narrator scrupulously refuses to speak as a man speaking of men, and discriminates 'a man, say – for it is a man who is here concerned. . .'. Finally, there is a small but significant comment on the words 'masculine' and 'feminine' which shows George Eliot's tentative examination of these confidently used terms. Daniel is described as being 'moved by an affectionateness such as we are apt to call feminine, disposing him to yield in ordinary details, while he had a certain inflexibility of judgment, an independence of opinion, held to be rightfully masculine' (Chapter 28). George Eliot's developing assumption of masculine, feminine and androgynous narrative voices, and her developing comparisons of masculine and feminine characters, alert her to the dangers of sexual categorization, and it seems appropriate that these disclaimers of masculine identity should occur in *Daniel Deronda*. In this novel the omniscient author's comment is subdued, Daniel's own conceptual analysis carrying some of the burden of general discourse in a way that none of George Eliot's earlier registers of consciousness was equipped to do. Moreover, in his character George Eliot assimilated earlier insights

10. It is tempting to refer this allusion to Herbert Spencer.

into the psychological and social conditions of women, and such permutations are very likely to have compelled close scrutiny of sexual differences and resemblances.[11]

George Eliot's authorial narrators share a changing but consistent language of reticence. She never wrote a novel which would allow or demand the convention of a fully autobiographical first-person narrator like those of Defoe, Richardson, Charlotte Brontë, Thackeray and Dickens. (She and Thomas Hardy are the only great Victorians who never use the autobiographical narrative convention.) She wrote one full first-person narrative as a short story, 'The Lifted Veil' (again like Hardy[12]). Unlike most exceptions, this one really does prove the rule. If we speculate on her reasons for never writing her version of *David Copperfield*, *Henry Esmond*, or *Jane Eyre*, there are several guesses to be made. Her own story was perhaps less tellable, even in outline, than those of the other great Victorians, and when we see how her reticent first-person narration often led back into glimpses of the personal past, it is possible to surmise that she preferred to dissociate the personal 'I', in which she could tell technical and moral truths, from invention and fiction. 'The Lifted Veil' is itself the story of an unusually expansive and prescient imagination. It is not only an analysis of an artist's vision, but one which is fully aware of the burdens of imagination, and closely related to her interest in Daniel Deronda's advisory, marginal, empathetic and self-repressive imaginative rôle. George Eliot's affection for multiple action and historical overview would probably have made the concentration on a first-person viewpoint restrictive and uncongenial. 'The Lifted Veil' supports this judgment in its very avoidance of the solipsism and uniscience of the conventional autobiographical form. Its hero, Latimer, is gifted or afflicted with telepathic insight, so not restricted to one viewpoint; he is clairvoyant, so not impeded by the veiled future. He is even allowed to do what George Eliot likes to do, and completes the story. Most first-person narrators, even Beckett's, stop short of their own deaths, but Latimer tells the story of his own ending, even though it is death. His unique advantages of vision are unquestionably presented as disadvantages, and they not only reverse the usual conditions of George Eliot's authorial narrators, but reject their affirmations and celebrations. The narrators in the novels narrate lovingly and sympathetically,

11. For instance, the analysis of historical consciousness in Dorothea is extended and elaborated in Daniel.

12. *The Poor Man and the Lady*, which was never published.

reticently, but warmly, addressing men and women who are usually assumed to be congenial and sympathetic. Latimer's narration in 'The Lifted Veil' is spoken from beyond the tomb, coldly, bitterly, and morbidly:

> Before that time comes, I wish to use my last hours of ease and strength in telling the strange story of my experience. I have never fully unbosomed myself to any human being; I have never been encouraged to trust much in the sympathy of my fellow-men. But we have all a chance of meeting with some pity, some tenderness, some charity, when we are dead: it is the living only who cannot be forgiven – the living only from whom men's indulgence and reverence are held off, like the rain by the hard east wind. While the heart beats, bruise it – it is your only opportunity. . . .

Latimer is the deviant; normally George Eliot's authorial narrators celebrate human communication and acknowledge the healing powers of telling and listening. As her characters remember, look forward, lie, tell the truth, gossip, and converse, they move between the extremes of confidence and reticence, like the formal narrators. In *Scenes of Clerical Life* there is the exchange of confessions by Tryan and Janet, in which telling engages with listening to elicit telling. In the last novel, *Daniel Deronda*, there are the final exchanges between Daniel and Gwendolen, in which the question of communication has become immensely more complicated. Gwendolen's telling engages her mentor, as she transfers a heavy burden and creates a powerful need:

> Against his better will, he shrank from the task that was laid on him; he wished, and yet rebuked the wish as cowardly, that she could bury her secrets in her own bosom. He was not a priest. He dreaded the weight of this woman's soul flung upon his own with imploring dependence. (Chapter 56)

and

> And all the while he felt as if he were putting his name to a blank paper which might be filled up terribly. Their attitude, his averted face with its expression of a suffering which he was solemnly resolved to undergo. . . . (ibid.)

and

> 'It could never be my impulse to forsake you,' said Deronda promptly, with that voice which, like his eyes, had the unintentional effect of making his

ready sympathy seem more personal and special than it really was. And in that moment he was not himself quite free from a foreboding of some such self-committing effect. His strong feeling for this stricken creature could not hinder rushing images of future difficulty. He continued to meet her appealing eyes as he spoke, but it was with the painful consciousness that to her ear his words might carry a promise which one day would seem unfulfilled: he was making an indefinite promise to an indefinite hope. (Chapter 57)

Gwendolen casts Daniel for the rôle of listener and mentor but when the rôles are reversed and she is made to attend to that story which the reader has already been fully told, Daniel tells and Gwendolen listens. The narrative irony created by the structural dualities precipitates expectation, tension, and climax. We know what she does not know, what has been beyond her imaginative timidities, her self-pre-occupations, her social ignorance, and her simplification of Daniel's rôle. She is shocked into recognizing that he has a story to tell, as the universe forces itself, in James's words, upon her narrow consciousness. She is pressed into a necessary displacement as Daniel's reticence is forced to speak. It is the most fully imagined case of reticence in George Eliot.

In *Scenes of Clerical Life* all the secrets can be finally told, but the novels contain a channel of private and untellable life – Arthur's, Hetty's, Maggie's, Tom's, Romola's, Tito's, Dorothea's, Casaubon's, Lydgate's. Attention is often drawn to the silences. No one would ever know what Dorothea thought of her wedding journey to Rome. Communication is often astounding, since isolation prevails: when Dorothea confides in Lydgate it is a rare illumination of a troubled darkness. Communication may bring no more than a momentary conjunction: Rosamond never forgets the moments of conversation with Dorothea, but it brings about no moral transformation. Mrs Bulstrode says, 'Look up, Nicholas', but he never makes a full confession to her, postponing it for a deathbed repentance. Inner life is not always accessible, even to the author and reader; Bulstrode's prayers are not narrated, because private prayer is not always candid. Grandcourt's circling depths are imaged, not related.

George Eliot's narrators are not always treated so centrally and tragically. When we assess her explorations of reticence, we must remember that they are often set beside talkativeness and freedom. Mrs Patten, Mrs Poyser and Aunt Pullet are three comic triumphs of George Eliot's virtuosity in local narrative display. But her comedy is never simply local after *Scenes of Clerical Life.* Mrs Poyser's brilliantly amusing stories and compressed fables – he was 'like a cock as thinks the sun's rose o' purpose to hear him crow' – are relevant to *Adam Bede's* moral and psychological concerns. Mrs Pullet's line of lachrymose valetudinarian anecdote, shown most elaborately in the set-piece story of old Mrs Sutton of the Twentylands and her asthmatic gentlemanlike cousin, is humorously displayed; but that characteristic narrative humour is unobtrusively used to precipitate discovery and climax – 'I never come along the road but he's a-scrambling out o' the trees and brambles at the Red Deeps' (*The Mill on the Floss*, Book Five, Chapter 5). George Eliot's fully characterized narrators and narratives are fully functional to the whole.

George Eliot develops a special use of reticence in her creation of those minor characters who carry with them the implications of unrevealed and complex life. In *Adam Bede*, Bartle Massey never tells his story; the curt mention of his earlier days, his misogyny, and his ways with men and dogs combine to make its presence and pressure detectable. Tom Tulliver's love for Lucy is hinted at in stray clues here and there, and quietly creates a pressure behind his control, distress, and intolerance. All characters cannot be developed, and George Eliot manipulates such reticence to make its implications work for economy, richness and complexity.

She does not always choose a reticent character to show the nature of reticence. A surprising case of secret life is that of Mr Brooke. Leaky-minded, verbose, endlessly confidential and self-explanatory, he has his one moment of telling and not telling which makes him a part of the novel's seriousness, passion, and vitality. He gives one brief revelation of a life he never talks about for all his loquaciousness. Like Sir Andrew Aguecheek's 'I was adored once too', which lifts him briefly out of comedy into pathos, this glimpse of Brooke's love-life is startling and expansive. It is provided by the serious question of Casaubon's proposal for Dorothea, to which he addresses himself as concentratedly and responsibly as he can – 'The fact is, I never loved any one well enough to put myself into a noose for them' (*Middlemarch*, Chapter 4).

George Eliot practises an art of reticence, pursuing it with passion. Her own vulnerability, privacy and silence, lie behind the reticence in her novels. There are links between characters who tell their stories, the narrator who does everything but tell his or her story, and the reticent author whose name never appeared on the cover or title-page. These connections have more than a biographical interest. George

Eliot's habits of structured reticence relate the fullness of her fiction to the ellipses of later fiction. Before George Eliot, all the stories are told by the end of the story. She, like Henry James, makes the medium of her fiction less porous than that of, say, Richardson or Jane Austen or Dickens. In *The Golden Bowl*, we never know whether Adam Verver shares Maggie's knowledge. In Alain Robbe-Grillet's *Jalousie* we never know if the reading should be that of jealous obsession with appearances, or of objective rendering of impenetrability. Novels have come to represent the reticences and silences of life outside novels. Artifice asserts its limits, and refuses to attempt completion and closure. George Eliot's novels use Victorian forms and conventions, but strain towards the conventions and forms of modernism.

1978

8
Objects and Environments

SILAS MARNER HAS ROAST PORK FOR SUPPER: OBJECT AND PLOT

George Eliot's handling of the inanimate world must be seen from several points of view. Although Victorian novels cannot be accurately classed together as wholly or similarly realistic, there is no doubt that George Eliot's presentation of objects is part of the qualified realism of her enterprise. Unlike Dickens, for instance, she does not animate objects but presents them with full attention to the physical differences between human beings and the world of things. She uses verisimilitude in an attempt to create structures and languages which investigate the relationship between people and their environments. She looks at the ways in which we 'belong to our belongings', to use the words and concept Thackeray put in the mouth of his old worldling Lady New in Chapter 28 of *The Newcomes*, when she instructs Ethel in the ways of the world. George Eliot is aware of the need to place individual identity in a closely specified social context in order to reflect on the continuity between the 'self' and its surroundings, dramatizing the 'cluster of appurtenances' from which humanity cannot be detached, as Henry James made his worldling, Madame Merle, point out to Isabel Archer when instructing her in the ways of the world.

What is realistic in George Eliot exists in the interests of analysis and judgment: it is not enough to say that her presentation of such things as dress, furniture, buildings, and other objects, is vivid and accurate. She is not a simple mimetic writer – if they exist – concerned with visible and

147

tangible surfaces, even though her surfaces are rendered with sensuous precision. She is concerned with the interaction of people and the inanimate world, with speculations about social and economic influences, and with the individual's imagination, aspiration, relationships, sense of society, and sense of self. Dickens, too, is far from being unaware of such interactions; he uses fiction in ways which are significantly distinct from those of George Eliot. For instance, he occasionally reflects on the ways in which human beings relate to each other through accessories, as he does at the beginning of *The Old Curiosity Shop*, where the narrator describes Nell asleep amongst the curiosities and observes that:

> We are so much in the habit of allowing impressions to be made upon us by external objects, which should be produced by reflection alone, but which, without such visible aids, often escape us, that I am not sure I should have been so thoroughly possessed by this one subject, but for the heaps of fantastic things I had seen huddled together in the curiosity-dealer's warehouse. These, crowding on my mind, in connection with the child, and gathering round her, as it were, brought her condition palpably before me. (Chapter 1)

Dickens's method, however, is to animate both things and environment through his prevailing style, rather than to show individual acts of animation of things by people.

George Eliot shares with Dickens and Thackeray a keen sense of the history of environments, and explicit narrative observations work together with dramatic renderings to create an archaeology of household objects, dress, architecture and institutions. Historical significances are usually observed together with individualized imaginative pressures. When she presents Mrs Tulliver, for instance, it is with an exact sense of the history of costume. In Chapter 2 of *The Mill on the Floss*, Mrs Tulliver's fan-shaped cap belongs to the period of the novel's action, and is a bygone fashion from the point of view of the author and her contemporary readers (which in turn becomes increasingly distanced for later readers). Mrs Tulliver's belongings, however, are not there simply to document history; her way with things is presented as part of a social context which is generalized but also particularized through comparison, contrasts and development. Her attitudes to dress, for instance, are grouped with those of other women whose social and economic assumptions resemble hers, but are distinguished by personal and social influences: Mrs Pullet can afford to dress more fashionably and extravagantly than Mrs Tulliver, as can Mrs Glegg, who chooses to be conspicuously frugal; Lucy Deane dresses expensively and conventionally, but is not intense about dress, while Maggie is shown in various attitudes of rebellion, austerity, and imaginative detachment. Each character is fully imagined in a social, economic, and psychological context, and the accumulation and interplay of their environments are judged and analysed.

Like other novelists, George Eliot uses objects as artistic properties which contribute to the presentation of character, plot, argument, and form. Since she seldom uses any elements of her novels simply, and the objects in her novels are thoroughly and complexly imagined, we cannot pick out accessory objects which function as crude props. When Henry James insisted in his Preface to *The Portrait of a Lady* that there are some characters which belong to the treatment, and some to the form, he might have applied the distinction to fictional objects. George Eliot's objects, like her characters, tend to belong both to treatment and to form. They are as fully imagined as objects can be, less fully imagined than characters can be, in the nature of things. As Marx observed:

> A commodity appears, at first sight, a very trivial thing, and easily understood. Its analysis shows that it is, in reality, a very queer thing, abounding in metaphysical subtleties and theological niceties. (*Capital*, Chapter 1)

George Eliot's most trivially functioning objects turn out to be highly complex.

To isolate the influential plot-properties in *Scenes of Clerical Life* is instructive. At every turn in the action, some appropriate object is picked out as instrumental. In 'The Sad Fortunes of The Reverend Amos Barton' a small but emphatic catastrophe is caused by spilt gravy at the dinner-party where Mr Bridmain and the Countess Czerlaski entertain Amos and Milly Barton, and a problem is solved by a mistake over a jug of cream, 'taken according to custom from last night's milk and specially saved for the Countess's breakfast' and 'a small jug of milk standing on the tray by the side of the cream, and destined for Jet's breakfast' but on one occasion forgotten by the unusually 'moithered' Nanny. In 'Mr Gilfil's Love Story' Caterina's destiny is settled by some manuscript music, which Lady Cheverel needs to have copied, and by a dagger taken from a cabinet in one of the galleries of Cheverel Manor. In 'Janet's Repentance' a violent two-stage quarrel involves Dempster's evening clothes, which he flings into the drawing-room, and a moral crisis is caused by Janet's discovery of a hidden spirit-decanter in a bureau. These crucial properties are part of a larger structure in which things determine destinies. The Bartons' poverty and Milly's hard work and anxiety are shown through domestic items of mending, clothes, food, furniture, and bills, which are all solidly specified. The Cheverels' wealth and connoisseurship are shown through architectural details, objects of luxury, cultural accessories, and collectors' items. The domestic routines of the Dempsters are precisely described, in objects and scenes which show a precarious balance between stability and instability, while the subject of alcoholism necessarily involves a number of precise details about drink. George Eliot's objects are determined by her presentation of special social problems. 'Amos Barton' is centrally concerned with the grim genteel poverty of a curate's family, firmly placed for us at the outset by a generalization which acquires precision and definiteness by the end of the story:

> Those were days when a man could hold three small livings, starve a curate a-piece on two of them . . . (Chapter 1)

The story itself joins the subject of malicious and ignorant gossip with that of a woman's death through pregnancies, hard work, anxiety and poverty, by an insistence on the ironic ordinariness of suffering. In 'Mr Gilfil' Caterina's tragedy is caused by the cruelties of social and economic barriers. All the important objects in 'Amos Barton' are instances and expressions of a killing poverty, and all the important objects in 'Mr Gilfil' are instances and expressions of a killing wealth. 'Janet's Repentance' is the most complex story of the three, aspiring towards a concern with moral conflict and process and, though some of the objects are obvious items, like the decanter, others reflect and reflect on a more subtle sense of relations between people and environment. Janet's frustrated and pathetic domestic life with Dempster and her later domestic benefactions and satisfactions with Tryan are complex in psychological significance and structure. What emerges, even in these early stories, is the impossibility of separating plot-objects from the imagined social and psychological contexts. The inanimate objects are crucial, but inextricable, parts of a thoroughly realized sense of time, place, economic constraints, and psychic life. People are seen as made by and as making their surroundings; relationships are energized by the life of things. Things are seen as aspects of social and personal processes – of giving, taking, working, needing, consuming, collecting, wasting and indulging. Not that the function of objects in plot is unimportant; the developments of plot are made to arise 'naturally' from environment. The quiet and understated tragedy depends on the weight of little things. George Eliot's concern with social determinism and her development of the unheroic tragedy of everyday life are worked out with the aid of things.

The artist is always at work. In all the scenes where things are important, George Eliot takes great care to particularize, to naturalize, and to make the part relate to the whole. The muddle over the milk and the cream is dramatized in detail and at length, as many household objects and routines are precisely and vividly recorded. The plot-objects are naturalized as part of a continuous chronicle of domestic life, in which contrasts and comparisons work dynamically. The story places the poverty of the Bartons in the context of a prosperous village life where other characters eat and drink in ease and comfort. Even the heavy authorial apostrophe is part of what Henry James called, in his Preface to *The Tragic Muse*, the novelist's 'art of preparations'; it immediately follows the general comments on starving curates and the specific details about Amos's strained stipend with its apparently – but only apparently – detached facetious details about the 'sweet history' of the 'real farmhouse cream' in the cup of tea Miss Gibbs hands to Mr Pilgrim. This is an art which disguises art because the art is secondary to the presentation of the human problem. Similarly, in the presentation of the episode of Dempster's evening clothes, there is a fully articulated drama, in which we are aware of the poignant domestication of marital tragedy, as Janet asks her husband to change for dinner, and as he brutally but naturally turns ceremonial costume into a weapon of war. The discovery of the decanter (an object which anticipates an even more influential object in *Middlemarch*) is completely integrated with large and small external events, and with the recording of physical, emotional, and moral life. Mr Pittman asks Janet to look through the letters in Dempster's bureau for a letter about a mortgage, when she is in a state of depression, partly accounted for by the particular grief and loneliness of bereavement, partly generalized in a brilliant insight into a woman's affective life as one of those 'vague undefinable states of susceptibility . . . states of excitement or depression, half mental, half physical – that determine many a tragedy in women's lives' (Chapter 25). Outer incident and inner life are interwoven in narrative and drama. The scene is then sharply focused, in details which create tension and surprise, and establish the substance and force of things:

> . . . she went at once to a bureau which stood in a small back-room, where Dempster used sometimes to write letters and receive people who came on business out of office hours. She had looked through the contents of the bureau more than once; but today, on removing the last bundle of letters from one of the compartments, she saw what she had never seen before, a small nick in the wood, made in the shape of a thumb-nail, evidently intended as a means of pushing aside the movable back of the compartment. In her examination hitherto she had not found such a letter as Mr Pittman had described – perhaps there might be more letters behind this slide. She pushed it back at once, and saw – no letters, but a small spirit-decanter, half full of pale brandy, Dempster's habitual drink.
>
> An impetuous desire shook Janet through all her members; it seemed to master her with the inevitable force of strong fumes that flood our senses before we are aware. Her hand was on the decanter; pale and excited, she was lifting it out of its niche, when, with a start and a shudder, she dashed it to the ground, and the room was filled with the odour of the spirit. (Chapter 25)

When we come to the novels, the sheer number of such influential objects greatly increases. To some extent the complex presences of plot-properties in *Scenes of Clerical Life* can stand as models for the later books, but there is a growing tendency for such objects to become more conspicuous in their work, more patterned in their organization, and more socially generalized and symbolic. In *Adam Bede*, the properties stay fairly small and inconspicuous, but a pattern emerges in their common failure to avert the tragic course of events. Hetty Sorrel's locket with its love-knots, a clandestine present from Arthur, is very like Caterina's secret object, the gold-framed miniature of Anthony Wybrow, also with a love-knot under its glass back, and it comes close to giving away Hetty's secret when it falls from her bead necklace at the Birthday Dance. The episode is fully rendered, in social and psychological significance. Like the cross and chains in *Mansfield Park*, the hidden expensive locket with Arthur's hair is incongruously yoked to the string of rustic dark-brown berries which can be visible. Adam's suspicion is quietened by illusory trust and social ignorance:

It looked too expensive for that – it looked like the things on white satin in the great jeweller's shop at Rosseter. But Adam had very imperfect notions of the value of such things, and he thought it could certainly not cost more than a guinea. Perhaps Hetty had had as much as that in Christmas boxes, and there was no knowing but she might have been childish enough to spend it in that way; she was such a young thing, and she couldn't help loving finery! But then, why had she been so frightened about it at first, and changed colour so, and afterwards pretended not to care? Oh, that was because she was ashamed of his seeing that she had such a smart thing – she was conscious that it was wrong for her to spend her money on it, and she knew that Adam disapproved of finery. It was a proof she cared about what he liked and disliked. (Chapter 26)

The revelation scene is frustrated, as of course it must be for George Eliot's plot to develop, the 'trifle' acting like a subtle influential pivot: influence is promised in order to be thwarted. The very disappointment of power has its own function, showing the psychological and social barriers so important in this novel. Another deceptive property is the slip of paper with Dinah's name, which Hetty turns up in her red-leather case when she is looking for 'something worth selling'. Though it turns her towards Dinah, that turn is not followed through and once more what might be powerful is thwarted by stronger circumstances. Another deliberately disappointed instrument is the little pink silk handkerchief which Arthur thrusts 'deep down into a waste-paper basket' when he expects Adam to come to the Hermitage, in Chapter 28. This trifle acts as a poignant clue, one of the very few signs – another is the ottoman – that the ironically named Hermitage is the secret theatre of Hetty's offstage seduction. The Rector's study provides another thwarted plot-property of this kind, its cultivated plenty provided the wrong environment for a confessional:

It was a small low room, belonging to the old part of the house – dark with the sombre covers of the books that lined the walls; yet it looked very cheery this morning as Arthur reached the open window. For the morning sun fell aslant on the great glass globe with gold fish in it, which stood on a scagliola pillar in front of the ready-spread bachelor breakfast-table, and by the side of this breakfast-table was a group which would have made any room enticing. In the crimson damask easy-chair sat Mr Irwine, with that radiant freshness which he always had when he came from his morning toilet; his finely-formed plump white hand was playing along Juno's brown curly back; and close to Juno's tail, which was wagging with calm matronly pleasure, the two brown pups were rolling over each other in an ecstatic duet of worrying noises. On a cushion a little removed sat Pug, with the air of a maiden lady, who looked on these familiarities as animal weaknesses, which she made as little show as possible of observing. On the table, at Mr Irwine's elbow, lay the first volume of the Foulis Æschylus, which Arthur knew well by sight; and the silver coffee-pot, which Carroll was bringing in, sent forth a fragrant steam which completed the delights of a bachelor breakfast. (Chapter 16)

In this novel the plot-objects come to nothing, partly because George Eliot reserves her tragic climax, partly because such trivial checks and obstacles bring out most clearly the subject of social segregation as the main instrument of tragic plot.

Moving further from the unheroic tragedies of unexceptional people, *The Mill on the Floss* shows the development of more conspicuous, portentous, and patterned plot-objects, like the boat in which Maggie and Stephen glide absently down the Floss, the Dutch ship which picks them up, the boat in which Maggie rescues Tom for a more fulfilling death, and the mass of loosened machinery in which George Eliot - unscientific for once[1] - drowns and unites brother and sister. The plot-objects are clearly related to each other by being placed in a series, one which also includes references to Noah's ark, Philip's joke about the boat that haunts the Floss, the St Ogg's legend, Maggie's dream, and the central presence of the river with its literal and symbolic meanings. In *Romola* the objects which precipitate crisis or turn action also tend towards conspicuous symbolism, like Tito's invisible light armour, Bardo's library, the book in which Baldassare fails to read, the dagger which kills Tito, and Tito's ring. In *Silas Marner* - which interrupted the composition of *Romola* - we return to a more muted and unheroic life. Though George Eliot has by now got into the swing of combining plot-properties with portentous and explicit symbolism, as in the central and powerful golden hoard, she returns in one important episode to the small and inconspicuous plot-properties of *Scenes of Clerical Life*. Like the domestic items in those early stories, the objects of the simple households in Raveloe are accumulated and pressed into a double service, socially expressive and instrumentally powerful. The three plot-objects which allow for the central action of Dunsey's theft, which leads to his death, Godfrey's marriage, and Silas's assimilation into the community, are linked in

1. Keith Brown, 'The End of *The Mill on the Floss*' (*Notes and Queries*, June 1964), p. 226.

collaboration. The objects are a piece of pork, a rare treat given to Silas by Priscilla Lammeter, a doorkey which he attaches to the kettle-holder in order to roast the meat, and 'a piece of very fine twine' urgently needed for the next day's work. He goes to get the twine after the primitive cooking apparatus has been set up, so that the door is left open to Dunsey's thieving entry. The linked domestic objects are quietly and fully expressive of Silas's social and psychic life, articulating the network of trifles which play their part in shaping lives. For Silas, the things are appropriate, minimal, common, and necessary. Other objects are influential in the story, including the pocket-knife used by William Dane to frame Silas for the first theft, the dangerous gold and Molly Cass's opiate. But even the gold depends for its influence on the ministration of humbler things. Their collaborative machinery shows George Eliot's powers of understatement and implication.

In the three late novels, *Felix Holt*, *Middlemarch*, and *Daniel Deronda*, plot-properties are conspicuous in power and presentation. *Felix Holt* is George Eliot's most sensational novel, and its properties are conventional and melodramatic: a ring, a watch, a seal, documents, and a lost pocket-book. George Eliot takes care, however, not to place too much weight on any one thing, diffusing and diminishing the weight of convention, accident and coincidence. In these novels, the machinery involves socially conspicuous objects which are in process of becoming literary plot-conventions – things lost and found, wills, legacies, codicils, heirlooms – partly because plotting becomes more important in these elaborate multiple actions, partly because of the influence of the Victorian Sensation Novel, partly because George Eliot's fiction becomes increasingly concerned with high life. In *Middlemarch* there is not only a pattern of legal apparatus – two dead hands clutching life through wills and testamentary changes – but an unusually melo-dramatic emphasis on discovery through an object, in the brandy-flask with 'a letter signed *Nicholas Bulstrode*' wedged into the loose cover. In *Daniel Deronda*, too, there are wills, and an elaborate pattern of jewel-lery and money – the turquoise necklace, the poisoned diamonds, Daniel's ring, and money lost in various forms of gambling. All these crucial plot-objects are also dominant and explicit symbols, developed and enlarged through accretion and the resonance of satellite imagery and mythological allusion. The objects are thoroughly expressive as social and moral items, tending to be categorized and contrasted as expensive and malignant, poor and beneficent. The complexity and subtlety of structure and nuance are admirable, though if we look back at *Scenes of Clerical Life, Adam Bede* and *Silas Marner*, there may seem to be some loss of richness and freedom as the artist grows more deliberate in her manipulations of things. In *Art and Reality* Joyce Cary observes that a symbol is strongest when the artist is least conscious of its meanings, and the late novels occasionally show a certain reductive clarity, or what Coleridge might call fixity and definiteness, in the treatment of plot-properties.

(2)

MR GRANDCOURT CHOOSES AN ORANGE: THE RANDOM OBJECT

Such reductiveness and explicitness are found only in objects used centrally in plotting. In many ways, object-world in the later novels possesses the richness, fluidity, and freedom which we value as aspects of George Eliot's qualified realism. In *Scenes of Clerical Life* there is a multiple functioning of things; the powerful objects belong to a densely created social environment from which they seem almost to be plucked at random. It is easy to imagine substitutes for those little jugs or the evening clothes. Nothing is more natural-seeming than that decanter with its pale liquid hidden behind the back of the lawyer's bureau. The fact of instrumentality is disguised in the ease of social documentation – though that is too inflexible a term for the products of George Eliot's sociological and psychological imagination. In the late novels there is a more specialized, segregrated, and heightened presentation of proper- ties used to direct action, but there remains a web of expressive things. The novelist imaginatively creates what Henry James calls his creature and 'his creature's conditions'.[2] At one extreme are the symbolic plot-levers like Daniel's ring or Gwendolen's jewels, and at the other are many little things which form the fine fabric of the envelope of character. Such objects perform the function of particu- larizing the actions of character and relationship. George Eliot took care to give her characters things to do, as they think, feel, and speak. Where her emphasis is placed on action, the properties in themselves may not rise into special significance. When Dorothea throws her gloves on to a table (in Chapter 30 of *Middlemarch*), or Celia carefully lays down the paper man she is making for the curate's children (in

2. 'The Lesson of Balzac' (*Atlantic Monthly*, August 1905), reprinted in *The House of Fiction* (ed. Leon Edel, London, 1957).

Chapter 5), or Catherine Arrowpoint tears a piece of paper into small pieces 'as if at a task of utmost multiplication imposd by a cruel fairy' (in Chapter 22 of *Daniel Deronda*), or when Gwendolen (in Chapter 23) pinches the edges of sheet-music, the objects appear to be chosen at random, as things in themselves. The emphasis is placed not on things but on expressive behaviour. This may be recurrent and characteristic, like Dorothea's informality and Celia's carefulness, or locally expressive of mood, like Catherine's and Gwendolen's unconscious and nervous fidgeting. Such subdued use of objects contributes to the natural-seeming surface of George Eliot's fiction, which subordinates art to nature.

Her realistic accumulations of character and environment are not ends in themselves. The novelist is thoroughly imagining behaviour and emotion, letting the reader form impressions unconsciously or half-consciously. Feeling may be acted out and not described. Environments are assimilated to character. Information is presented piecemeal, and unobtrusively.

For instance, in Chapter 54 of *Daniel Deronda* George Eliot presents a characteristic exchange between Gwendolen and Grandcourt:

'I like yachting longer than I like anything else,' said Grandcourt; 'and I had none last year. I suppose you are beginning to tire of it. Women are so confoundedly whimsical. They expect everything to give way to them.'

'Oh dear, no!' said Gwendolen, letting out her scorn in a flute-like tone. 'I never expect you to give way.'

'Why should I?' said Grandcourt, with his inward voice, looking at her, and then choosing an orange – for they were at table.

The orange is a typical random object. It is socially apposite, since this is a necessary and local commodity, 'At dinner he would remark that the fruit was getting stale, and they must put in somewhere for more.' The orange is appropriate but not irreplaceable, and the specification just sufficient for the behavioural point to be made. Grandcourt is given this small and inconspicuous object in order to conclude the conversation, with coolness, and calculation. He is made to move away from the involvement of conversation to the indifference of act. The orange is the property which registers the characteristic smooth brutality of his snub. It is in scenes like this that George Eliot's presentation seems to be at its most dramatic, but is most novelistic, since the novel permits both a closer and a more transient focus than the theatre.

The objects used in such novelistic dramatization are not always as rapidly and fleetingly singled out as Grandcourt's orange. In Chapter 22 of *Daniel Deronda*, where Catherine Arrowpoint tells her parents about the projected *mésalliance* with Klesmer, the dialogue is almost unobtrusively punctuated by her father's play with his cigar:

> The father took his cigar from his mouth, and rose to the occasion by saying, 'This will never do, Cath.'

and

> 'Your marrying is quite out of the question,' said Mr Arrowpoint, rather too heavily weighted with his task, and standing in an embarrassment unrelieved by a cigar.

and

> 'Harry Brendall will get through it all in no time,' said Mr Arrowpoint, relighting his cigar.

The object, through accessory substance and business, also organizes dialogue, stressing beginning, middle, end, and anti-climax. But most prominent is the registration of feeling: awkwardness, dumbness, embarrassment, and helplessness are given a physically expressive outlet, which excellently trivializes the actor, who clutches at the cigar like a straw. The cigar itself is unimportant, as is clear from another scene, in Chapter 25, when Grandcourt is also provided with an expressive cigar:

> Grandcourt said nothing, but pressed the newspaper down on his knees and began to light another cigar. Lush took this as a sign that he was willing to listen, and was the more bent on using the opportunity;

and

> Lush's tone had gradually become more and more unctuous in its friendliness of remonstrance, and he was almost in danger of forgetting that he was merely gambling in argument. When he left off, Grandcourt took his cigar out of his mouth, and looking steadily at the moist end while he adjusted the leaf with his delicate finger-tips, said –
> 'I knew before that you had an objection to my marrying Miss Harleth.'

and

Grandcourt made no immediate answer, and only went on smoking.

The manuscript of *The Mill on the Floss*[3] shows an earlier use of the cigar as a property, in a scene between Philip Wakem and his father, in Book Six, Chapter 8. Here, George Eliot uses a cigar to punctuate the passage where Wakem abruptly resumes a conversation about Maggie, after he has left Philip in anger but returns in peace. He enters 'with a cigar in his mouth', begins to talk with it held out in his hand, a little later takes to it again, and marks his concluding capitulation by throwing the end away. George Eliot cut out all this cigar-play, probably because she felt it to be redundant, since the scene gives Wakem plenty to do in the way of movement and gesture. Moreover, this cigar has none of the expressiveness of the Arrowpoint and Grandcourt business, where it provides the only physical action for one character's constraint and the other's restraint.

The novels are filled with such particularized accessories, contributing to character, scenic vividness, and social density. Sometimes the object represents a social habit, like smoking, drinking, eating, or dressing. Sometimes it indicates a very personal envelope of appurtenances, like Philip Wakem's pencil, with which he plays and displays nervous energy, or Catherine Arrowpoint's and Gwendolen's similar and yet distinct business with sheets of music. One of George Eliot's special qualities is her unobtrusive use of this detail. If we compare her with Dickens, who vigorously animates the accessories, and tends also to stylize them, or with Zola, who treats them in a factual and documentary way, or with Thackeray, who consciously accumulates a satiric inventory, we find that her trademark is the implicit presentation of things. This is her constant method, but it is certainly not her only method. She also uses explicit and even conspicuous presentation, and at times mixes overt analysis with covert detail.

(3)

LISBETH BEDE CLEANS HER BEDROOM AND NEGLECTS HER KITCHEN: OBJECT
BECOMES SYMBOL

All objects are social and personal signs. Sometimes the significance is

3. See *The Mill on the Floss*, Clarendon Edition, p. 375 (fns. 4 and 6) and p. 376 (fns. 1 and 3).

quietly implied, as in the examples of Grandcourt's orange and Philip's pencil. Sometimes the author writes a scene which concentratedly presents and places the character's relationship to the surrounding things. The women in *Middlemarch* usually show some degree of sartorial self-consciousness, ranging from the assumptions of Rosamond Vincy about her trousseau, to Harriet Bulstrode's shift from fashionable and expensive costume to appropriately austere Quaker wear for forgiveness and shared penance. The critical reader can extract the sartorial pattern and abstract a sense of social and psychic customs and rituals, which are heightened within the work of art, but reflect, and reflect on, customs and rituals outside literature. At times George Eliot refuses to leave the implications to be picked up by reading inference, and makes the pattern clear and strong. The orange which Grandcourt chooses is left to speak in mute language for itself, but Gwendolen's jewellery is completely and dynamically characterized. We see her appearance from the very first sentence of the novel, through the consciousness of other characters and then through her own awareness: not consistently, as in Jane Austen, but more variably, George Eliot assimilates the surfaces and environments which make and are made by her characters to the intellectual and affective life of those characters. In the early chapters of *Daniel Deronda*, the free indirect style and dramatic dialogue are fully used to present people inhabiting the world of things. The things most personal to Gwendolen in these first introductory stages are her personal belongings, her clothes, jewellery, and various objects she takes with her on her travels. The first conspicuous thing is her turquoise necklace, whose history plays an important part in the larger history of Gwendolen, Daniel, Grandcourt, and the novel as a whole. The necklace is introduced in Chapter 2 of *Daniel Deronda* as one of 'some ornaments which she could sell to a dealer', then singled out as 'an Etruscan necklace which she happened not to have been wearing since her arrival'. Its subsequent adventures are well-known: it is sold, repurchased[4] anonymously by Deronda and transformed into a sacred object signifying Gwendolen's developing sense of his moral persuasion and influence. He returns the necklace in an early attempt to dissuade her from the temptation to live by risk and at other people's expense. In Chapter 24, the transformation of the object is carefully dramatized. Gwendolen asks

4. Not without some change of mind on George Eliot's part. The manuscript 1st and 2nd editions have 'pawn' and 'redeemed' for 'part with' and 'repurchased', which replaced them in the Cabinet Edition.

her mother to sell her ornaments, in order to get money and also to mark her feeling that she is starting a new life of deprivation: 'Governesses don't wear ornaments.' She makes an exception of the necklace, and her mother's reply, 'No, dear, no; it was made out of your dear father's chain,' makes clear the nature of Gwendolen's former indifference. Not only is she beginning to treasure this object, but she is beginning to treasure objects, as she has never done before. A previous thinness of attachment and a new development in caring are shown in the detail about her father's chain. The narrator draws our attention to the emotional shift by focusing on the object, as Gwendolen looks at it while speaking tenderly to her mother. It has not only an important plot-rôle but a conspicuous part in that slow process of imaginative symbol-making which the narrator calls 'constructive imagination'. Gwendolen's change is something she is aware of, but with a revealing acceptance of incomprehension:

> But the movement of mind which led her to keep the necklace, to fold it up in the handkerchief, and rise to put it in her *nécessaire*, where she had first placed it when it had been returned to her, was more peculiar, and what would be called less reasonable. It came from that streak of superstition in her which attached itself both to her confidence and her terror – a superstition which lingers in an intense personality even in spite of theory and science; any dread or hope for self being stronger than all reasons for or against it. Why she should suddenly determine not to part with the necklace was not much clearer to her than why she should sometimes have been frightened to find herself in the fields alone: she had a confused state of emotion about Deronda – was it wounded pride and resentment, or a certain awe and exceptional trust? It was something vague and yet mastering, which impelled her to this action about the necklace. There is a great deal of unmapped country within us which would have to be taken into account in an explanation of our gusts and storms. (Chapter 24)

Gwendolen's course is still far from settled and her next act of symbol-making is dangerously brash; in Chapter 27 she refuses to wear earrings and says black is the only wear for refusing an offer. Her response to the necklace, which is to become extended and complicated in constructive comparisons with other jewels, is an instance of George Eliot's interest in the construction of a personal symbolism by her characters. There are many occasions in the novels when the growth of symbol is conducted with the kind of narrative irony we find in Shakespeare, where the identification of symbolism is shared by author and reader, bypassing the character. Familiar instances of this process are the mirrors and windows in *Adam Bede*, *Middlemarch* and *Daniel Deronda*, the river in *The Mill on the Floss*, space and light in *Middlemarch* and the horses in *Daniel Deronda*. All these symbols develop through simple objects and a metaphorical extension. George Eliot – like Henry James after her – liked to internalize metaphor and symbol, and many of the key symbols begin within the reflections made by the characters. It is Dorothea, for example, inspired by strong feeling and vague comprehension to use symbolism, who observes that she can't say precisely what her faith is, but can suggest imagistically that it consists of a desire for:

'. . . what is perfectly good, even when we don't quite know what it is and cannot do what we would, we are part of the divine power against evil – widening the skirts of light and making the struggle with darkness narrower.' (*Middlemarch*, Chapter 39)

In *Daniel Deronda* Gwendolen's ability to imagine is shown as she haltingly learns to make connections between Daniel's apparent bastardy and Grandcourt's illegitimate children, and between casinos and capitalism, and in her capacity to sanctify objects. She acquires values through converting things into carriers of value. Jane Austen made Fanny Price – prototype of the Victorian heroine – the guardian of the Mansfield memory, preserving discarded objects with loving and sanctifying imagination. The capacity for treasuring things is in George Eliot, as in Jane Austen, a central illustration of imaginative capacity to see similarity in dissimilarity, to take the part for the whole, to comprehend the world outside the self.

Mrs Tulliver is an example of metonymic blindness: as we see in Book One, Chapter 2 of *The Mill on the Floss* when Mr Tulliver uses the example of the waggoner's mole, her literal-mindedness flounders and he gives up – 'I meant it to stand for summat else' – in an excellent definition of imagistic construction. Tom inherits something of his mother's unimaginativeness, as is clear in his refusal to play when Maggie tries out her heroic fantasy about meeting lions (in Book One, Chapter 5). George Eliot is by no means inclined to show symbol-making only in intellectually sophisticated characters. Mrs Tulliver may not know a rhetorical mole from a real one, but she laments over her household gods with the full force of symbolic imagination. Silas Marner's fetishistic worship of his objects is the unconscious imaginative activity of a mind scarcely animated, let alone creatively stirred. Silas is carefully drawn as a simple man whose sense of past and future has been paralysed by a personal and religious shock. His attitudes to his loom, his gold and silver, and his brown earthenware pot show both the distortion and diminution of loving relationship and its survival. He creates a ritual, as we all do, through the inheritance of larger ritual, like the ceremonies of eating and relaxing, and the personal interpretation and extension, shown in his sanctification of the broken pot, in gratitude, affection, and memorial. In vital existence, objects are sanctified through human connections, as souvenirs, presents, and icons; George Eliot implies through Silas and his personal possessions, that the channels of loving can be kept unlocked, even when human associations are minimal, through the sanctification of things.

For Lisbeth Bede, the human associations with things are strong, as she carries out the usual social rituals after her husband's death, when his corpse lies in their bedchamber. An elaborately patterned scene, in Chapter 10 of *Adam Bede*, makes use of a split set which shows Lisbeth's half-conscious use of ritual, with its sacred objects. Lisbeth is throughout doing two things: obeying an existing ritual, which has grown up through the basic rhythms and ceremonies of living and dying, and bringing to its channels of comfort and support in grief her own particular needs and variations. Some of the attendant objects and ceremonies are prescribed: the cleaning of the bedroom, the laying-out of the body, and the darkening of the room. Others are personal, arising naturally from what is customary: the mending of the torn curtain, and perhaps the locking of the door. Ritual is kept alive from imaginative participation, proved by such improvised and personal activity. Some of this is made explicit, some is implied:

At five o'clock Lisbeth came down-stairs with a large key in her hand: it was the key of the chamber where her husband lay dead. Throughout the day, except in her occasional outbursts of wailing grief, she had been in incessant movement, performing the initial duties to her dead with the awe and exactitude that belong to religious rites. She had brought out her little store of bleached linen, which she had for long years kept in reserve for this supreme use. It seemed but yesterday – that time so many mid-summers ago, when she had told Thias where this linen lay, that he might be sure and reach it out for her when *she* died, for she was the elder of the two. Then there had been the work of cleansing to the strictest purity every object in the sacred chamber, and of removing from it every trace of common daily occupation. The small window which had hitherto freely let in the frosty moonlight or the warm summer sunrise on the working man's slumber, must now be darkened with a fair white sheet, for this was the sleep which is as sacred under the bare rafters as in ceiled houses. Lisbeth had even mended a long-neglected and unnoticeable rent in the checkered bit of bed-curtain; for the moments were few and precious now in which she would be able to do the smallest office of respect or love for the still corpse, to which in all her thoughts she attributed some consciousness. Our dead are never dead to us until we have forgotten them: they can be injured by us, they can be wounded; they know all our penitence, all our aching sense that their place is empty, all the kisses we bestow on the smallest relic of their presence. And the aged peasant-woman most of all believes that her dead are conscious. Decent burial was what Lisbeth had been thinking of for herself through years of thrift, with an indistinct expectation that she should know when she was being carried to the churchyard, followed by her husband and her sons; and now she felt as if the greatest work of her life were to be done in seeing that Thias was buried decently before her. . . .

After the ritual has been completed, with this full affective response, clearly narrated and substantiated through the particulars of the woman's actions in the environment, there is a brilliantly felt lapse into inertia. The ritual cleaning and ceremony and activity are completed through their opposites: care is followed by neglect, ceremony by disarray, domestic work by languor:

She had locked the door, and now held the key in her hand, as she threw herself wearily into a chair that stood out of its place in the middle of the house floor, where in ordinary times she would never have consented to sit. The kitchen had had none of her attention that day; it was soiled with the tread of muddy shoes, and untidy with clothes and other objects out of place. But what at another time would have been intolerable to Lisbeth's habits of order and cleanliness, seemed to her now just what should be: it was right that things should look strange and disordered and wretched, now the old man had come to his end in that sad way: the kitchen ought not to look as if nothing had happened. Adam, overcome with the agitations and exertions of the day after his night of hard work, had fallen asleep on a bench in the workshop; and Seth was in the back-kitchen making a fire of sticks that he might get the kettle to boil, and persuade his mother to have a cup of tea, an indulgence which she rarely allowed herself.

There was no one in the kitchen when Lisbeth entered and threw herself into the chair. She looked round with blank eyes at the dirt and confusion on which the bright afternoon's sun shone dismally; it was all of a piece with the sad confusion of her mind – that confusion which belongs to the first hours of a sudden sorrow, when the poor human soul is like one who has been deposited sleeping among the ruins of a vast city, and wakes up in dreary amazement, not knowing whether it is the growing or the dying day – not knowing why and whence came this illimitable scene of desolation, or why he too finds himself desolate in the midst of it.

George Eliot makes it plain that Lisbeth has some awareness of the decorum of her acts, in the observation, 'it was right that things should look strange and disordered'. She also makes it plain that such clarity exists in the full affective context of confusion, 'it was all of a piece with the sad confusion of her mind'. The finely placed ambiguity of 'sad' joins the narrator's compassionate medium with the record of the character's emotion, and both are extended and generalized through the final image of the ruined city, bringing us into the imaginative sense, which lies beyond Lisbeth's personal preoccupations, of the human condition of loss, distress, and bewildered alienation. This is surely a perfected example of George Eliot's blend of feeling and knowing, a model of a death scene where particularities avoid the stock demands of sentimentality, and where generalization marks the mode of imaginative enquiry and investigation. Social habits, religious ritual, and personal need are dramatized in order to be understood through the things; the things which are animated by custom, duty, love and need are inseparable from the human being. This is one of many answers given by George Eliot to the questions formulated by Henry James in *The Portrait of a Lady*: 'What shall we call our "self"? Where does it begin? where does it end?' (Chapter 19) and 'What do you call one's life? . . . One's appearance, one's movements, one's engagements, one's society' (Chapter 22). James's most social creature, experienced and hardened, formulates a truth when she tells the still ignorant Isabel, deluded by dreams of the unconditional, that the self 'overflows into everything that belongs to us – and then it flows back again'. Madame Merle demonstrates the malignancy of reification, the destruction of love by the bad object-stuff that flows back. Lisbeth and Silas Marner show the association with things at its most nourishing and life-enhancing.

(4)

George Eliot is doing more than recording and investigating the
relationship of the self to the envelope of environment. Although there
is a recent tendency to reject the social criticism of Victorian fiction as
complacent and restricted, the existence of such a critical attitude
cannot be denied. In many ways, George Eliot, like Jane Austen before
her and Henry James after her, is irritating to radical taste because she
is neither uncritical of materialism and aggrandisement, nor totally
and lucidly political. Like Dickens, she has a conservative fear of a
separation of social revolution from moral revolution, and Felix Holt's
radicalism is a term used with caution, irony, an invisible question
mark and re-definition. But the tale is greater in its display and
implication than the conscious didacticism of the author, and nowhere
is this plainer than in *Daniel Deronda*. There are moments in earlier
novels where she stands on what for her was a dangerous verge
between conservatism and social rejection: in *Adam Bede* the scenes
where gentry meet the villagers in what are superficially festive unions
in the organic community are imbued with an ironic sense of gaps and
gulfs; in *Middlemarch* the unmilitant labourer, Timothy Cooper,
refuses to join with his fellow-workers and attack the railway survey,
but still utters a political challenge which no one in the novel can
answer and which the 'omniscient' narrator calls 'an undeniable
truth':

> 'Aw! good for the big folks to make money out on,' said old Timothy
> Cooper, who had stayed behind turning his hay while the others had been
> gone on their spree; – 'I'n seen lots o' things turn up sin' I war a young un –
> the war an' the peace, and the canells, an' the oald King George, an' the
> Regen', an' the new King George, an' the new un as has got a new ne-ame –
> an' its been all aloike to the poor mon. What's the canells been t'him?
> They'n brought him neyther me-at nor be-acon, nor wage to lay by, if he
> didn't save it wi' clemmin' his own inside. Times ha' got wusser for him sin'
> I war a young un. An' so it'll be wi' the railroads. They'll on'y leave the
> poor mon furder behind. But them are fools as meddle, and so I told the
> chaps here. This is the big folks's world, this is. But yo're for the big folks,
> Muster Garth, yo are.' (Chapter 56)

Like Dorothea, George Eliot did not always see what could be done about social injustice and inequality, and her novels do not provide ideal, or even idealistic, social solutions. *Daniel Deronda*'s concern with a political ideal turns away from the condition of England to look at the historical consciousness of a man with the opportunity of a political vocation impossible for a woman, but in a foreign, vague, and indeterminate region. However, the novelist is socially critical: she makes that metaphorical connection between gambling and capitalist speculation, and draws the strongly satirical presentation of English politics in the portrait of Mr Bult. The novel offers no solution and very little discussion of the events it mentions as lying outside Gwendolen's selfishly restricted consciousness, like the American Civil War and the Lancashire cotton famine; but it contains an examination of materialism which implies a radical positive whose implications go beyond anything George Eliot had presented earlier. The examination is largely implicit, but it shows the novelist's use of her form for the expression of grave social dissatisfactions. Like many of the characters in the novels of Henry James, who assimilated so much, while rejecting so much, from her art, the characters in *Daniel Deronda* are shown as fatally acquisitive, materialist, and hierarchical.

When Gwendolen has decided to sell herself to Grandcourt, whose very name expresses rank and wealth, her relatives have an interested discussion of the selling and the profits:

> 'I should like to know exactly what sort of places Ryelands and Gadsmere are,' said Mrs Davilow.
>
> 'Gadsmere, I believe, is a secondary place,' said Mr Gascoigne; 'but Ryelands I know to be one of our finest seats. The park is extensive and the woods of a very valuable order. The house was built by Inigo Jones, and the ceilings are painted in the Italian style. The estate is said to be worth twelve thousand a-year, and there are two livings, one a rectory, in the gift of the Grandcourts. There may be some burthens on the land. Still, Mr Grandcourt was an only child.'
>
> 'It would be most remarkable,' said Mrs Gascoigne, 'if he were to become Lord Stannery in addition to everything else. Only think: there is the Grandcourt estate, the Mallinger estate, *and* the baronetcy, *and* the peerage,' - she was marking off the items on her fingers, and paused on the fourth while she added, 'but they say there will be no land coming to him with the peerage.' It seemed a pity there was nothing for the fifth finger.
> (Chapter 28)

Like all the questions in this novel, from the first sentence onwards, this speculation is innocent and has to wait for a full answer. It echoes a preparatory remark on the theme of property, in which Gwendolen's young sense of humour flaunts its daring ignorance, 'I wonder what sort of behaviour a delightful young man would have?', a grave question lightly answered, 'I know he would have hunters and racers, and a London house and two country-houses, – one with battlements and another with a veranda. And I feel sure that with a little murdering he might get a title.' The narrator draws our attention to the nature of her irony, 'of the doubtful sort that has some genuine belief mixed up with it' (Chapter 9). The author's irony, however, is more profound. Mrs Davilow's dangerous question is echoed later, as Grandcourt is walking with Gwendolen in the conservatory of one of the splendid seats in the novel, Brackenshaw Park, when he asks, 'Do you like this kind of thing?' and the duplicity of the slang phrase is carefully pointed out by the narrator, who comments that Gwendolen says 'Yes' without considering what '"kind of thing" was meant – whether the flowers, the scents, the ball in general, or this episode . . .'. The dangerous openness of 'sort of behaviour' and 'kind of thing' comes to be particularized and recognized by Gwendolen. She enjoys fully the sense of self in a grand environment, and there is a series of scenes, like the episode in the conservatory, in which George Eliot places the character's process of social identification. She enjoys the fallen grandeur of Offendene, seizing vaguely on its 'romantic' promise, as 'a good background for anything'. 'Anything' is eloquent. She is self-consciously exultant as she passes through a long suite of rooms in Quetcham Hall: 'She had never had that sort of promenade before, and she felt exultingly that it befitted her: any one looking at her for the first time might have supposed that long galleries and lackeys had always been a matter of course in her life.' Once more, the colloquial vagueness of 'that sort' opens out ironically, suggesting the lack of understanding and appraisal. Gwendolen is afraid of wide horizons, in nature and culture, and mistakes the length and breadth of great houses for an environment that fits her. She is, however, to be fitted uncomfortably to the place, to be constricted, to have exultancy turn into fear and subjection. George Eliot's ironies and tensions in this display of character and environment intensify before the Grandcourt marriage. Gwendolen jokes, almost for the last time, as she reminds her mother of the advantages of the marriage:

'And you shall sorrow over my having everything at my beck - and enjoying everything gloriously - splendid houses - and horses - and diamonds, I shall have diamonds - and going to court - and being Lady Certainly - and Lady Perhaps - and grand here - and tantivy there - and always loving you better than anybody else in the world.' (Chapter 31)

The whole chapter is a socially and sexually climactic drama of Gwendolen's sense of self and environment. George Eliot creates a little sympathetically clouded weather, but lets Gwendolen appreciate 'the grand outlines' and other natural and man-made beauties of the park as the married couple drive into Ryelands. She is going to discover the answer to her mother's question, and George Eliot presents her mounting tension as a mixture of expectations:

> She was really getting somewhat febrile in her excitement; and now in this drive through the park her usual susceptibility to changes of light and scenery helped to make her heart palpitate newly. Was it at the novelty simply, or the almost incredible fulfilment about to be given to her girlish dreams of being 'somebody' - walking through her own furlong of corridors and under her own ceilings of an out-of-sight loftiness where her own painted Spring was shedding painted flowers, and her own fore-shortened Zephyrs were blowing their trumpets over her; while her own servants, lackeys in clothing but men in bulk and shape, were as nought in her presence, and revered the propriety of her insolence to them: - being in short the heroine of an admired play without the pains of art? (Chapter 31)

This is cast deliberately in the form of yet another question. Out of many details, we must notice the return of those lackeys so casually mentioned as part of the scenery in the Quetcham episode. George Eliot brings out Gwendolen's illusions and the nature of her mistaken sense of centrality, by the theatrical image. She also prepares clearly for background to turn into foreground, and the sexual simplicity of 'men in bulk and shape' is part of the understatement of the novel's treatment of sexuality, the more violent for its very suggestiveness. The process and procession is elaborated; Gwendolen is greeted by 'a brilliant light in the hall - warmth, matting, carpets, full-length portraits, Olympian statues, assiduous servants'. The matter-of-fact inventory has its own pressure. Later, Gwendolen is 'led by Grandcourt along a subtly-scented corridor, then into an anteroom where she saw an open doorway sending out a rich glow of light and colour'. Once more there is a spurious openness, and the sensuous details. Beyond the doorway lie what Grandcourt calls 'our dens', in another superb stroke of ambiguous slang, perfect in the context of the novel's insistent animal imagery.

In the room there are images of reflection, as she 'saw herself repeated in glass panels with all her faint-green satin surroundings', an echo of the mirror images and the characteristic colour of her early appearances. The scene is set for the letter from Lydia and the marvellously aggressive presentation of the diamonds. But this is much more than strong scene-setting: George Eliot is concluding a series of images of a woman's misplaced sense of self and a desired environment. After this, the succeeding places and backgrounds are never to be easily misread by Gwendolen. I do not suggest that she ever comes to reflect on the full social significance of George Eliot's experiment with her person, place, and her sense of personhood and place, but the significances are there for the reader. George Eliot answers certain questions for Gwendolen, and for her mother, who is indeed to sorrow over her daughter's expensively purchased possessions, but she answers them even more fully for the critical reader.

This pattern is repeated throughout the novel, where every person and every group of people are carefully and dynamically placed in particularized settings. As with the small objects, the houses, estates, and furnishings have a social generalization and personal applications. Grandcourt's setting shows a rare example of George Eliot's controlled animation of still-life – a word which she has used before in *Felix Holt*, where Esther Lyon makes mistakes and achieves recognitions through observing her self and other selves in relation to their environments and clusters of appurtenances. The word is used deliberately of Grandcourt's surroundings:

> On the second day after the Archery Meeting, Mr Henleigh Mallinger Grandcourt was at his breakfast-table with Mr Lush. Everything around them was agreeable: the summer air through the open windows, at which the dogs could walk in from the old green turf on the lawn; the soft, purplish colouring of the park beyond, stretching towards a mass of bordering wood; the still life in the room, which seemed the stiller for its sober antiquated elegance, as if it kept a conscious, well-bred silence, unlike the restlessness of vulgar furniture. (Chapter 12)

There are many other examples of this kind of assimilation of character to environment, a designation of objects by character and character by objects, which has various aspects. The Grandcourt example is sinister: his own stillness merges with the still-life to diminish humanity. George Eliot's reifications are always subtle, never grotesque, but no less frightening for the muteness. The novel accumulates a number of contrasting environments, which not only extend and characterize the human characterization, but also accrete a cross-section of society. There is the fallen grandeur of Offendene, to which Gwendolen returns with a more educated sense of the meanings of grandeur, poverty and fall. There is the cultivated slice of Chelsea dwelling inhabited by the Meyricks, described first in a rare set-piece, from the narrator's point-of-view, but subsequently particularized as occasion and character demand:

> The small front parlour was as good as a temple that morning. The sunlight was on the river and soft air came in through the open window; the walls showed a glorious silent cloud of witnesses – the Virgin soaring amid her cherubic escort; grand Melancholia with her solemn universe; the Prophets and Sibyls; the School of Athens; the Last Supper; mystic groups where far-off ages made one moment; grave Holbein and Rembrandt heads; the Tragic Muse; last-century children at their musings or their play; Italian poets, – all were there through the medium of a little black and white. The neat mother who had weathered her troubles, and come out of them with a face still cheerful, was sorting coloured wools for her embroidery. Hafiz purred on the window-ledge, the clock on the mantelpiece ticked without hurry, and the occasional sound of wheels seemed to lie outside the more massive central quiet. (Chapter 20)

Sometimes the presentation is fairly bland, as in the case of Gadsmere, 'the secondary place' of Grandcourt's second household, Lydia Glasher and their children, which is a beautiful example of George Eliot's refusal to melodramatize setting. We might expect more harshness in this environment for guilt and misery, but the description is cool and matter-of-fact, since the emphasis is placed on Lydia's indifference to mere place:

> Imagine a rambling, patchy house, the best part built of grey stone, and red-tiled, a round tower jutting at one of the corners, the mellow darkness of its conical roof surmounted by a weather-cock making an agreeable object either amidst the gleams and greenth of summer or the low-hanging clouds and snowy branches of winter: the grounds shady with spreading trees: a great cedar flourishing on one side, backward some Scotch firs on a

broken bank where the roots hung naked, and beyond, a rookery: on the other side a pool overhung with bushes, where the water-fowl fluttered and screamed: all around, a vast meadow which might be called a park, bordered by an old plantation and guarded by stone lodges which looked like little prisons. Outside the gate the country, once entirely rural and lovely, now black with coal-mines, was chiefly peopled by men and brethren with candles stuck in their hats, and with a diabolic complexion which laid them peculiarly open to suspicion in the eyes of the children at Gadsmere – Mrs Glasher's four beautiful children, who had dwelt there for about three years. Now, in November, when the flowers-beds were empty, the trees leafless, and the pool blackly shivering, one might have said that the place was sombrely in keeping with the black roads and black mounds which seemed to put the district in mourning; – except when the children were playing on the gravel with the dogs for their companions. But Mrs Glasher under her present circumstances liked Gadsmere as well as she would have liked any other abode. The complete seclusion of the place, which the unattractiveness of the country secured, was exactly to her taste. (Chapter 30)

Throughout the novels, the environments are animated sooner or later by the characters' sense of their relationship to place, and this is seemingly more elaborate and sustained in *Daniel Deronda* than in any of the earlier work. Examples of the emotional and moral symbolism of place are plentiful in *The Mill on the Floss*, *Middlemarch* and *Felix Holt*, though there are rather more set-pieces of description in *Scenes of Clerical Life* and *Adam Bede*. *Middlemarch* has such superbly appropriate properties as Lowick, and such affective assimilations of person and place as the description of Dorothea in Rome, but the exploration of environment in *Daniel Deronda* seems to be conducted on a large scale and with a sustained pattern of parallel, contrast, particularization and generalization. The reason for this shift of scale is, I believe, George Eliot's central treatment of the Jamesian question, 'What shall we call our "self"?', as an aspect of her critical and satirical presentation of England's lack of culture and lack of values, and as a contrast to the Jewish culture. In some ways, the novel turns its back on social detail, like the Hyde Park riots or trade-unionism. It is, however, George Eliot's most contemporary novel, set in the decade immediately preceding its composition, and it deals most critically with the individual's sense of environment. That environment is animated and organized, as an element in the novel which is as important and as complex as the psychological realities of character from which it cannot be separated. The social problems of class and capital are not illustrated in historical detail as they are in *Felix Holt* and *Middlemarch*, but social concepts are everywhere explored. The chosen subject of social and cultural comparison involved a much more thorough examination of the relationship between the individual and society than George Eliot had attempted in any previous novel.

1979

9

Chapter 85 of *Middlemarch*:
A Commentary

Like every chapter of *Middlemarch*, this one dilates and contracts. In its brief space[1] it shows George Eliot's powers of analysis, drama, form, language and allusion. It is an organ to the whole – in Coleridge's words – but it has its own shape and growth.

It begins with the quotation from Bunyan's *The Pilgrim's Progress*, which shows the complexity of George Eliot's use of motto:

> 'Then went the jury out, whose names were Mr Blindman, Mr No-good, Mr Malice, Mr Love-lust, Mr Live-loose, Mr Heady, Mr High-mind, Mr Enmity, Mr Liar, Mr Cruelty, Mr Hate-light, Mr Implacable, who every one gave in his private verdict against him among themselves, and afterwards unanimously concluded to bring him in guilty before the judge. And first among themselves, Mr Blindman, the foreman, said, I see clearly that this man is a heretic. Then said Mr No-good, Away with such a fellow from the earth! Ay, said Mr Malice, for I hate the very look him. Then said Mr Love-lust, I could never endure him. Nor I, said Mr Live-loose; for he would be always condemning my way. Hang him, hang him, said Mr Heady. A sorry scrub, said Mr High-mind. My heart riseth against him, said Mr Enmity. He is a rogue, said Mr Liar. Hanging is too good for him, said Mr Cruelty. Let us despatch him out of the way, said Mr Hate-light. Then said Mr Implacable, Might I have all the world given me, I could not be reconciled to him; therefore let us forthwith bring him in guilty of death.'

The modulation is fluent: the account of Faithful's trial in the motto

---

1. It is in fact the second shortest chapter in the novel. If one does not count the mottoes of the respective chapters, only Chapter 79 is shorter.

does not name the accused, so that his naming in the first sentence of the narrative bridges and completes. A further and economical link is the attribution to author; this is made in the opening sentence of the narrative, so is not attached to the motto. As well as modulation, there is the making of narrative tension: if we do not immediately identify the anonymous personal pronoun in the motto, we find it in the narrative. (If we do, there may still be a slight pause of expectation.) George Eliot begins with another author's particularity, using it to edge her way toward her own particulars. (Her modes of generalization are many and varied.) The first paragraph is a daring dilation, in such a short and condensed chapter. It is beautifully built. Bunyan bridges motto and text. The reference in the first sentence is made dynamic by one of the novelist's skilfully placed questions, addressed to the reader and to human nature . . . 'who pities Faithful?' The question arrests us not simply by being a question, but by its surprise – we are likely to expect to pity the victim of such a jury, but by a subtle moral turn we are told why the pity is not appropriate. The turn takes us further into generalization as the commentator explains, with firm confidence, the nature of that 'rare and blessed lot' which is the certainty that we are denounced only for the good in us. Then follows a further balancing generalization, through antithesis, about the pitiable lot of the man who suffers denunciation without any conscientious defence. Then the second paragraph takes us from this process of graduated generalization to the particular case of Bulstrode's consciousness.

The Bunyan extract, dwelt on in the motto and the narrative, has other functions too. It draws attention sharply to the moral clarity of the issues before us. It announces the ruling theme of the chapter – moral consciousness or conscience. It is a little matrix of imagery: the legal metaphors of 'tribunal', 'advocacy', 'judgment', 'warranted', 'pronouncing' and 'condemnation' which describe Mrs Bulstrode's implicit rebuking presence spring from it, and use an allegorical and semi-allegorical method which is one of George Eliot's many ways of dramatizing the life of mind and feeling. (We may notice it particularly in this chapter because of the motto, but it is present from the beginning of her work to the end, and prominent elsewhere in *Middlemarch*.) The function of the motto which I want to stress is its duality: it is appropriate to the narrative tone and temper, in the fullest sense, and more narrowly and locally appropriate to Bulstrode. There is a sadly but strongly ironic point in having this phase in the life of a hypocrite (Faithful's opposite, and Bunyan's degenerate successor in faith) conducted under the aegis of *The Pilgrim's Progress*. George Eliot uses religious imagery in all her novels, and very prominently in this one, but what I want to draw attention to is the local potency of imagery here. The imagery of Bunyan's vivaciously named jurors and Faithful's fate underline what is happening to Bulstrode. Some of his opponents may be seen, by him or by us, or by Lydgate, as 'ugly passions'; George Eliot's display of passions in the scene of public condemnation in the streets and the Town Hall (Chapter 71) is a Victorian conversion of Bunyan's method. But it also allows George Eliot, or the narrator (if we wish to make this discrimination), to direct our awareness of character with the sense of superior direction. This second paragraph is a masterpiece of the free indirect style, and the imagery belongs at once to the simplifying traditions of Bulstrode's puritanism as well as to the larger resonance of George Eliot's moral personifications.

The sense in which the style colours the double point of view of character and narrative guidance is stable and subtle. Bulstrode's pompous, superficial and false assumptions of language shade into, or are covered by, the narrative's sobriety and solemnity. He 'withers' under his own consciousness, and his life is 'stricken'. In the third sentence of this paragraph the narrator uses two metaphors which combine to make us move from one to the other with a slight jolt: 'the acts which he had washed and diluted with inward argument and motive, and for which it seemed comparatively easy to win invisible pardon – what name would she call them by?' This glide into the free indirect style is another specimen of George Eliot's combination of dramatization and superior direction, as of her linking and bridging. The word 'washed' may at first sight seem to belong only to the Biblical imagery of Bulstrode's consciousness (the language of baptism and washing in the blood of the Lamb), but it is strongly qualified by 'diluted' and is drawn into the orbit of the narrator's moral definiteness. To call the effect irony is too crude: it is as if an equivocal association is briefly offered and then withdrawn. Water washes, and washing is good. But the metaphorical action of dilution, since it is the dilution of acts, is not good. There is a tug or tension here between what seems to belong to Bulstrode's consciousness – its 'equivocations', as they are clearly called at the beginning of this sentence – and that which is unequivocal and inescapable. It seems to belong to the stern language of George Eliot's old evangelicalism and the cant of Bulstrode. The narrative keeps moving us from cant to truth. There is another pull of tension in the metaphor 'shrouded' in the next but one sentence: 'He felt shrouded by her doubt: he got strength to face her from the sense that she could not yet feel warranted in pronouncing that worst condemnation on him.' He is clearly engaged in the dubious activity of finding protection and cover in deadly garments; once more the application to him is in keeping with his stylistic register, but also suggests a level of linguistic application to which he is blind. The narrative direction makes us perceive his blinkered, dangerous, mistaken selection in imaging, and the larger implications to which he cannot reach. The last example comes in the last two sentences of this condensed paragraph:

> Some time, perhaps – when he was dying – he would tell her all: in the deep shadow of that time, when she held his hand in the gathering darkness, she might listen without recoiling from his touch. Perhaps: but concealment had been the habit of his life, and the impulse to confession had no power against the dread of a deeper humiliation.

Again, there is a reliance on the traditional imagery of deep shadow and gathering darkness, the language of Bible and hymn. And it makes a strong emotional appeal, an appeal which is transiently felt by the reader as it internalizes Bulstrode's own self-pity and indulgent fantasy. The narrative guidance is inexorable, and we are pulled back from the dramatizing images to a sense of their fiction. The first 'perhaps' belongs to his equivocations and to his customary habit of deceptive procrastination. The second 'Perhaps', emphatically repeated and isolated solemnly behind the colon, leads us to the enlarged sense of the unreliability of the first 'perhaps', and of the imagery and fantasy of a gentle death-bed and forgiveness. We already know, from much explicit commentary and from the moral action, how Bulstrode's mature deeds have been schooled by younger foredeeds.

What is emphasized by the imagery and diction of the free indirect style is also made plain by the internal narrative. Like all George Eliot's characters, Bulstrode is given his characteristic mode of narrative. It is a negative mode, a reticence which shrinks from painful narration of the past, both in memory and in confession. In an earlier chapter[2] we have seen how Bulstrode is made to endure a crisis in which he is oppressed and obsessed by memory, in a turning back of his

2. Chapter 61.

wadded consciousness to those stories of the past which he has inhibited. The return of Raffles, with his threat to tell the secrets, makes Bulstrode's memories rise to haunt him. (At the point of revelation, they are disclosed to the reader.) We have also seen[3] how he does not need to confess to his wife: the town's gossip almost reaches her, but the story is eventually told to her, 'very inartificially', by her brother, Vincy. It is not until we get to Chapter 85 that we feel the moral weakness of Bulstrode's continued refusal to tell:

> The duteous merciful constancy of his wife had delivered him from one dread, but it could not hinder her presence from being still a tribunal before which he shrank from confession and desired advocacy.

The weakness of this fear and the procrastination are made crystal clear, but so too is Bulstrode's cause of fear. The free indirect style forces us to move from the personal white-washing and dilution of his self-pity and self-deception to the verdict of the narrator. This verdict is that of a moral consensus silently or directly evoked, as in the chapter's first question. The style also makes an affective medium for revealing his feelings, without too much interference from moral analysis and judgment. Just as we cannot stay within the narrow language and action of his dramatized consciousness, so we cannot wholly stay apart, distant and detached. The narrative cannot be described in the terminology of 'distance': it moves to and fro; it dilates and contracts. Its contraction makes us feel the nature of the character's feelings. For instance, in the phrase 'that sad refuge, the indifference of new faces', the narrator expresses a pity which is authorial and in character. 'Sad' contains no complexity, but belongs to either viewpoint. The quiet but shocking words, 'the indifference of new faces', are hard to pinpoint. They concentrate the implications of this man's future, the 'end' of his 'stricken life', in the relentless plain statement. What is said reverses what one usually expects from change and newness, but is an exact forecast here. The other example of George Eliot's plain style comes in the following sentence, 'The duteous merciful constancy of his wife,' etc. The style dares to make this threefold pile of abstractions, 'duteous', 'merciful', and 'constancy'; because they are so pressed together, we cannot simply run along the sentence but have to pause and weigh each word. The

3. Chapter 74.

accumulation, plainness, and slow pace make us look at each abstraction and review it in the light of all we have seen of Harriet Bulstrode. Again, plain and simple language says something surprising. Like 'who pities Faithful?' and 'the indifference of new faces', the collocation of abstract moral qualities forces us to respond. The language is not transparent, and we ponder its opacity. One by one, almost as if they are personified qualities, like those of Bunyan, we look at Duty, Mercy, and Constancy, accepting each one and the hard fact of their combination. We had the sublime moment of acceptance when Harriet, appropriately attired in the austere costume of pity, showed her mercy and constancy. By the time we reach this chapter it all seems less sublime, belonging to the hard psychological realities of this life, this contemplated exile, this silence, fear and fantasy of bad faith, this withering to death. The word 'duteous' forces a new concept on Bulstrode and on us. The generalizations are animated, as so often in George Eliot. They are often a source of her animated portrayal of a consciousness which is fully shown. It is there in its moral action, in its feeling and passion, and in its internal narrations and analyses.

The most violent generalization in the whole chapter also fixes Bulstrode's fear: 'That she should ever silently call his acts Murder was what he could not bear.' His movement of mind is wonderfully evasive. The word 'Murder' is almost personified by its capital letter, in this context of allegorical vitality. It is not presented as the word he can ever call his acts, but as the word he could not bear her 'ever' and 'silently' to call them. The action of this shrouded, dying, but painfully still alive consciousness is a powerful example of George Eliot's portrayal of the inner life. She presents restriction, evasion, equivocation. We move into, within, and out of, a shrouded consciousness.

The emotional life of Harriet is presented more simply, from the outside, since, unlike Bulstrode's, it *is* largely articulated. We should notice George Eliot's notation of time here. Like most of the chapters in the novel, this one generalizes and summarizes the movement of time, but also dwells on a particular time and place at some point. George Eliot has a fine capacity to generalize the time which passes, and to do so with psychological particularity, as in the second paragraph here.

In the third paragraph the very rapidity of the motion is both an image and an appeal: 'she could live unconstrainedly with the sorrow that was every day streaking her hair with whiteness and making her eyelids languid.' This is generalized and sensuous, both in its physical detail – especially significant in the case of this woman – and in its reminder of the speed of the body's responsive deterioration. But George Eliot does not show husband and wife as entirely separate. This is a marriage. He cannot confess, and in the dialogue which ends the chapter, and which brilliantly combines psychological drama with important plot-making, we proceed painfully through reluctance and silence to some few necessary moments of telling. Bulstrode has to tell her about Lydgate's refusal to accept the money, and about Dorothea's help, both bitter pills for him to swallow. The bitter taste is renewed by the telling and the silent listening of Mrs Bulstrode. There is another instance of quiet, plain, but effective language. George Eliot uses the dead metaphor of 'wincing': in the seventh paragraph he is seen 'wincing under her suggestion'. The ninth paragraph, in which Mrs Bulstrode reads Lydgate's letter, begins with the words, 'The letter seemed to cut Mrs Bulstrode severely.' The continuity of imagery is locally felt, and here it joins two pains. It shows her suffering, at this moment, as stronger than his; but his sense of her suffering then exacerbates his own. It is a small detail of style, but an example of the strength of language in the novel. The animation of image, as so often in George Eliot, is here felt not through startling novelty or originality, but through feather movements. This sense of a revival of deadened language and deadened response demonstrates the special activity of her language. This is the language of fiction fully energized. It shows the human consciousness, from outside and inside, in isolation and in relationship.

1980

10

George Eliot on Imagination

THE LETTERS, ESSAYS AND POEMS

As George Eliot created character, she imagined Imagination. Her images of individual human life perform imaginative actions: they image, generalize, relate, harmonize, unify, sympathize, invent, and make. This is to generalize actions which the novelist particularizes: since George Eliot is a psychologically realistic novelist, she creates a large range of human variations, and one of her great contributions to the art of fiction is a dynamic and mobile particularization of the motions of the mind. It would be most accurate to say that her characters *attempt* to image, generalize, relate and unify. She catches effort on the wing, showing Imagination as it struggles to achieve, as it does badly, well, and better. Her concept is psychological and ethical. She imagines Imagination as the power to grow and extend the self, and sees it as an instrument of personal and social survival. Like Jane Austen before her, George Eliot shows the difficulties and dangers of Imagination in such characters as Dorothea Brooke and Daniel Deronda. Like James Joyce after her, she takes pains to show the inner action of unimaginative minds in such characters as Amos Barton, Hetty Sorrel, Silas Marner, and Rosamond Vincy. She also shows, with meliorist intent, the development and improvements of imaginative activity, in Adam Bede and Gwendolen Harleth. I have not found that her concept of imagination changes greatly in explicit formulations, but what grows finer and subtler is her art of representing imaginative processes. This art expanded in power as it was practised, as the artist reflected on the practice, learning more about mind as she made and meditated on her models of mind, and as she made and meditated on her own imaginative forms of fiction.

Though her novels use explicit as well as implicit observations and analysis, their mode is impassioned and particular. Theory and idea are almost always thoroughly 'incarnated', to use George Eliot's own word. To abstract concepts from the particularities of art is to recognize most fully art's special powers of making and investigating. The portrayal of imagination is an important aspect of George Eliot's fiction, and a subject on which she ponders in fiction. She shows the dynamism and particularity of creating images, or forecasting experience for instance, in a medium which is dynamic and particularized. The experiments and investigations of literature are in some ways like the experiments and investigations of science, as George Henry Lewes recognized, when he insisted that imagination was the basis of science and of art (*Principles of Success in Literature*, Chapter III). Her art enquires and analyses.

Before looking at the novels, however, I want to recall her letters, essays, and poems, in which discussion and definition of ideas is discursively rational, abstract, and explicit. The word 'imagination' occurs frequently in George Eliot's letters. From the early letters I choose three examples, two to Maria Lewis, one to Martha Jackson:

> When I was quite a little child I could not be satisfied with the things around me: I was constantly living in a world of my own creation, and was quite contented to have no companions that I might be left to my own musings and imagine scenes in which I was chief actress. Conceive what a character novels would give to these Utopias. (16 March, 1839; *Letters*, I, p. 22)

> My imagination is an enemy that must be cast down ere I can enjoy peace or exhibit uniformity of character. I know not which of its caprices I have to dread – that which incites it to spread sackcloth 'above, below, around', or that which makes it 'cheat my eye with blear illusion, and beget strange dreams', of excellence and beauty in beings and things of only 'working day' price. (17 September, 1840; *Letters*, I, pp. 65-6)

> Imagination herself being only a combining faculty and entirely dependent on our much depreciated senses, I am hopeless that she could depict to you

my condition, and employ for the last three weeks, for right gladly do I
believe that you have no materials in your memory wherewith she might
construct a type of them. (4 March, 1841; *Letters*, VIII, p. 7)

In these observations, solemn or mock-serious, George Eliot is
beginning to meditate on problems of the primary imagination, as this
is defined by Coleridge in Chapter XIII of *Biographia Literaria*. She
picks out the following aspects: a tendency to make self-centred
fantasy; an aspiration towards sympathy and relationship; wish-
fulfilling illusion; the shaping and connecting force of feeling; a power
to transcend the senses and convey difference and otherness. All these
features are reproduced in the dramatized inner lives of George Eliot's
characters, born fifteen years after these precocious ruminations. The
clarity with which she saw this psychological machinery, and its
ethical significance, is important in her personal life-story and in the
story of her storytelling.

All her early observations on the primary imagination apply also to
the secondary imagination, as defined by Coleridge in the same
chapter. Bad art can be indulgent, inturned, and self-occupied, as can
the art produced by what Coleridge called the Spinozistic deity and
Keats the egotistical Sublime. The creation of truth and deception is
relevant in art as in life. The almost casual image of spreading the
sackcloth is an everyday equivalent of Coleridge's brilliant observation that imagination modifies by 'a predominant passion' (*Biographia
Literaria*, Chapter XV) and of George Eliot's own comment in her
'Notes on Form in Art' (*Essays of George Eliot*, ed. Thomas Pinney);
'what is fiction other than an arrangement of events or feigned
correspondences according to predominant feeling?' All these early
formulations of imaginative power apply not only to the energies, good
or bad, of the minds of her *dramatis personae*, but to her novels as wholes,
in their variety, unity, extensiveness, inclusiveness, and passionate
direction.

George Eliot's poems are indifferent wholes but treasure-houses of
detail, as Henry James might have said. The very failures in
particularity of feeling and language make her verse an awkward and
accidental anthology of good ideas. All the things which make it bad as
poetry – its illustrativeness, its explicitness, and its abstraction –
highlight generalization. In *The Spanish Gypsy*, she creates a poet, Juan,
a minor character and an object for analysis. She uses the traditional
image of the mirror to bring out the poet's sensitive reflection of the

world outside, but her view of his reflective power does not stress realism so much as negative capability:

> A crystal mirror to the life around,
> Flashing the comment keen of simple fact
> Defined in words; lending brief lyric voice
> To grief and sadness; hardly taking note
> Of difference betwixt his own and others';
> But rather singing as a listener
> To the deep moans, the cries, the wild strong joys
> Of universal Nature, old yet young.
> Such Juan, the third talker, shimmering bright
> As butterfly or bird with quickest life.

This points to the poet's affective sensibility, his penetration to a common emotional experience. It sounds rather too simple and naïve a view of lyric power, reminiscent of woodnotes wild, but another point of view, that of the Host, usefully draws attention to language, if somewhat superficially:

> Pooh, thou'rt a poet, crazed with finding words
> May stick to things and seem like qualities.

One hopes that this is deliberately crude: the list of conceits that follows - a 'moon out of work, a barren egg' - to describe a pebble, is close to Lewes's examples of barren and clever conceits that tell us nothing about the thing being imaged; 'A work is imaginative in virtue of the power of its images over our emotions: not in virtue of any rarity or surprisingness in the images themselves' (*Principles of Success*, Chapter III).

On a later occasion, Juan himself expresses the sense of imaginative deception in fantasy, though the statement is interestingly complicated by the recognition of affective shape:

> I speak not as of fact. Our nimble souls
> Can spin an insubstantial universe
> Suiting our mood, and call it possible,
> Sooner than see one grain with eye exact
> And give strict record of it. Yet by chance

> Our fancies may be truth and make us seers.
> 'Tis a rare teeming world, so harvest-full,
> Even guessing ignorance may pluck some fruit.

Juan oscillates between these two points – the direction and construction of prevailing passion, and the chameleon poet's imaginative identification with a world outside self. Once more, there is a Keatsian sense of the poet's withdrawal of character, the annihilation of self:

> Juan is not a living man by himself:
> His life is breathed in him by other men,
> And they speak out of him. He is their voice
> Juan's own life he gave once quite away.
> Pepíta's lover sang that song – not Juan.
> We old, old poets, if we kept our hearts,
> Should hardly know them from another man's.
> They shrink to make room for the many more
> We keep within us.

He can emphasize the brilliant arbitrary nature of untethered invention, poetry at its most speculative and free:

> I can unleash my fancy if you wish
> And hunt for phantoms: shoot an airy guess
> And bring down airy likelihood – some lie
> Masked cunningly to look like royal truth
> And cheat the shooter, while King Fact goes free;
> Or else some image of reality
> That doubt will handle and reject as false.
> As for conjecture – I can thread the sky
> Like any swallow, but, if you insist
> On knowledge that would guide a pair of feet
> Right to Bedmár, across the Moorish bounds,
> A mule that dreams of stumbling over stones
> Is better stored.

The last of her comments, usefully undissolved in the poetic medium, brings out the idea of the unifying and engrossing image. The gypsies dread to lose their Chief, because to lose him is to lose a unifying and cohesive image:

> All life hung on their Chief – he would not die;
> His image gone, there were no wholeness left
> To make a world of for the Zincali's thought.

George Eliot doesn't always establish her concepts solidly. In 'How Lisa Loved the King', for instance, there is a sentimental approval of Lisa's affective simplifications. We begin by hoping for the friction or contradiction between fantasy and actuality found in *Adam Bede* or *The Mill on the Floss*, but Lisa is denied the instructive contrast provided for Arthur, or Hetty, or Maggie. Her lily-coloured dreams are given an appropriate object. Still, the aesthetic argument is clear: the dream and image are motivated, coloured and unified by feeling:

> Young Lisa saw this hero in the king,
> And as wood-lilies that sweet odours bring
> Might dream the light that opes their modest eyne
> Was lily-odoured, – and as rites divine,
> Round turf-laid altars, or 'neath roofs of stone,
> Draw sanctity from out the heart alone
> That loves and worships, so the miniature
> Perplexed of her soul's world, all virgin pure,
> Filled with heroic virtues that bright form,

And as so often in George Eliot, something is retrieved. We move on to an identification of imagination and love, which can't be wished away:

> . . . great Love his essence had endued
> With Pedro's form, and entering subdued
> The soul of Lisa, . . .

Even the embodiment of vision has its moments:

> Sweet Lisa homeward carried that dire guest,
> And in her chamber through the hours of rest
> The darkness was alight for her with sheen
> Of arms, and plumèd helm, and bright between
> Their commoner gloss, like the pure living spring
> 'Twixt porphyry lips, or living bird's bright wing
> 'Twixt golden wires, the glances of the king
> Flashed on her soul, and waked vibrations there

Of known delights love-mixed to new and rare:
The impalpable dream was turned to breathing flesh,
Chill thought of summer to the warm close mesh
Of sunbeams held between the citron-leaves,
Clothing her life of life.

George Eliot images the transformations of love or imagination, and in doing so makes the observation that imagination can work through the senses, 'impalpable dream was turned to breathing flesh', and the recognition that imagination moves from the familiar to the strange, 'known delights love-mixed to new and rare'. This is the act of imagining, the mind's power over the sensations, the dynamic movement of thought and image, the extension from the known to the unknown, the kindling of fresh experience.

The aesthetic discussions in the poetry deserve fuller treatment. I must however mention the emphasis on work and embodiment – found also in Lewes – in 'Stradivarius', and the debate about art's scope and relevance and power, vigorously raised and sadly dissolved, in 'A College Breakfast-Party'. Perhaps the most developed comment in the poetry comes in the autobiographical sonnet-sequence, 'Brother and Sister'. In the last three sonnets George Eliot deals with the imaginative extension of self in human relationships, a subject which is prominent in the novels. Here there are several interesting emphases: the brother learns to perceive and benefit from the world outside personal impulse, and though the story is told in unsurprisingly sexist terms, the implications can stand for any relationship:

We had the self-same world enlarged for each
By loving difference of girl and boy:
The fruit that hung on high beyond my reach
He plucked for me. . . .

and

Thus boyish Will the nobler mastery learned
Where inward vision over impulse reigns,
Widening its life with separate life discerned,
A Like unlike, a Self that self restrains.

And the process is seen in reverse, as the girl partakes of the boy's pleasures, broadening her scope in entering his world; partly through love and sympathy - 'His sorrow was my sorrow', partly through a sexual extension - exchanging dolls for marbles and tops, partly through a rejection of the private world of enclosed and indulgent dreams of self:

> Grasped by such fellowship my vagrant thought
> Ceased with dream-fruit dream-wishes to fulfil;
> My aëry-picturing fantasy was taught
> Subjection to the harder, truer skill
>
> That seeks with deeds to grave a thought-tracked line,
> And by 'What is,' 'What will be' to define.

These observations are typical of George Eliot's continuing concern with imagination as it works in and outside art. I do not think we can derive from them, or from other comments, a consistent or systematic theory of imagination. These are, at best, cohering notions, fragmentary and at times contradictory. It has been suggested that we can trace a course from a realistic theory of fiction to a more formalist one, or that there is a division between her theory of lyric and her theory of narrative imagination,[1] but this seems to me very doubtful. Even within a single essay, she is capable of shifts or contradictions: in her earliest essays, 'Poetry and Prose, From the Notebook of an Eccentric' (1846-7; reprinted in *Essays of George Eliot*, pp. 13-47), we find her emphasizing the imprint of individual temperament and feeling, 'morbid sensitiveness in his feeling of the beautiful', as well as formulating a highly conscious and rational concept of art as the product of a contemplated perfect whole.[2] Each of these views is clearly provisional and suggestive, and each is placed carefully in a partially dramatized and narrated form. (The 'editor' of the essays, and their 'author', Macarthy, are Marian Evans's fictionalized narrators, the one anonymous, the other given a fuller identity, as

---

1. See Thomas Pinney, Introduction, *Essays of George Eliot*, p. 9.
2. For instance:
I love to think how the perfect whole exists in the imagination of the artist, before his pencil has marked the canvass, - to observe how every minute stroke, every dismal-looking layer of colour, conduces to the ultimate effect, and how completely the creative genius which has conceived the result can calculate the necessary means. (*Essays of George Eliot*, pp. 17-18)

I have observed in Chapter 7). The frame and the enclosed writings stand halfway between essay and fiction, and can usefully remind us of the variety of forms and formulations from which her ideas – rather than her idea – can be derived. She is speculating informally, but although her comments in letters and notebooks are introspective and casual, they are often also scholarly and sophisticated. She must have read widely enough in Romantic and pre-Romantic poetic theory[3] to be able to write so allusively and ironically about the 'combining faculty'; the reference could suggest an acquaintance with the discussions of Wordsworth and Coleridge, in Wordsworth's Prefaces and Appendix to the *Lyrical Ballads* and the *Biographia*, or with the associationist theories of imagination, in Hartley, Alison, Whiter, or with a number of other eighteenth-century aestheticians. The remark about imagination's combining power and reliance on the senses may not be ironic: Lewes, in the mid-'sixties, insisted that 'Imagination can only recall what Sense has previously impressed' (*Principles of Success*, Chapter III). In her essay 'Silly Novels by Lady Novelists' (October 1856; *Essays of George Eliot*, p. 310), George Eliot refers easily to lady novelists who 'relieve their eyesight by occasional glimpses of the *noumenon*', but there is nothing directly Kantian or Coleridgean in her explicit comments. Certain threads of interest continue, and relate to each other. The extracts I have quoted, whether concerned with 'ordinary' or 'extraordinary' imaginative experience, would give a misleading impression if taken in isolation, but we can put together such explicit observations and relate them to the speculation conducted in her fiction.

(2)

THE NOVELS

When Lawrence advised us to trust the tale, not the artist, he was contrasting the truthful particulars of art with the tendentious and abstract nature of theory and dogma. But even when we consider theory, the embodiments of idea in art can valuably enlarge and qualify the ideas defined or argued outside art. In George Eliot's novels, we find all the aspects of imagination discussed in her letters,

3. Meyer H. Abrams in *The Mirror and The Lamp* (London, 1960) shows that Coleridgean and pre-Coleridgean views of imagination co-existed in nineteenth-century poetic theory.

essays, and poems. The emphasis is psychological and ethical. The concern is with primary and secondary imagination. There is often explicit and general comment on imaginative acts of mind, but it is either given personality and particularity as part of authorial commentary, or internalized and dramatized as an aspect of imaginative awareness. We find a prominent concern with affective form, as characters construct or perceive in consequence of strong feeling. We find an interest in the tendency, narrative and dramatic, to create harmonies and wholes. We find an awareness of the selfish acts of creativity, selective, exclusive, false, and dangerous. We find a continued exploration of the efforts of imagination, which is never taken for granted. To imagine is to extend self, or to grasp the world outside self, or to face what is uncongenial and undesirable, and George Eliot knows that such adventures of the spirit are hard for all striving human beings.

The idea of affective unity is made explicit in *Middlemarch*: 'there is no human being who having both passions and thoughts does not think in consequence of his passions – does not find images rising in his mind which soothe the passion with hope or sting it with dread' (Chapter 47). This is more precise and subtle than the brief early comment on imaginative sackcloth, as we should expect. It is also more precise than a more generalized and extended account of the same process in Lewes's *Principles of Success*, where he emphasizes imaginative stimulus of feeling, or speaks, in Coleridgean terms, of Shakespeare's 'predominantly emotive' mind, and his intellect 'always moving in alliance with the feelings, and spontaneously fastening upon the concrete facts in preference to their abstract relation' (Chapter I). George Eliot is particularizing the alliance of mind and feelings. She explicitly makes a causal link between image and passion. The alliance of intellect and feeling was delineated long before *Middlemarch*, in *Scenes of Clerical Life*. Janet Dempster is the character who first embodies subtle insights into impassioned construction and image-making, but it is interesting that George Eliot began with negative rather than positive examples of imagination. Amos Barton is the least imaginative and sensitive of her central characters; no one in this story has much constructive power, apart from the village gossips, whose collective imagination makes its fascinating, false, and superficial constructions contrast strongly with the quiet and uneventful story George Eliot imagines to rouse our sluggish and passive sympathies. Amos has very little awareness, even in his attachments, and George

Eliot shows how desperately he clings to the environment and symbols of his love as he says goodbye to his parish and his wife's grave. Without the solid objects which furnished his affective life, he lacks even that imaginative memory which George Eliot, like Wordsworth, saw as necessary for our sense of continuity, identity, and projection.

However, in 'Janet's Repentance', George Eliot creates an elaborate image and action in which imagination is dramatized as it is analysed. First, we are presented with imagery which is internalized. It strikes the reader, in vivid particularity and appropriate embodiment, but it is clearly shown as belonging to the character's inner life. Like that spread of sackcloth, the images of depression show Janet's depressed imagination at work:

> Her ideas had a new vividness, which made her feel as if she had only seen life through a dim haze before; her thoughts, instead of springing from the action of her own mind, were external existences, that thrust themselves imperiously upon her like haunting visions. The future took shape after shape of misery before her, always ending in her being dragged back again to her old life of terror, and stupor, and fevered despair. Her husband had so long overshadowed her life that her imagination could not keep hold of a condition in which that great dread was absent – and even his absence – what was it? only a dreary vacant flat, where there was nothing to strive after, nothing to long for. (Chapter 16)

and

> The daylight changes the aspect of misery to us, as of everything else. In the night it presses on our imagination – the forms it takes are false, fitful, exaggerated; in broad day it sickens our sense with the dreary persistence of definite measurable reality. The man who looks with ghastly horror on all his property aflame in the dead of night, has not half the sense of destitution he will have in the morning, when he walks over the ruins lying blackened in the pitiless sunshine. That moment of intensest depression was come to Janet, when the daylight which showed her the walls, and chairs, and tables, and all the commonplace reality that surrounded her, seemed to lay bare the future too. . . . (Ibid.)

and

> Everywhere the same sadness! Her life was a sun-dried, barren tract, where there was no shadow, and where all the waters were bitter. (Ibid.)

George Eliot uses the word 'imagination', but the analysis is implicit. We see the shaping power of feeling. Janet's feelings determine imagery and narrative. Images become 'vivid', thoughts are externalized, the story of the future is shaped by the selections of misery, stupor and terror. George Eliot not only chooses appropriate image and event, but places image and event clearly and carefully in the character's creative and reflective consciousness. Analysis and feeling are blended. 'The ideas had a new vividness' is a generalization which moves into the particularized language of the 'dim haze'. The comment that Janet's thoughts 'were external existences' is a generalization which becomes concrete in the imagery of 'springing from the action' and 'thrust themselves imperiously'. George Eliot is imagining what, how and why Janet imagines. The action is dynamic and mobile. Janet's perception of her new images depends on her sense of the past; her thoughts are seen as active, referred back to previous experience not contained in a 'present'. The future is imagined as a story, summarized imagistically; the flatness and generality of 'shape after shape' and the abstraction of named passions, 'terror, stupor and despair' are enlivened and bridged by the specific action of the dragging back. In the second passage, the action is even plainer. There is a clear statement of imaginative pressure and shaping. There is the important recognition that imagination must work on the external materials. And the externals are not wholly passive, but determine the shaping. Passion constructs but construction is affected by materials. Daylight and night-time produce differing shapes and images. This is an early example of something crucial in George Eliot's imagining of imagination: she sees not only the inner action but the outer 'reality' which is given, not chosen.

This insight is nowhere made explicit, but it is everywhere embodied. Maggie Tulliver can make dream-worlds until the given materials become intransigent. I nearly said that she made dream-worlds 'easily enough' until the materials changed, but this isn't so, and one of the innumerable small subtleties in George Eliot's narrative analysis of imagination – and of Maggie – is the comment that Maggie found imaginative constructions tiring, and liked to use literature as an auxiliary aid.[4] But Maggie, who needs their consolations and illusions,

---

4. For instance, in a manuscript passage which does not appear in the novel we have the comment 'so that she could always have something new to read and not have the trouble of fancying things out of her own head' (*The Mill on the Floss*, Clarendon Edition, p. 42. fn. 6).

takes some pleasure in telling stories, not only to herself, but also to other people – to Lucy, who listens willingly, and to Tom, who inherits his mother's literal-mindedness. Mrs Tulliver can't grasp the symbolic function of imagery or metonymy, as Mr Tulliver can, though without being able to formulate their puzzling nature; Tom can't see that Maggie's little fantasy about his fighting lions is a potent expression of her love, hope, and need. It takes her heroism and their union in death to educate his sluggish imagination because he is like Marlowe's Faustus, unable to change his mind through imagination and so needing experience to do it for him. Not that George Eliot doesn't also realize that imagination can function erratically: Adam Bede can have a vision of good work in the form of roads and woods, but has to be pushed by the violent tragic action of Hetty's infanticide into a vision of human suffering. Like Marlowe and Shakespeare, George Eliot liked to show the spots of unimaginative resistance in powerful minds. Certain material is especially difficult to reconstruct.

The Mill on the Floss contains another interesting insight into George Eliot's first treatment of the artist's imagination, shown directly and explicitly. (Unless we count 'The Lifted Veil', where George Eliot's only first-person narrator who is not George Eliot is given the professional task of writing his own story.) Philip Wakem is made to express an idea which is at least as interesting as any that come after, but which never reappears, though it must have been, and continued to be, a valued insight. Philip is a discontented artist, frustrated and depressed by his inability to execute. His discontent with art is excellently mingled with his physical and psychological discontent, with his body, his sexuality, his love for Maggie. He is equipped with an intelligent sense of his own bias. When he tells Maggie, for instance, how he has felt the 'vibration of chords in your nature', which he feels 'the want of' in Stephen, he adds the qualification, 'But perhaps I am wrong; perhaps I feel about you as the artist does about the scene over which his soul has brooded with love . . .' (Book Seven, Chapter 3). Perhaps George Eliot planned the continuation; perhaps she was led into it by the simile of the artist. In any case, Philip's final generalization emerges from his feeling and thinking, to suggest the connection between the artist's extension of self and the lover's:

'You have been to my affections what light, what colour is to my eyes – what music is to the inward ear; you have raised a dim unrest into a vivid consciousness.[5] The new life I have found in caring for your joy and sorrow more than for what is directly my own, has transformed the spirit of rebellious murmuring into that willing endurance which is the birth of strong sympathy. I think nothing but such complete and intense love could have initiated me into that enlarged life which grows and grows by appropriating the life of others; for before, I was always dragged back from it by ever-present painful self-consciousness. I even think sometimes that this gift of transferred life which has come to me in loving you, may be a new power to me.' (Book Seven, Chapter 3)

The 'gift of transferred life': George Eliot never improves on this phrase. It is not the image alone which is important, but the insight. Philip is made to fix the artistically significant aspects of his experience, in the transformation of vagueness into vividness, in the transformation of self-consciousness into imaginative sympathy. And nowhere else does George Eliot formulate this most sensitive process of moving out of self through 'that enlarged life which grows and grows by appropriating the life of others'. We can see too how the aesthetic and the ethical merge in her concept of imagination. Philip tells Tom and Maggie the story of Philoctetes, an intelligent choice of story-telling for an artist-character who slowly sees the connection between his wound and his bow.

In *Silas Marner* we return to the history of a less powerful imagination. Unlike Amos Barton, Silas is made to reveal the inner action and continuity of a passive mind. Amos wasn't really shown at work; Silas is. Once more, the affective pressures are fully demonstrated, but in the case of Silas they cause stupor and oblivion. George Eliot showed the conflation and confusion of memory and imagination in the blurred narrative framework of *The Mill on the Floss*, and it is typical of her insight that she showed Silas suffering an arrest of memory and fantasy. He can look neither before nor after, and his catalepsy is a striking image for his imaginative state. (This is really why it vanishes after Eppie comes along, though George Eliot neatly provides the little detail about his medicinal smoking.) *Silas Marner* returns to the subject of imaginative materials. Silas stops imagining, and is brilliantly shown as offering no personal assertion in the face of the outer world. So it takes over:

5. Hazlitt emphasizes the vividness of imaginative particularity in his essay 'On Poetry in General' (1818).

So, year after year, Silas Marner had lived in this solitude, his guineas rising in the iron pot, and his life narrowing and hardening itself more and more into a mere pulsation of desire and satisfaction that had no relation to any other being. His life had reduced itself to the functions of weaving and hoarding, without any contemplation of an end towards which the functions tended. The same sort of process has perhaps been undergone by wiser men, when they have been cut off from faith and love – only, instead of a loom and a heap of guineas, they have had some erudite research, some ingenious project, or some well-knit theory. Strangely Marner's face and figure shrank and bent themselves into a constant mechanical relation to the objects of his life, so that he produced the same sort of impression as a handle or a crooked tube, which has no meaning standing apart. (Chapter 2)

I know of no clearer illustration of a process never made fully explicit by George Eliot, but frighteningly and authoritatively expressed by Henry James's Madame Merle when she instructs Isobel Archer in the ways of reification:

'What shall we call our "self"? Where does it begin? where does it end? It overflows into everything that belongs to us – and then it flows back again.' (*The Portrait of a Lady*, Chapter 19)

This is Marx's reification, and it is instructive that the central aggressive thing which contaminates the life-flow of Silas is the gold of his hoard. He withdraws the activity of self – interestingly, having suffered betrayal and exile from lies, he begins to try to believe in the power of evil, as source of the lie, and can no longer tell the true stories of past and future. As so often when one tries to simplify George Eliot in interpretation, intransigent details push back the activity of the critic's imagination. Although she suggests that Silas is reduced, and has stopped contemplating ends, he does in a sense perform imaginatively when he treats his hoard as a living companion. Yet, in a way, this is perhaps imagined by the novelist as an almost automatic process, in which the object-world becomes over-animated after the withdrawal of a man's minimal animation. Perhaps we should not make the reification sound too sinister. Silas keeps the channels of love flowing, after all, in his personifications and fetishisms, though George Eliot may have imagined his imaginative communion with the brown pot in order to introduce something more benign than money. Two things stand out: the continued interest in the relationship of inner life and environment, and the loving, thorough, imaginative presentation of Silas's mind. George Eliot can make the apparently simple mind as interesting as the sophisticated and more inventively creative mind of the artist. Nothing in the human imagination was alien to her imagination.

In *Middlemarch* the imaginative artist is Will Ladislaw. The prolonged action of Chapter 47 shows the generation of Will's feeling:

Having silenced Objection by force of unreason Will walked to Lowick as if he had been on the way to Paradise, crossing Halsell Common and skirting the wood, where the sunlight fell broadly under the budding boughs, bringing out the beauties of moss and lichen, and fresh green growths piercing the brown. Everything seemed to know that it was Sunday, and to approve of his going to Lowick Church. Will easily felt happy when nothing crossed his humour, and by this time the thought of vexing Mr Casaubon had become rather amusing to him, making his face break into its merry smile, pleasant to see as the breaking of sunshine on the water – though the occasion was not exemplary. But most of us are apt to settle within ourselves that the man who blocks our way is odious, and not to mind causing him a little of the disgust which his personality excites in ourselves. Will went along with a small book under his arm and a hand in each side-pocket, never reading, but chanting a little, as he made scenes of what would happen in church and coming out. He was experimenting in tunes to suit some words of his own, sometimes trying a ready-made melody, sometimes improvising. The words were not exactly a hymn, but they certainly fitted his Sunday experience:–

O me, O me, what frugal cheer
My love doth feed upon!
A touch, a ray, that is not here,
A shadow that is gone:

A dream of breath that might be near,
An inly-echoed tone,
The thought that one may think me dear,
The place where one was known,

The tremor of a banished fear,
An ill that was not done –
O me, O me, what frugal cheer
My love doth feed upon!

Passion finds appropriate imagery; it constructs and forecasts scene and action; it makes an imaginative whole out of inner hopes and love and outside context. It also shows the selective process as a falsification: Will's loving anticipation – in lyrical narrative – of 'frugal cheer' which will nourish him, muted though it is, in accord with his kind of loving, does not match reality. This is a particularly elaborate example, because Ladislaw is one of the rare characters in George Eliot's novels who attempts artistic creation. The 'real' poem his author provides for him redeems him from being just an artistic jack-of-all-trades, and his experience of several arts gives substance to his Lessing-like preference for poetic imagination:

> 'Your painting and Plastik are poor stuff after all. They perturb and dull conceptions instead of raising them. Language is a finer medium.' (Chapter 19)

The theory is placed in the solvent of a fictional medium, stated by Ladislaw's restless bias, and ironically answered by Naumann's, 'Yes, for those who can't paint.' Similarly particularized is the Hartleian (and Wordsworthian) definition of poetic sensibility:

> 'I wonder what your vocation will turn out to be: perhaps you will be a poet?'
> 'That depends. To be a poet is to have a soul so quick to discern, that no shade of quality escapes it, and so quick to feel, that discernment is but a hand playing with finely-ordered variety on the chords of emotion – a soul in which knowledge passes instantaneously into feeling, and feeling flashes back as a new organ of knowledge. One may have that condition by fits only.' (Chapter 22)

The last example of George Eliot's imagining of the artist's imagination is from *Daniel Deronda*. The pains of negative capability were first expressed – or at least discussed – in the first published essays already referred to, 'Poetry and Prose, From the Notebook of an Eccentric', where a writer's abnormal state of consciousness was imagined. The fragmented and provisional form, half-essay, half-story, made an appropriately tentative medium for Marian Evans's own melancholy, self-consciousness, doubt and ambition, as well as being an appropriately undeveloped and unfinished expression of Macarthy's troubled temperament. She returned to a similarly febrile self-preoccupation in 'The Lifted Veil', where clairvoyance and telepathy act as correlatives for diseased and wretched imagination. In both these fictions, she plays with the idea of imaginative potentiality and imaginative failure. In Daniel and Mordecai, she at last finds a healthy outlet for imaginative morbidity in Mordecai's second-sight and Daniel's empathy. They are two sides of the one coin: Mordecai's vision and obsession, clearly delineated and impelled by faith and tradition, Daniel's dangerously available negative capability.[6] George Eliot recorded in a letter of 4 June, 1848 (*Letters*, I, p. 264) her own experience of a dwindling of identity, 'It seems to me as if I were shrinking into that mathematical abstraction, a point – so entirely am I destitute of contact that I am unconscious of length or breadth.' It is her morbid version of Keats's sense of annihilation in the presence of the crowding identities of a crowded room, clearly related to many images of disenchantment, and probably a personal source for Daniel Deronda's imagination, created as the right repository for Mordecai's vision and purpose, but also fully and subtly delineated as psychological experience. George Eliot no doubt puts into the conception of Daniel her own sense of the strains and fatigues of negative capability. Not for Daniel – or his author, as far as we know – the blissful relief of sinking into darkness, to rest, like Virginia Woolf's Mrs Ramsay, from the demands of love and imagination. George Eliot shows Daniel as experiencing the dangers and difficulties of his imagination, both in that action in which he responds over-sensitively to irreconcilable demands, and in moments of uncommitted response. Daniel's repose is dangerous: just before he rescues Mirah from attempted suicide, he has been experimenting in meditation:

> He was forgetting everything else in a half-speculative, half-involuntary identification of himself with the objects he was looking at, thinking how far it might be possible habitually to shift his centre till his own personality would be no less outside him than the landscape, – when the sense of something moving on the bank opposite him where it was bordered by a line of willow-bushes, made him turn his glance thitherward. (Chapter 17)

In this analysis of negative capability, George Eliot first shows the passive withdrawal of self which receives the sensuous imprint of the

6. Both are contrasted with the imagination of Gwendolen, whose blend of memory and forecast, morbidity and health, susceptibility and solipsism, is explicitly described as constructive (Chapter 27).

natural scene, then makes the sudden transition to human need. It is a model of imaginative receptivity and action, seeming to apply fully to life and to art. It reminds me of a more humorous and muted episode in Jane Austen's *Emma*, where Emma relaxes her imaginist's zeal for a moment, pleased with her own mind, enjoying the non-committed contemplation of small external impressions: 'the butcher with his tray, a tidy old woman travelling homewards . . . two curs quarreling . . .' (Vol. II, Chapter 9). Jane Austen observes the satisfied idling of her powers, 'A mind lively and at ease, can do with seeing nothing, and can see nothing that does not answer', then immediately provides material on which her heroine's imagination sets to work. There may even be a link between Emma and Daniel in the portrayal of Mary Garth in *Middlemarch*, in the scene where she 'revolves' in her mind the images of other peoples' illusions, and takes some pleasure in her own capacity to accept and see the world as it is. Daniel's empathy has many shifts and significances, and George Eliot records its dangers and its discontents in many passages of dramatized analysis. At times he is in danger of lacking the definitions of identity; at times, like Mary Garth, he almost falls into the trap of scepticism which is one of the moral dangers of negative capability and detachment. (George Eliot notices cynicism as a danger which Mary escapes, thus reminding us of its proximity.) For Daniel, the temptation is to be over-receptive, but on one occasion he is shown as personally preoccupied. This scene, like the scene in *Emma*, is remarkable as showing the creative mind in an atypical mood, but for Daniel there is no enjoyment:

> Many nights were watched through by him in gazing from the open window of his room on the double, faintly pierced darkness of the sea and the heavens: often in struggling under the oppressive scepticism which represented his particular lot, with all the importance he was allowing Mordecai to give it, as of no more lasting effect than a dream – a set of changes which made passion to him, but beyond his consciousness were no more than an imperceptible difference of mass or shadow; sometimes with a reaction of emotive force which gave even to sustained disappointment, even to the fulfilled demand of sacrifice, the nature of a satisfied energy, and spread over his young future, whatever it might be, the attraction of devoted service; sometimes with a sweet irresistible hopefulness that the very best of human possibilities might befall him – the blending of a complete personal love in one current with a larger duty; and sometimes again in a mood of rebellion (what human creature escapes it?) against things in general because they are thus and not otherwise, a mood in which

Gwendolen and her equivocal fate moved as busy images of what was amiss
in the world along with the concealments which he had felt as a hardship in
his own life, and which were acting in him now under the form of an
afflicting doubtfulness about the mother who had announced herself coldly
and still kept away. (Chapter 50)

This is an imaginative crisis. Daniel suffers the nervous anxiety of
divided consciousness, George Eliot analyses and images his un-
pleasantly mobile self-awareness, as he sways from one state to
another, feeling scepticism, dreamlike unreality, satisfying energy,
sweet hope and rebelliousness. It is at the other pole of imaginative
experience from the relaxed negations of that scene on the Thames:
George Eliot tells us that he was 'getting into that state of mind in
which all subjects become personal'. This is the imagination unable to
relax, concentrate, or work. In Daniel, George Eliot imagines most
fully and complexly the various stages in an individual imaginative
life, showing a quivering oscillation between the poles of too much
empathy and too much personal preoccupation, the one marked by an
emptying of the psyche, the other by an uncomfortable fullness.

Nowhere else, I think, does George Eliot show such minute and
delicate details and variations. Perhaps one of the difficulties of
Daniel's embodiment lies in this total exposure of introspection. Here
in negative and positive forms are the pressures of feeling, imaginative
incapacity, confusion, and power. His imagination finds congenial
materials, a balance of inner urge and outer demand. Here is the
problem of the extension of the self, shown not in speculation, as in
Philip's letter to Maggie, but in process. Daniel is not an artist like
Ladislaw and Latimer, but his furtherance of Mordecai's vision shows
how George Eliot is trying to extend the idea of the artist into the idea
of the imaginative man of action. In 'A College Breakfast-Party' Osric
and Guildenstern argue about the social relevance and significance of
art, Guildenstern 'shattering Osric's point/That sensibilities can move
apart/From social order'. Guildenstern's defence is spirited and
intelligent, an impassioned attack on the aesthetic imagination as it
makes its vivid images and constructs its unities:

> 'Is your beautiful
> A seedless, rootless flower, or has it grown
> With human growth, which means the rising sum
> Of human struggle, order, knowledge? – sense

Trained to a fuller record, more exact –
To truer guidance of each passionate force?
Get me your roseate flesh without the blood;
Get fine aromas without structure wrought
From simpler being into manifold:
Then and then only flaunt your Beautiful
As what can live apart from thought, creeds, states,
Which mean life's structure.'

Guildenstern insists that imagination must be more than aesthetic,
and has its origin in the context of social love. The debate ends in
uncertainty, as the Hamlet character insists that Guildenstern has not
'annulled his thesis that the life of poesy . . . Has separate functions'.
Laertes suggests asking the makers:

'See if their thought
Be drained of practice and the thick warm blood
Of hearts that beat in action various
Through the wide drama of the struggling world.'

The Hamlet figure, who seems to be closest to George Eliot, is left
alone and dubious, but ends by having a dream which he decides to
withhold 'as yet', perhaps admonished by shades who warn him that

visions told in haste
Part with their virtues to the squandering lips
And leave the soul in wider emptiness.

Perhaps it is not too idly speculative – at least it seems idealistically
appropriate – to suggest that the withheld dream imagined for this
Victorian Hamlet is reflected in Daniel Deronda. Daniel may not
be the most fully fleshed of her characters, but he has the most
thoroughly imagined imagination. He is imagined as imagining a
vocation beyond that of the artist, which attempts a synthesis of the
artistic and the social imagination. The end of the novel, 'grand and
vague' as Blackwood said, is an imprecision which has its own force.

7. 'A College Breakfast-Party', originally called 'A Symposium', is dated April 1874 in
the Cabinet Edition. At that time George Eliot was beginning *Daniel Deronda*.

We are left with Daniel's imagination bracing itself for action. Vision is given its material: both self and society may be enlarged. George Eliot is at last trying to imagine the heroic imagination. As Coleridge might say, her imagination, working through the models of fiction, is 'struggling to idealise' (*Biographia Literaria*, Chapter XIII).

Daniel imagines tentatively, but idealistically, like his author. As George Eliot imagined his ideal intention, she was obviously anxious not to remove it from the ordinary likelihoods of experience. A small but significant insertion in the manuscript shows her insistence on caution. He tells Gwendolen that he 'is possessed' with the idea of restoring a political existence to his people; and the insertion qualifies this ideal when Daniel says, 'At the least, I may awaken a movement in other minds, such as has been awakened in my own' (Chapter 69). For Daniel, as for George Eliot, the story is incomplete. But it is possible to over-emphasize the openness of the novel's ending. The narrative is broken off, for narrators and listeners inside and outside the novel, but the ethical conclusion is secure and complete. There is no closure in action, but a definite closure in ethical argument. Daniel and Gwendolen have their direction firmly established. Ideal vision is narrated, even allowed an awareness of its ideality, but only up to a point. Many common hazards, lapses, and complications are ignored, in order to achieve the moral certainty. The grand and vague ending permits the statement of grand and precise ethical ends. The narrative closures of *Middlemarch* are open to defects and complications, insisting on historical relativism and determinism; Daniel's nobility and Gwendolen's redemption resound more emphatically and ideally than Dorothea's muted and restricted contribution.

It is good to find, in George Eliot's final comments on imagination, a recognition of the problem of combining vision and likelihood. She had shown her awareness of the importance of materials and environment in imagining the imagination of Maggie Tulliver, Silas Marner, and Dorothea Brooke. She had shown her awareness of the obsessions and selections of human passion in Janet and all subsequent images of imagination. In those early letters she had shown her knowledge of the temptations of imaginative invention and construction. In the last essays of *Theophrastus Such* she summed up and surpassed these insights, in a sensitive acknowledgment of the artist's imaginative struggle to idealize and to register intransigence. Theophrastus Such observes that for the responsible artist there is no such thing as creative freedom, 'a fine imagination . . . is always based

on a keen vision, a keen consciousness of what *is*.' Vision is limited by
knowledge:

> . . . powerful imagination is not false outward vision, but intense inward
> representation, and a creative energy constantly fed by susceptibility to the
> veriest minutiae of experience, which it reproduces and constructs in fresh
> and fresh wholes;[8] not the habitual confusion of provable fact with the
> fictions of fancy and transient inclination, but a breadth of ideal association
> which informs every material object, every incidental fact with far-
> reaching memories and stored residues of passion, bringing into new light
> the less obvious relations of human existence. The illusion to which it is
> liable is not that of habitually taking duck-ponds for lilied pools, but of
> being more or less transiently and in varying degrees so absorbed in ideal
> vision as to lose the consciousness of surrounding objects or occurrences;
> and when that rapt condition is past, the sane genius discriminates clearly
> between what has been given in this parenthetic state of excitement, and
> what he has known, and may count on, in the ordinary world of experience.
> (*Impressions of Theophrastus Such*, 'How we come to give ourselves false
> testimonials, and believe in them')

George Eliot's last novel – like much of her work – may not create
the perfect balance between idealistic rapture and ordinary expectations which she admired in Dante. She never imagined that this
balance was easily achieved. That discontent which modern readers
have felt with the complacency or simplicity of the idealistic strain in
George Eliot and other Victorian novelists would not have surprised
the novelist who invented that failed writer, Macarthy, her first artist
character, unable to bridge the gap between ideal and actual society:

> He moved among the things of this earth like a lapidarian among false
> gems, which fetch high prices and admiration from others, but to him are
> mere counterfeits. He seemed to have a preternaturally sharpened
> vision. . . . The unsightly condition of the masses – their dreary ignorance –
> the conventional distortion of human nature in the upper classes – the
> absence of artistic harmony and beauty in the details of outward existence,
> were with him not merely themes for cold philosophy, indignant philippics,
> or pointed satire; but positively painful elements in his experience, sharp
> iron entering into his soul. (*Essays of George Eliot*, p. 15)

8. This phrase 'fresh and fresh' does not appear to be a mistake since it also occurs in
Chapter 19 of *Daniel Deronda*.

Before and after the novels, in essays using fictionalized forms and more discursive and explicit statement, George Eliot voiced the dilemma of the imaginative artist, caught between the impulse to recreate and the impulse to utter the whole truth about things as they are.

1980